ECOLOGY, SOCIETY, & THE QUALITY OF SOCIAL LIFE

ECOLOGY, SOCIETY, & THE QUALITY OF SOCIAL LIFE

Edited by
William V. D'Antonio,
Masamichi Sasaki
& Yoshio Yonebayashi

Transaction Publishers
New Brunswick (U.S.A.) and London (U.K.)

Copyright © 1994 by Transaction Publishers, New Brunswick, New Jersey 08903

All rights reserved under International and Pan-American Copyright Conventions. No part of this book may be reproduced or transmitted in any form or by any means, electronic or mechanical, including photocopy, recording, or any information storage and retrieval system, without prior permission in writing from the publisher. All inquiries should be addressed to Transaction Publishers, Rutgers—The State University, New Brunswick, New Jersey 08903.

Library of Congress Catalog Number: 93-44900
ISBN: 1-56000-722-2 (paper)
Printed in the United States of America

Library of Congress Cataloging-in-Publication Data
Ecology, society, and the quality of social life / edited by William V. D'Antonio,
    Masamichi Sasaki, Yoshio Yonebayashi.
        p. cm.
    Includes bibliographical references and indexes.
    ISBN 1-56000-722-2 (paper)
    1. Man—Influence of environment—Congresses.   2. Quality of life—
Congresses.   3. Human ecology—Congresses.   I. D'Antonio, William V.   II.
Sasaki, Masamichi S.   III. Yonebayashi, Yoshio, 1941–
HM206.E25   1994
304.2—dc20   93-44900
                                                                           CIP

To
the memory of

Paolo Ammassari
1931 - 1991

President
International Institute of Sociology
1989 - 1991

TABLE OF CONTENTS

Chapter

INTRODUCTION

All of the works in this volume were originally prepared for and presented during the 30th World Congress of the International Institute of Sociology (IIS) which was held in Kobe, Japan in August of 1991. Established in 1893, IIS is the oldest continuous sociological association. The 30th Congress, the first ever held in Asia, had as its theme "Ecology, World Resources and the Quality of Social Life."

This volume contains thirteen of the keynote papers presented at the Congress, selected because of the way they reflect the theme, "Ecology, Society and the Quality of Social Life." The twelve chapters that constitute the main body of the book present a range of theoretical ideas, methodological issues, and empirical findings, while the Appendix represents the work of a public figure, the governor of Hyogo Prefecture, where Kobe City is located. It is at once a recognition of the relevance of sociology to the body politic, and the statement of a public policy designed to confront the challenge to ecology and quality of life at the regional level created in turn by policies developed at the national level to meet international economic competition. Thus, in an interesting way, this and the other papers reveal the growing global interdependence and the crisis emerging out of the failure so far of the world's nation states to effectively meet the challenge of that interdependence.

The world's ecological problems call out for and demand our attention now; they are at least as serious for developed as for developing nations. The Kobe Congress intended that sociologists from all over the world now finally recognize the critical nature of these problems and turn their attention to assisting in the process of achieving viable and lasting solutions. These solutions may well involve developing models that will suggest the kinds of sacrifices needed to preserve and even improve the quality of social life in complex, new and distinct ecological/societal relationships. To do so it is necessary to steer sociology and its study of human social relationships in a global direction. And while the chapters of this book do not emphasize the point, it is important to keep in mind that sociologists have to learn to work across disciplines and across national boundaries, and in concert with public officials. We must be modest enough to recognize that ours is but one among many contributions needed to begin to turn things around. At the same time, we must not have a failure of nerve in confronting the immensity of the challenges that lie ahead.

Just how much of this goal the Congress achieved remains an open question. Part of the answer may be found in the degree to which this volume stirs interest and debate among sociologists and related scholars, leading to action on their part in this area. Like the United Nations Earth Summit, held in Rio de Janeiro in June 1992, perhaps the Congress's theme alone suggests a growing awareness of the emergency at hand. In the context of the diminution of the East-West conflict, perhaps humankind will now have the time to turn its attention where it is most needed. With its establishment of a set of cardinal principles for sustainable development, the 1992 Earth Summit certainly identified the cost/benefit picture vis-à-vis economic and environmental issues. The question of the quality of social life needs to be added to the equation. We may then ask the question, "Economic development, to enhance the quality of social life, at what cost?" Environmental protection, to enhance the quality of social life, at what cost? And who will pay? These were the issues at the Earth Summit, and these are issues to which sociologists are urged now to turn their attention.

The Congress appealed to sociologists from throughout the world to deal with its theme from both theoretical and empirical perspectives. During the Congress the extent of the accumulated research findings regarding the *quality of social life* was described and observed. But, whether these findings can be integrated with ecology and world resources—both of which, despite their significant weight as global issues, are relatively new to sociology and have not yet been appropriately positioned in the sphere of sociological paradigm—remains to be seen.

The papers accepted for this volume are organized as follows: A global perspective of the subject matter, "Ecology, Society and the Quality of Social Life" is presented by Anthony Giddens in his paper, "Industrialization, Ecology, and the Development of Life Politics." Giddens's overview is followed by two papers which specifically address the issues of ecology and environment: Riley E. Dunlap and William R. Catton, Jr. present their assessment of the history and state of environmental sociology in "Toward an Ecological Sociology: The Development, Current Status, and Probable Future of Environmental Sociology," and Edgar F. Borgatta paints an attention-getting picture of population and environmental resource problems in "Sociology and the Reality of the Press on Environmental Resources."

Attention then turns to several papers which deal specifically with the issue of Quality of Life or Quality of Social Life, with frequent references to its relationship to the environment and world resources. The late Paolo Ammassari couches his evaluation in terms of social relationships in "Ecology and the Quality of Social Life." Turning to empirical perspectives, the next two papers discuss the study of the Quality of Social Life: Alex Inkeles,

"Industrialization, Modernization and the Quality of Life," and Erwin K. Scheuch, "The Puzzle of 'Quality of Life.'" The next three chapters look at the Quality of Social Life from the perspectives of Social Movements and Social Policies: S. N. Eisenstadt, "New Social Movements and Alternative Modes of Development," T. K. Oommen, "Social Movements and Social Policies: A Misplaced Priority in Social Research," and France Govaerts, "Quality of Life, Development Policies and Female Children and Adolescents."

Closely related to environmental and quality of life issues is the subject of development, which is the topic of the next two papers: G. Széll, "High Technology: Industrialization and Problems of Development," and Raymond Boudon, "The Grandeur and Decadence of the Development Sciences: A Study of the Sociology of Knowledge."

Finally, the last paper, by Akinsola Akiwowo, "Human Social Relations and Environment Change: A Global Perspective," presents an alternative global perspective of the theme at hand.

The appendix contains a paper by Toshitami Kaihara, the Governor of Japan's Hyogo Prefecture, "A New Paradigm for Regional Policies: The Challenge of Hyogo Prefecture." Intended as an empirical illustration of many of the principles described in the main body of this volume, Kaihara's work describes an actual regional implementation of social policy in the twelfth largest of Japan's forty-seven states or prefectures.

To expand upon the content of each of this volume's chapters and to assist the reader in identifying the underlying threads which tie each together, the following describes each chapter and their interrelationships in greater detail.

In his paper on "Industrialization, Ecology and Development of Life Politics," Giddens argues that fundamental structural changes occurring in societies in recent years require a "profound conceptual rethinking of modern social analysis." Given that modernity "signals massive change," Giddens describes how the world of late modernity is one characterized by a degree of chaos and feelings of dislocation. He argues that tradition is waning, becoming only one of many alternative lifestyles, a process he terms the "radicalization" of modernity. In the context of the "globalization" of the institutions of modernity, Giddens points out that this is a "conflictual process which accentuates identity as opposed to producing cultural homogeneity." Giddens discusses the "disembedding" of modern institutions (the lifting out of social relationships and their recombination across time-space distances); "institutional reflexivity," a conceptual characteristic of modernity involving the constant use of information to organize and reorganize environments of action; the fact that sociological investigations yield results which become part of the things they studied; the fact that we now live in a "secular risk culture" in which risk is basic to organizing personal life and analyzing global futures; the "sequestration of experience" in which many of life's crises are now shielded from our everyday view; and a new political program, "Life Politics," which asks the question: "How shall we live in conditions of late modernity?" Giddens suggests that we must develop an ethical formulation of how we should live our lives in a globalized world. All these issues are placed in a context of "methodical doubt," which has come to be a principle of modernity. Giddens stresses that population problems are fundamental to late modernity and that all these phenomena are strongly influenced by the electronic media. Many of these themes will be revisited in subsequent chapters; in particular, the role of the media, the profound quality of social change in our time, that nothing is sacred in late modernity, that we must abandon the idea that everything will turn out all right and that the movement of world history is toward some kind of resolution of human problems, and finally the need for a profound rethinking of sociological concepts.

Riley E. Dunlap and William R. Catton, Jr. bring the reality of environmental sociology to us in their chapter. Beginning with a history of sociology's neglect of the environment, Dunlap and Catton first describe the Dominant Western Worldview (DWW) in which humankind was (is) seen as master of its destiny, as fundamentally different from all Earth's other creatures, and living in a world of unlimited opportunity (resources). The physical environment was seen as irrelevant to social life: "the Durkheimian legacy suggested that the physical environment *should* be ignored, while the Weberian legacy suggested that it *could* be ignored." Dunlap and Catton then go on to illustrate the succeeding stage exemplified by the "Human Exemptionalism Paradigm," in which humankind is still unlike all other animals but now with a cultural heritage in which "social and cultural environments are the crucial context for human affairs," while the "biophysical environment is largely irrelevant." In this stage, social problems are still "ultimately soluble." The DWW and to a lesser extent the HEP were anthropocentric stages and thrived on the Earth's apparent resource abundance. Here again, as Giddens pointed out, humans thought they could solve all their own problems. Dunlap and Catton suggest the need to patently reject the prevailing paradigm in favor of a new one: the New Ecological Paradigm (NEP) where humankind is still exceptional (culture, technology, etc.), but is now "one among many species that are interdependently involved in the global ecosystem." Here "purposive human actions have many unintended consequences" and "humans live in and are dependent upon a finite biophysical environment" with "potent physical and biological restraints." Finally, the NEP recognizes that "ecological laws cannot be repealed." Dunlap and Catton go on to describe in some detail how thinking about ecology and the ecosystem have evolved within sociology, not entirely successfully, over the past forty years, making it clear that today sociology is missing many funding opportunities by ignoring the biosphere. Sociologists, as "avowed experts," are called upon to act decisively and to retool concepts, theories and methods to achieve an ecological sociology.

Placed in the context of a modern version of the Malthusian formulation, Edgar F. Borgatta's chapter centers on the issues of population and its press on environmental resources. Borgatta's analysis suggests strongly that world population will increase in a narrower time frame than many forecast and that this will accelerate the pressures on the environment and the limited world resources (such as cultivable land, fresh water, clean air vs. desertification, deforestation). Borgatta argues that natural and human-made disasters are unlikely to attenuate the population explosion and its attendant press on the environment. He suggests, however, that the technical basis for fertility control exists now and at a comparatively "trivial" cost; that the issues which remain therefore are cultural ones. Borgatta also provides a sobering picture of the extent of our waste disposal problems, asking who will pay and indeed who can afford to pay for the cleanup. Finally, Borgatta points out that the press on environmental resources will continue until there are *major* policy shifts. Like Giddens and Dunlap and Catton, Borgatta states that sociologists are "well-qualified to attend to the problems of social behavior" and therefore must turn their attention to these crises.

Focus now shifts somewhat away from environmental issues and toward the quality of life or quality of social life debate. The late Paolo Ammassari argues that "quality of life" in the 1960s came to be identified with aimless economic growth, well exemplified by Los Angeles with its high material living standard but physically polluted and socially deteriorating environment. Quality of Life then began to be associated with ideas like "way of life" or "level of living" or "life satisfaction." Per Capita GNP was developed as an indicator of quality of social life but proved to be inadequate as a concept. Slowly, we have come to recognize some of the evaluative aspects of quality of life; that it is culture-bound, value-dimensioned and prescriptive of a good state of affairs. Ammassari suggests that a new definition of the quality of *social* life is in order, one that involves good social relationships. He points to the moral vs. ethical dimensions of social relationships, the former being self-oriented and the latter being collectivity-oriented. Recall that Giddens calls for an ethical formulation of life in a globalized world. Ammassari goes on to point out that the "dominance of social relationships based on ethical obligations has developed with the mass-consumer society and its over-exploitation of the biosphere/ecosystem, causing all to deteriorate." Referring to environmental sociology, he notes that the discipline has traced the "effects of sociology on the physical environment rather than assessing the impact of natural environments on social life," asking, in turn, "How do a degraded environment and resource depletion impact social life?"

Inkeles brings a variety of empirical measures to bear on his analysis of the relationship between Industrialization, Modernization and the Quality of Life. His chapter begins by describing how industrialization, with its move away from agriculture into manufacturing and services, is the vehicle for modernization, involving technological, economic and social change. Inkeles sees modernization as a "tightly structured syndrome," pointing out that, from a statistical standpoint, ten indicators work best in factor analysis to describe modernization, with Per Capita GNP being the best. Inkeles describes two approaches to judging or assessing quality of life: objective indicators, which can be subdivided into physical (e.g., housing square footage) and legal rights (i.e., social and political conditions); and subjective indicators, obtained by asking people how satisfied they are with their lives and specific aspects of their lives. These perceptions of their quality of life are important since people act upon them. Inkeles then asks about the causal sequence; that is, does modernization bring about improved quality of life? He posits that modernization often results in vast improvements in quality of life, citing as supporting evidence that maternal mortality in childbirth is 11 per 100,000 in the developed areas of the world, as compared with 607 per 100,000 in the less developed areas. These and other demographic and survey data, when juxtaposed with people's subjective perceptions, appear congruent when national response propensities are taken into consideration. Presenting other data, including comparisons within industrial nations and across the range from the most to the least industrialized, Inkeles shows that "the relations of many of the objective and subjective indicators are much more complex than is generally imagined, and indeed the facts are often counter-intuitive."

Erwin K. Scheuch, in the next chapter, also focuses on the evaluation of quality of social life, though many of his perspectives differ from those of Alex Inkeles. Scheuch begins by noting that despite apparent economic growth, many now protest that our quality of life is declining. Thus, what are the value dimensions? Welfare was supposed to mean collective happiness, but does it also mean individual happiness? Scheuch cautions that the social indicator movement is really making predictions and that social predictions are often wildly off. Scheuch maintains that it is not possible to derive a "number" which describes both individual and collective quality of life; that a shift toward measuring individual quality of life, based on subjective feelings about life conditions, is leading to the development of quality of life indices. As far as Per Capita GNP is concerned, Scheuch argues that while it is a lagged indicator, it is generally "pretty imperfect," due, in part, to differing cultural standards. Scheuch also cautions that the interpretation of attitudinal or subjective data requires a great deal of additional contextual knowledge and that the results can be seen only as very rough approximations (e.g., rank orderings). Like many other authors in this volume, Scheuch targets the influence of the media, noting that it can strongly influence perception. To illustrate how the media may influence perception, Scheuch notes that within a six year period, the public's attitudes toward the environment became 50% more negative than they had been. Questioning whether the environment itself could possibly have declined in quality so dramatically in six years, Scheuch hypothesized that the change was due to media influence, or as he put it, media "agenda setting." With Inkeles, Borgatta and others, Scheuch reviews an array of demographic and survey measures of quality of life, subjects them to rigorous theoretical and methodological critiques, and notes the gaps between these and more qualitative measures. Still he acknowledges that the evidence points to a growth in options for increasing numbers of persons, encouraging a kind of individualism within an "ordered diversity," and with some very traditional ideas of quality still very much intact.

A chapter by S. N. Eisenstadt on "New Social Movements and Alternative Modes of Development" opens the section on social movement and social policies. He asks, "What is meant by modernization, particularly as it spreads throughout the world?" He sees a reformulation of modernization, of modern civilizations. One expression of this phenomenon is the formation of new types of formal social movements. Beginning with the protest movements of the 1960s and coming up to the recent ecological movements, Eisenstadt shows that these no longer have "conflictual-ideological" focus on the "center" and its reconstitution, but now extend the "systemic range of social life and participation" and signal a shift from emphasis on increased standard of living to quality of life. "All this is brought about by the changing relations among state, economy, and society and their growing globalization." All this, too, is reinforced by the mass media. What does this mean? Eisenstadt points to the weakening of the formerly rigid, homogeneous definition of life patterns (e.g., the boundaries of the family and community); the dissolution of major roles (occupational, family and gender roles); a redefinition of roles (especially occupational and citizenship roles—consider, for example, the high-level executive with leftist political views); and the "development of various structural enclaves in part as counter-cultures, in part as components of new culture." Finally, Eisenstadt shows us that there is greater and greater dissociation among the occupational, cultural and political spheres of life; that different social strata no longer have different cultures; rather, they participate in the mass culture.

In his paper, Oommen sets as a main thesis the common goal of both social movements and social policies to be that of improving the quality of human social life. He acknowledges the many forces, such as military juntas and religious fundamentalists, that oppress and suppress social movements, but sees the latter as potentially effective weapons "of the weak against the strong," especially in heterogeneous multi-party states. But he is quick to recognize the difficulties of bringing that potential to reality. Oommen also discusses the transformation of social policy in the context of a move from homogeneous to heterogeneous state-societies in which more and more individuals and groups demand more and more of the state's resources, often "going beyond the material needs and aspirations of the vulnerable groups."

In the context of environment issues, Oommen chides the Wallersteinian world system model as accounting for only the human world (cf. the HEP) while ignoring the non-human environment. Oommen notes that the new paradigm must embrace the "ecological perspective as an alternative to modernization." "Authentic development implies quality of life but development is only sustainable by regulating energy consumption, ecological degradation and environmental pollution." The limits to growth require a new cognition regarding quality of life. Oommen argues that quality of life, as a universal concept, needs to be "demystified, concretized in the historicity of context to which it is applied." Finally, Oommen describes the elements necessary to construct an "authentic index of the quality of social life," including the "changing role of the state and its harnessing of social movements as an instrument of social transformation"; the evolution of social policy from a state-maintaining to a change-inducing tool"; and the recognition that both social movements and social policies contribute to quality of life.

France Govaerts narrows her focus on the quality of life to female children and adolescents. For her the primary indicators of quality of life are "access to health, nutrition, education, conditions to exercise with dignity social-human and economic roles, training to survive and earn income, and activities which make time more valuable." Focusing her attention on all women, but female children and adolescents in particular, Govaerts first cautions that we cannot rely upon data depicting national averages; that rampant discrimination is actually embedded within these aggregated data. Govaerts goes on to identify two specific phenomena which play a major role in the continuing discrimination against females: totalization, whereby identity is denied to "specific population categories," and the exclusion of these population categories from certain fundamental roles. For instance, most data address children in the aggregate; however, this kind of aggregation distorts reality and obscures hidden inequalities. Disaggregation will reveal significant differences embedded within the data, i.e., between girls and boys. Govaerts argues that economic and social-human development policies can correct these imbalances and provides examples of several Asian countries which have so far done the best job of identifying the problem and taking action to correct it. Govaerts, too, argues that fundamental structural changes are needed; that "improvements must come through education, health services and income-generating activities"; that we must "mobilize all existing services to produce valid data and programs which include girls and women as the main orientation of development policies." She urges that "by obtaining higher social status, greater freedom of action, more economic and cultural resources, women will escape the vicious circle of disease, illness and poverty and numerous childbirths which close to them those roles in society which are necessary to improve their conditions." It is incumbent upon sociologists to carry out research with the methodological safeguards that will reveal the biases, inequalities and discrimination against female children, and thus increase the probability of a more balanced quality of life for all young people.

Though several of the preceding authors have made development a part of their discussions, G. Széll and Raymond Boudon focus more specifically on the issue. For Széll, the prospects for ecology and the quality of social life depend on "a broad public debate and local action—'Think globally, Act locally.'" Technology assessment and forecasting are anew of vital importance. He posits that disarmament and arms conversion are mandatory if we are to cope with our ecological crises; only then will the economic resources be available. We must, Széll insists, "decide consciously about our future, not leave it in the dark, to market forces." Here we revisit the falsity of the idea that everything will work out fine for humankind. Széll asks, what is quality of social life? "Is it higher productivity? more profits? or is it more freedom, liberty, autonomy, democracy for the individual and society at large? or do we already live in the best of all possible worlds?" Like other authors in this volume, Széll argues that "A democratic and ecological future will not come by itself, but we have to fight for it against many vested interests and narrow-minded citizens." Széll's approach is regionally rather than globally oriented. Realization of these goals must come about in each region, "according to its needs and historical and cultural specificities." This approach represents a departure from many of the other authors who argue for a global perspective. Széll also delineates Beck's two choices, authoritarian technocracy or ecological democracy, noting that the former appears more likely now but that "counter-strategies are in place" to work toward ecological democracy. With regard to sustainable development (by UN definition, "a global development which equilibrates ecology and human needs"), Széll offers that "uniting ecology, resources and the quality of social life is proposed because it expresses an orientation towards endogenous, sustainable development," at the regional (not local) level. With reference to high technology, Széll argues that it *can* save energy and resources and thus has the "potential to increase quality of social life, preserve world resources and ecology," but cautions that it can also waste energy and resources. Finally, asserting that the "ecological crisis is the greatest challenge in human history," Széll maintains that the "only alternative then is a socially oriented technology."

Raymond Boudon begins his chapter by asking why the development sciences suffered the beginnings of a decline in the 1970s. He sees the answer as lying in two main ideas within the sociology of knowledge: extrapolation, and the fact that knowledge does not reflect what is real. Boudon illustrates extrapolation by posing a four-color pyramid with four individuals sitting each in front of one side of the pyramid (and unable to see the other sides). When asked what color the pyramid is, an individual will likely respond that it is the color of the side that individual sees. This example carries over to the fact that knowledge does not reflect what is real, but rather is composed of the answers a subject gives, keeping in mind that the form of the question can dictate or contribute to determining the answer, which can result in false beliefs. Given this background from the sociology of knowledge, Boudon states that "development sociologists and economists have sought the *principal* factor responsible for development." But this pursuit presupposes that a principal factor actually exists! Boudon suggests that the language of factors be renounced; that too many given assumptions often muddle reality. By way of concrete example, Boudon discusses the case of Colombia's development at length, arguing that the principal factor approach is defective here and in many other instances as well. Referring again to the principal factor approach and others, Boudon argues that "such 'laws' or 'theories' should be restated as *models*," with sufficient caution appended, such as "If all the conditions of *A* are assumed to be present, then it *might be* that *B*...," representing what Boudon calls a "mutable relation." With models, then, which cannot directly guide political action, science and the social sciences can clarify, but not guide action.

Akinsola Akiwowo's chapter presents what we might be tempted to call an "alternative perspective" on the subject matter of this volume. Though it perhaps reflects a unique or unusual way of looking at the world, at least to some Westerners, it nevertheless reiterates much of the content we have seen in the preceding eleven chapters. Akiwowo proposes the formulation of a world society which he calls *asuwada*, the "purposive clumping of diverse existences." Here we revisit globalization, seen, in this instance, from what Akiwowo calls an African cosmological view of humankind's destiny. This view sees humankind as introducing "over time, fresh and revolutionary ways of improving the quality of life of humans and other living things." Calling upon a variety of literary sources, Akiwowo paints a picture of world society, of globalization, in an imaginative and compelling way. He concludes by stating that "whatever development policies we formulate should be for all mankind, not separate policies for different continents and peoples."

The founder of the International Institute of Sociology, Rene Worms, believed strongly that sociology's focus should be both cross-national and cross-disciplinary. In addition, he believed it essential that public figures (governmental, business and professional) should have a central place in IIS congresses. This would permit them to interact with sociologists and thus gain a better idea of what they may have to contribute to solving major social problems too often thought to be the province of the natural sciences and technology. The opportunity was also seen as important to sociologists who should be interested in public policy matters.

In the case of the Kobe Congress, we were fortunate to have a paper presented by the governor of Hyogo Prefecture, Toshitami Kaihara. The congress site, Kobe, is one of the key cities of the Prefecture, and so it was fitting that the governor presented a paper on "A New Paradigm for Regional Policies: The Challenge of Hyogo Prefecture." The governor displayed a keen understanding of the potential utility of sociology and the other social sciences in confronting and resolving major problems that have arisen in Japan and other developed nations as a result of the economic revolution that followed World War II.

After describing how Japan's economic revolution had been planned and controlled from the center, Tokyo, Governor Kaihara explained how this central planning, while vital to Japan's growth, had impacted negatively on regional and local sectors. Decline of neighborhood associations and of a sense of community, combined with a new tendency toward egocentrism, and the disruption of rural and urban life by the shifts in and new densities and locations of populations, were all factors leading to a standardization of life focused on the economy above all other elements.

To counter this, Kaihara proposed that regional governments (prefectures) take responsibility for developing a new paradigm, modeled on the idea of a gemeinschaft, "a communal society in which all members feel bonded by mutual dependence and trust." He asserted that economic power must be contained by fostering a community in which people are encouraged and taught to live in peace and harmony with their neighbors and with the surrounding environment. This, said Kaihara, would produce a "Richness of Mind" that he envisioned as a truly rich quality of life.

Governor Kaihara proceeded to outline the actions being taken in Hyogo Prefecture to implement this paradigm, and in the process "help correct the regional imbalances arising out of the overdependence on economic development in recent decades.

The reader will find in this work many of the ideas, theories and prescriptions posed by the preceding authors. Indeed, this appendix represents an excellent example of the empirical attention to and implementation of many of the sociological observations made in the twelve chapters constituting the body of this volume. The paper serves then as an exemplar of the vision of IIS's founder Rene Worms, of bringing sociological knowledge to bear for the improvement of the human condition. To the extent that the essays in this book make even a small contribution toward that end, we will have continued to honor the memory of the founder of the IIS.

Chapter 1

INDUSTRIALIZATION, ECOLOGY, AND THE DEVELOPMENT OF LIFE POLITICS

Anthony Giddens

University of Cambridge

One can say that the time at which we live, the closing years of the 20th century, is a period of social change, probably as profound as any that has occurred since the late 18th century. This is not just a case of *fin de siècle*, not just a case of a consciousness of moving from one century to another; it is an awareness of structural changes in modern societies that are probably as fundamental as those that ushered in the period of modernity.

To analyze social change in the late 20th century, we need a rethinking of sociological concepts perhaps as profound as that which initiated sociology in the first place in the 18th century. When we speak of ecology, high technology, feminist movements, peace movements—it might seem as though we simply add more problems onto those already existing in sociology.

However, there is something much more profound at issue than that. To develop a way of approaching the themes of this Congress, one needs to elucidate concepts which are substantially different from those which have dominated sociological thought over the past two centuries. What I would like to do here is to provide some indication of what this conceptual rethinking might be.

All sociologists are familiar with the idea that we live in an industrial society—that modernity means industrialism, or it means capitalism, or it means technological change. But, when we confront the problem of modernity today, looking back at the processes of change over the past two hundred years in modern societies, we can see that to equate modernity with industrialism or with capitalist society is in a certain respect superficial. To look at modernity today means reconsidering these orthodox characterizations, to see what underlies them. There are certain more profound transformations signaled by the advent of modernity than the orthodox labels, such as industrial society, capture.

What is modernity? Modernity for me is simply the system of modern institutions, the type of social order instigated by the changes which occurred from about the late 18th century on in Europe and then became worldwide. Why is modernity so crucial to us? Because modernity does signal *massive* change. There has never been any civilization in prior history where the pace of change, the depth of change, the degree to which it reaches into day-to-day life, and the scope of change, have been as large as in the circumstances of modernity.

To ask what modernity is, then, is to ask about a tremendous infrastructural dynamism which modern societies have set in motion. Two concepts might be introduced to characterize this dynamism, concepts which underlie the orthodox characterizations of industrial society, capitalism, and so forth. First of all, since its initiation, modernity (modern institutions) has been bound up with transformations of time and space. To analyze the dynamism of modernity is to theorize such time-space transformations. The organization of time and the organization of space are fundamental to the dynamic character which modernity has assumed.

To analyze in turn time-space transformations, there is a notion which I term the "disembedding" of modern institutions. It can be argued that modernity, from its origins, serves to disembed social relationships. "Disembedding" means the lifting of social relationships out of a particular context—out of the particularities of time and space—and their recombination across indefinite time-space distances.

The metaphor of disembedding is preferable to the metaphor of differentiation, which sociologists have very often followed in distinguishing modern from pre-modern societies. Differentiation suggests the increased complexity of a modern society as compared to traditional ones, but the break between the pre-modern and the modern is much more radical than such a notion suggests. By disembedding, therefore, I propose that the advent of modernity radically alters our relationship to time and space and initiates a process whereby the locality is tied, in a dialectical way, to transformations at distance.

Action at distance is one of the key characteristics of modernity, and the orthodox characterizations like capitalism capture some aspects of that. Capitalism obviously is a disembedding mechanism in the sense in which capitalistic markets are global markets or implicitly global markets. But disembedding goes much beyond capitalistic structures and is a key feature of the dynamism of modernity.

The second characteristic to be proposed is what I term "institutional reflexivity." Institutional reflexivity means that with the advent of modern institutions knowledge about social life is no longer knowledge about an external, given environment of action, but increasingly comes to constitute what that environment of action is. Institutional reflexivity means the constant use of information to organize and reorganize the environments of action which that information describes.

In the thought of Marx, of Durkheim, and even of Max Weber, we see the idea that, as we get more knowledge about society, so our control over the social world increases; and as we get more knowledge about the material environment, so our control over that environment grows. The enlightenment idea was that more knowledge equals more effective, rational understanding and control of the world in which we live. We know now, in the late 20th century, that this characterization of modernity was mistaken. We know now that information and concepts and findings which we develop about social life routinely re-enter social life and reconstitute it, producing erratic consequences.

The world of "late modernity" is not the world which the 19th-century thinkers anticipated. One of the chief reasons for this is the phenomenon of institutional reflexivity. More knowledge does not inevitably lead to more rational control. We can see this if we consider the Weberian model of the "iron cage." For Weber, we are doomed to live increasingly in a bureaucratized, technicized universe which holds us in a machine-like grip. But that is *not* the experience of late modernity, the experience of the late 20th century. The modern world may feel like that in some areas, but in other areas it feels more like a runaway world. We see phenomena like the revolutions in Eastern Europe, unanticipated even by the most stringent specialists who studied the East European countries. We contort a world of dislocation, running out of our domination as human agents. This erraticism is part of the very experience of modernity—not a world in control but a world out of control, or if you like, a mixture; certain sectors seemingly within our control, others which escape our control. This fractured world is the world of late modernity and paradoxically one of the very reasons for this fracturing is the constant intrusion of knowledge back into the environments it was coined to describe. Knowledge, as it re-enters the social and material environments of action, escapes the control of its initiators.

Any sociological investigation carried out today—for example into the nature of marriage—routinely becomes part of the environment under which marital relationships are contracted and personal life undertaken and thereby serves to alter the nature of those environments. This is not a feedback system; it does not obey the principles of cybernetics. It is not a system with a regulator becoming more and more controlled through that regulator. On the contrary, it is a system in which the regular intrusion of knowledge tends to fracture, tends to throw apart, phenomena which previously we thought we understood. The unpredictability of the contemporary world, therefore, paradoxically in some part derives from our knowledge about it, and that knowledge becomes more and more constitutive of the environments of action in which we live. This applies to the material world as well as to the social world and, as we now find, the very core of what seems to be technical knowledge about the material world, namely the natural sciences, itself rests upon a principle of doubt.

Enlightenment thought once believed science equals progress, science equals greater control of the material world. We now know, or can be *fairly* certain, because even this can be doubted, that science rests upon a procedure of methodical doubt, that science *is* methodical doubt, that therefore, according to the premises of natural science, there is nothing of which we can be certain, and there is nothing which we can prove.

If one asks about the phenomenon of global warming, for example, one asks about a phenomenon which is socially created, which is created through the intrusion of knowledge, but about which, certainly in current circumstances, it is impossible to decide. If one reads the literature on global warming, one might decide to believe one side or the other, but there is no final authority which will adjudicate. The phenomenon is an open one; it is a risk environment created by late modernity. All one can say with any certainty about global warming is that one cannot be certain it is not occurring, and certain practical consequences might flow from that.

A world of institutional reflexivity therefore is a highly mobile world which eventually strips away the last remnants of tradition. A world of institutional reflexivity is a world of methodical doubt in which, existentially for everyone, there are no final authorities.

What seems to be just an esoteric problem of science, the issue of methodical doubt as scientific procedure, actually is a principle of modernity. There is no single behavioral trait which we cannot say might not be, in principle, revisable in the light of more information. This applies to principles of diet, it applies to principles of bodily presentation, it applies to the intimacies of personal life, and it applies to global futures.

Disembedding and institutional reflexivity are both to be taken as indigenously characteristic of modernity since its origins. In the *current* period of transformation, the late 20th century, we see further changes emerging. One could understand many aspects of the earlier phase of modernity using enlightenment thought, and that is what sociology was essentially based on. As we enter the period of what I term not "post-modernity" but "late modernity," we see that these characteristics—disembedding and institutional reflexivity—become increasingly profound, and for us they produce a feeling of tremendous disorientation. They underline the need for a conceptual rethinking in modern social analysis which must go well beyond the mention of terms like "environment," "ecology," "the women's movement," and so forth.

What is the difference between classical modernity and what I term "late modernity"? One can sum up the difference in two characteristics. There are two sets of changes, particularly over the past thirty or forty years, which have altered the institutions of modernity and have altered their global impact.

The first set of changes I describe as the "radicalization" of modernity. The radicalization of modernity means that the principles of disembedding and institutional reflexivity penetrate the heart of our personal daily lives. We live in a world which is increasingly stripping itself free from tradition; a world in which, where tradition remains, tradition is one choice among other possible lifestyle options. The more modernity becomes radicalized, the more a traditional pattern of behavior becomes an option, becomes something subject to methodical doubt, i.e., something which has to be justified against other lifestyle options. One still has, of course, traditional cultures where tradition is tradition, but the more modernity becomes radicalized, the more any type of tradition is no longer tradition *in that sense*. Tradition then becomes one possible style of life among others, where the individual or group who sustains that tradition, for example religious fundamentalism, acknowledges that it is one possible mode of life among others and therefore in some sense has to be justified.

Where does religious fundamentalism come from? Religious fundamentalism is the other side of the radical, methodical doubt which modernity introduces. It is very difficult to live in a world where nothing is sacred, but the principle of radical doubt, the principle of institutional reflexivity, insists that nothing is sacred. To live in a world where nothing is sacred is psychologically difficult, and in some ways institutionally difficult, and we can understand the appeal of religious fundamentalism against such a backdrop because it gives one a coherent defense of tradition which does not need to address, in the same degree, the problem of methodical doubt which any other kind of defensive tradition does. It is a more closed form of defense of a traditional mode of life.

Thus, the first thing that has happened over the past thirty or so years is the radicalization of the institutions of modernity, penetrating our day-to-day lives, stripping away most of the traditions which continue to exist. Secondly, this is happening on a global level.

Globalization is the second fundamental concept with which all sociologists today must deal. First is the radicalization of the institutions of modernity; the second is the globalization of the institutions of modernity. The idea of globalization is a familiar one because it is part of our own day-to-day reflexivity. Hence, when one says the notion of globalization must be a key concept for sociology, one must work out what that concept actually is; how it should be understood. Globalization is not to be understood as the development of unified world systems. One must not equate globalization with a Wallersteinian world system. One must not equate globalization with a development of world systems as such. Globalization is a much more subtle but much more profound process than such characterizations would presume.

I would like to propose that to conceptualize globalization, one should understand globalization as an accentuating of a characteristic that I have treated as fundamental to modernity in the first place: transformation of time and space. Globalization is essentially the importance of action at distance upon social life and it is crucial to see that globalization is a dialectical phenomenon. Globalization transforms locality. It transforms personal life while at the same time being a set of processes transforming global systems as such; i.e., an event which happens in the global arena can have local consequences, but those local consequences might be quite the opposite of the global phenomena, even though they are causally tied to them.

If, for example, one considers the phenomenon of local nationalism, the expansion of local cultural identity which we now see all around us in the late 20th century world is dialectically tied to globalization, to the universalizing of certain kinds of economic and political relationships. It is a counter-reaction to those tendencies, but causally tied to it. Globalization therefore is contradictory. Globalization fragments. Globalization marginalizes. Globalization is a conflictual process which accentuates identity rather than simply producing McDonald's everywhere or producing cultural homogeneity.

Globalization, then, in sum, is the transformation of time and space, the increasing significance of action at distance on our lives, but conversely the increasing significance of local life for global futures; these things constantly having paradoxical, fractured, or conflictual outcomes, so that what happens in one area of the world might produce the opposite result in another, but nevertheless is an example of a globalizing phenomenon. Globalization over the past twenty or thirty years has been strongly influenced by the electronic media and by the development of instantaneous communication so that it is not the same as the expansion of capitalism in the earlier phase of modernity. It is not simply an extension of the international division of labor or international capitalistic markets. The phenomenon of instantaneous communication is at the core of the transformations which link the local and the global.

We all know now the connections between the local and the global—that these have to be understood as dialectical connections. For sociology the problem is to come to terms with the world in which, for the first time in human history, the intimacies in our personal life are bound up with global futures, and global futures are bound up with the intimacies of our personal activity. No other society in human history has ever had this characteristic, and to the degree to which sociology insists upon the notion of society, the nation-state as its core emphasis, it is not able to analyze this new dialectic, the dialectic of the local and the global or the dialectic of the personal and world futures. All debates about ecology, about the transformation of the so-called environment, have to be located in the context of this novel dialectic which needs, in turn, a series of novel concepts to try to understand.

Many implications stem from the emergence of a world in which for the first time one sees this massive connection between the local and the global in the context of institutional reflexivity. First of all, one consequence of these transformations, the emergence of what I term "late modernity," is the development of what I want to call a "secular risk culture" which affects personal life as well as global futures. By a "secular risk culture," I do not mean what the German sociologist Ulrich Beck calls a "risk society" precisely. I do not mean a society in which risk has become more fundamental. I mean a society in which the concept of risk becomes basic for organizing personal life and for analyzing global futures. The concept of risk is about time and about space. The idea of risk emerged in the early period of modernity in relation to insurance, where insurance is a mode of organizing time, of organizing the future. The more one sees the radicalization, the globalization of modernity, the more the organization of time and space is crucial to us, and the concept of risk is a concept which allows us to "colonize" the future. Colonizing the future means organizing future time and trying to make it into a territory of the present. Risk is a calculation and one can never calculate risk with any precision in most risky environments—it is a risky notion to calculate risk.

Risk is a mode which organizes our colonization of the future, whether it is in respect to individual life, as individuals would colonize the future in terms of deciding what to eat, how to act, how to live. It is a concept, however, which also applies on the global level. To live in a secular risk culture means abandoning all forms of providentialism, abandoning the idea that things will turn out all right in the end; i.e., that the movement of world history is towards some kind of resolution of human problems. Marx said human beings only set themselves such problems as they can resolve. That was a false theorem. To live in our world, a secular risk culture, is to recognize that risks are real and that no providential intervention will save humanity or will save us on a personal level. There are many implications of this for the conduct of social movements and for traditional interpretations of politics in the modern world.

Second, in the world of late modernity, just as on a global level, there is a secular risk culture. On a personal level, for us the self becomes a reflexive project. The self participates in the reflexivity of late modernity. To have a self in conditions of late modernity is to have a narrative of one's identity, a narrative which looks into one's past and anticipates a colonized future for the individual. The reflexive project of self is a fundamental change of self-organization from any traditional culture. The more the reflexive project of self becomes central, the more it becomes true that the idea of lifestyle becomes a technical-sociological concept. The more the self is a reflexive project, the more one has to choose among lifestyle options as a mode of organizing one's own personal activity.

The idea of lifestyle, therefore, becomes a sort of sectoral form of activity in terms of which one organizes self and social relationships. We are forced to choose between lifestyles in a context of methodical doubt. To choose among lifestyles in a context of methodical doubt is anxiety-ridden, an anxiety-ridden phenomenon which, however for us, is an obligation. There is no option except to decide.

A good example to think about this is diet. We tend to think of diet as meaning slimming, reducing one's body weight. But diet actually came into existence with the globalization of food production, from about the 1940s and 1950s onwards. With the globalization of food production, one has food from all over the world which is present and one can choose between it at any time of the year. One is no longer limited to local markets. Globalization of food production is a disembedding process *par excellence*. Once this has occurred, then diet becomes a lifestyle phenomenon and even if one stays with a traditional diet—say one is in Japan and eats raw fish and this is a well-established mode of eating—one cannot but recognize that this is one possible lifestyle option among others. It is no longer simply a tradition; it is a lifestyle option among other lifestyle options. The technical significance of lifestyle for us, which connects the reflexive project of self, is therefore fundamental.

The third characteristic of the development of late modernity is what I term the "sequestration of experience." By the sequestration of experience I mean that as modernity accelerates, as the institutions of modernity become more and more deep-rooted and extensive, whatever the conflicts they produce, so institutionally there develops a separation between day-to-day life and various moral, existential questions which life throws up for us. The sequestration of experience is expressed institutionally in the development of the hospital, the mental asylum, the transformation of nature, and the privatization of sexuality. These changes are changes which take out of our view, which take out of ordinary life, crisis situations which all human beings must experience. If one concentrates on just one, with the invention of the hospital serious illness becomes physically sequestered from view and separated off from the orthodox conduct of day-to-day life. Sequestration of experience means the separation of existential-moral issues from day-to-day life which takes on a routinized character. This is why when we actually confront a situation of moral crisis, it is often a genuine climactic crisis for the individual because these things are not experienced or dealt with as part of the moral tissue of day-to-day life. Modernity, if you like, is a control system which separates off questions which morally affect our lives but which are left, as it were, on the physical margins of our lives.

As a result of all this, we have a transformation of the political agenda of late modernity. To understand this transformation, one must make a distinction between two types of political agenda. The first type of political agenda I term "emancipatory politics." The second type of political agenda I term "life politics" or the "politics of lifestyle."

"Emancipatory politics" means the core components of politics as understood in the classical period of modernity. Emancipatory politics is a politics of freedom. It is a politics which obeys norms of justice, equality and freedom from exploitation. Emancipatory politics is a politics which pits some groups against other groups. It is a politics of the rich against the poor, the first-world nations against the third-world nations, women against men, blacks against whites. Emancipatory politics is an organizing medium of democracy in the world of modernity. It is very clear that emancipatory politics is fundamental to late modernity, as we see from the revolutions in Eastern Europe or from instances of radical democratization around us. The appeal of emancipatory politics is still fundamental to what the modern world holds out as a possibility for us.

More and more, however, emancipatory politics becomes infiltrated by and exists alongside a new political program. This new political program is the program of "life politics." The program of life politics is a program of political endeavors and political involvements which stems from the structural characteristics of late modernity. Life politics is a politics with no others. Life politics is not a politics of us against them, of one group against another group. It is not a politics which obeys a logic or a value system of justice, equality, freedom from oppression. Life politics poses for us and is organized around the question: How shall we live in a world of high reflexivity in which global futures and local lives are increasingly intertwined? Life politics is a politicization, a recovery of ethical questions about the nature and conditions of human life which certainly include our relations to nature, but which also include a whole other set of issues. Life politics is a politics which asks the question, How shall we live in conditions of late modernity? and regards as open most questions which previously were fixed by tradition. Life politics is a renewal of ethics. It involves ethical conflicts and it involves ethical conflicts around a recovery of those arenas of activity which have been pushed out of our lives by the sequestration of experience.

The sequestration of experience hides death, hides sexuality, hides self identity, hides the morality of sickness, hides the morality of reproduction from us. But this is something which cannot be achieved in human life. These things push back as ethical questions for us. As they push back as ethical questions which have to be justified, one has the emergence of new political agendas. One way of thinking about what life politics is, is through the arena of reproduction.

Reproduction ties together a series of ethical issues, concerns issues of what it is to be a person, what our responsibilities are to future generations, what kind of sexual identity we should have, what kinds of sexual ethics we should follow. Reproduction ties together all these questions. It ties together intimacies of the self because the decision to reproduce is a personal decision. It ties together global futures because as reproduction (population problems are a fundamental issue in late modernity) becomes restructured, through the intrusion of social organization and technical decision-making, into an arena which used to be a natural environment of human action, now there is no necessary connection between sexual intercourse and the reproduction of children. There is no connection anymore between heterosexual marriage and the raising of children. These things, in principle, are separate from one another. The more these are transformed by socialized knowledge, the more they become part of the arena of institutional reflexivity; the more a whole series of ethical issues about reproduction comes to form part of a new political agenda, and those who follow the debates about abortion, about reproductive technologies and so forth, can see how intense this new political agenda is.

Sociologists must address, conceptualize, and think about the agenda of life politics, not just as a question of environment, not just as a question of resources, but as a question of how, globally, we can develop an ethical formulation of how we should live our lives in a globalized world, a series of ethical formulations which cannot just depend on tradition but must in some sense be justified—how to reach a world of what Rorty calls a "global cosmopolitan conversation" between differential lifestyles in a context of care for the earth and care for others, in which violence is extruded and the force of the better argument is used as a basis for a global cosmopolitanism. That is the issue which the future of humanity confronts.

Chapter 2

TOWARD AN ECOLOGICAL SOCIOLOGY:
THE DEVELOPMENT, CURRENT STATUS, AND
PROBABLE FUTURE OF ENVIRONMENTAL SOCIOLOGY

Riley E. Dunlap and William R. Catton, Jr.

Washington State University, Pullman

Although this paper's major focus will be to describe the emergence and current status of the field of environmental sociology, a new and still small specialization that represents a deviation from sociology's tendency to ignore environmental problems, much of it will deal with reasons for the widespread neglect of such problems in the larger discipline. In particular, we will analyze the fundamental assumptions or "paradigm" underlying our discipline which appear to serve as a set of "blinders" that makes it difficult for sociologists to perceive the societal significance of natural resources or environmental problems. We will then argue that this set of assumptions, which we term the "human exemptionalism paradigm," needs to be replaced by an "ecological paradigm" that recognizes the ecosystem-dependence of human societies, including modern industrialized societies. The conscious employment of this alternative perspective appears necessary if sociology is to make meaningful contributions to the study of global environmental change, a topic of increasing importance to scientists, policy-makers and citizens throughout the world. Replacing human exemptionalism with an ecological paradigm will not only increase the salience of environmental sociology, but may ultimately yield a truly "ecological sociology."

SOCIOLOGY'S NEGLECT OF THE ENVIRONMENT:
OUR DISCIPLINARY TRADITIONS AND EXEMPTIONALIST PARADIGM

Over a decade ago we pointed to the obvious fact that sociology was rather slow in recognizing the significance of environmental problems, and virtually ignored them until the larger society—stimulated by ecologists and environmental activists, both with assistance from the mass media—had clearly defined environmental quality as a "social problem" (Catton & Dunlap 1978a). Why was sociology so slow in seeing the societal significance of such problems, which were often local in scope, and why has it been so slow in responding to the recent widespread concern with global environmental problems (see Newby 1991 on the latter)? The answer, we think, lies in some fundamental assumptions upon which our discipline was established and continues to operate. Unconscious acceptance of these largely implicit assumptions has, in effect, blinded sociologists to the importance of environmental problems and the reality of changing ecological conditions. To understand these assumptions we need to examine the socio-cultural context in which our discipline developed, as well as traditions and perspectives that are peculiar to the field itself.

The Dominant Western Worldview[1]

Sociology has been deeply influenced by the Western culture in which it originally developed. This culture is strongly anthropocentric, viewing humans as separate from and above the rest of nature. Western people's ability to act upon the resultant belief that nature exists primarily for human use was dramatically increased by the scientific and technological developments of recent centuries. These developments, combined with the abundant resources discovered by Europeans in the New World, generated an "industrial revolution" that profoundly changed not only Western societies but eventually nearly all of the rest of the world (Catton 1980; Crosby 1986). Resource abundance and technological advancement fueled dramatic economic growth and development, and generated an optimistic expectation of perpetual progress in industrial societies—particularly in the United States. It is within the context of this anthropocentric and optimistic "Dominant Western Worldview" (DWW) that our discipline took root, and not surprisingly sociologists have at least implicitly adopted the assumption that ongoing technological development, economic growth and progress are the normal state of affairs, and can be expected to continue indefinitely (Catton & Dunlap 1980).[2]

Changes in how and where people lived, especially the massive shift toward industrialism and urbanism and away from agriculture, reinforced the notion that modern societies were becoming increasingly independent from their physical environments. In fact, life in industrialized societies created the impression that not only was the physical environment a perpetual and inexhaustible source of abundant natural resources, but that humans could manipulate and control that environment to suit their needs.

Sociological Traditions[3]

In addition to the inherently optimistic orientation about continued human progress that sociology adopted from Western culture, various factors unique to our discipline have reinforced sociologists' tendency to ignore the role of physical environment. To establish their new discipline, our founding fathers strongly asserted the uniqueness of our subject matter and perspectives. Of critical importance was Durkheim's emphasis on the "objective reality of social facts" and the irreducibility of such facts to the psychological properties of individuals. A corollary of this *sui generis* conception of social phenomena was the dictum that the *cause* of social facts must always be found in other social, as opposed to psychological, facts. The resultant "anti-reductionism taboo" also legitimated sociological rejection of biological and physical variables as potential explanations of social phenomena (Durkheim 1950).

Up until the early 20th century it was common for theorists to offer explanations of social phenomena in terms of biological, geographical and other physical factors. Because they often suggested that biological factors such as heredity or physical conditions such as climate were the *primary* de-

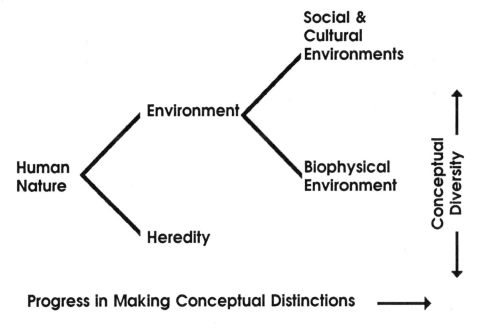

Figure 1. Differentiation of variables that influence human behavior

terminants of human affairs, such writers came to be criticized as biological or geographical "determinists." Encouraged by anti-reductionism, sociologists have been especially adamant in rejecting these views, to the point that the charge of determinism is now levelled (incorrectly in our view) at those who suggest that biological or environmental factors have *any* degree of influence on human affairs (Franck 1984; Benton 1991).[4]

The combined effects of sociology's anti-reductionist and anti-determinist "phobias" can be seen in our discipline's reaction to two crucial conceptual distinctions among the factors presumed to influence human affairs. First, when biological knowledge developed sufficiently to allow for the distinction between heredity and environment as sources of variation in human behavior patterns, the anti-reductionist taboo and reaction against biological determinism encouraged sociologists to reject "biologist" in favor of "environmentalist" explanations (Burch 1971, pp. 14-20). Further progress led to the distinction between socio-cultural and biophysical environments, but again, anti-reductionism and reaction against geographical determinism led sociologists to neglect biophysical in favor of socio-cultural environments (Klausner 1971, pp. 4-8). Thus, each time a conceptual distinction was made among potential explanations of human behavior, anti-reductionism and anti-determinism led sociology to ignore the "lower" class of variations—first biological, then physical—to focus on the "emergent" class of social variables (see Figure 1).

A second major tradition in sociology has also contributed to the discipline's tendency to ignore the physical environment. Inherited from Weber and elaborated by Mead, Cooley, Thomas and others, this tradition emphasized the importance of understanding the ways in which people define their situations if one is to explain their actions. Assuming that "the reality of a situation is in the definition attached to it by the participating actors," this perspective implied "that the physical properties of the situation may be ignored" (Choldin 1978, p. 353). This was because an actor's "definition of the situation" was assumed to be so influenced by surrounding actors as to be virtually independent of the situation's physical characteristics. Physical properties became relevant *only* if they were perceived and defined as relevant by the actors—i.e., transformed into "social facts." This "social definition" perspective therefore complemented the Durkheimian tradition in leading sociologists to ignore the physical environment.

In short, the impact of these disciplinary traditions concerning the physical environment can be summarized as follows: the Durkheimian legacy suggested that the physical environment *should be* ignored, while the Weberian legacy suggested that it *could be* ignored, for it was deemed unimportant in social life. Should one violate these traditions and suggest that the physical environment *might* be relevant for understanding human behavior or social organization, one risked being labelled an "environmental determinist." While these traditions are understandable, given sociology's quest for disciplinary autonomy in its infancy, the result is that mainstream sociologists even now use the term "environment" to mean something quite unlike what it means in most other disciplines and in public discourse. For non-sociologists, "environment" means our physical surroundings—the biosphere or a local portion of it. In contrast, within sociology the term is used quite differently to refer to social and cultural factors external to the entity being examined.[5]

The Human Exemptionalism Paradigm[6]

As a result of the socio-cultural context in which it developed and the unique traditions it evolved in its quest for disciplinary autonomy, sociology developed a largely implicit set of assumptions about the presumed irrelevance of the physical world to modern industrial societies. While seldom made explicit, this set of taken-for-granted background assumptions has influenced the way in which sociologists approach their subject matter and practice their craft. As such, they appear to represent a fundamental "paradigm," or a "lens" through which we view the world, one that appears to us to underlie the more commonly noted sociological paradigmatic cleavages— e.g., the conflict and order, or the social facts, social definition and social behavior distinctions (see, e.g., Ritzer 1975).

Thus, it is our position that the vast majority of sociologists share a common, but increasingly obsolete, "fundamental image of the subject matter" of their discipline. This shared image or paradigm can be described by a set of background assumptions which, taken together, seem to comprise a "common core of agreement" existing among sociologists (Ritzer 1975). It must be emphasized that these assumptions are so taken for granted that they are virtually never made explicit; yet, they clearly influence the practice of sociology and, we think, account for our discipline's slow recognition of the significance of environmental problems. Inherited from the Dominant Western Worldview, these assumptions are listed in Figure 2, along with a similar summary of the DWW. Taken together, they constitute a paradigm that is anthropocentric, technologically optimistic, and profoundly unecological.

The image of human societies conveyed by these assumptions is one which emphasizes the "exceptional" nature of our species stemming from our cultural heritage, including language, social organization and technology. For that reason we originally labelled them the "Human Exceptionalism Paradigm" (Catton & Dunlap 1978a, pp. 42-43). However, we did not wish to deny that *Homo sapiens* is an "exceptional species"; rather, we were denying that these exceptional characteristics "exempt" humans from ecological principles and environmental influences and constraints. For this reason we have more recently termed this set of assumptions the "Human Exemptionalism Paradigm" (or HEP).

In short, we are arguing that our discipline is premised on a set of background assumptions or paradigm that has led sociologists—regardless of their particular theoretical persuasion (functionalism, Marxism, interactionism, etc.)—to treat human societies *as if* they were exempt from ecological

	Dominant Western Worldview (DWW)	Human Exemptionalism Paradigm (HEP)	New Ecological Paradigm (NEP)
Assumptions about the nature of human beings:	DWW_1 People are fundamentally different from all other creatures on Earth, over which they have dominion.	HEP_1 Humans have a cultural heritage in addition to (and distinct from) their genetic inheritance, and thus are quite unlike all other animal species	NEP_1 While humans have exceptional characteristics (culture, technology, etc.), they remain one among many species that are interdependently involved in the global ecosystem.
Assumptions about social causation:	DWW_2 People are masters of their destiny; they can choose their goals and learn to do whatever is necessary to achieve them.	HEP_2 Social and cultural factors (including technology) are the major determinants of human affairs.	NEP_2 Human affairs are influenced not only by social and cultural factors, but also by intricate linkages of cause, effect, and feedback in the web of nature; thus purposive human actions have many unintended consequences.
Assumptions about the context of human society:	DWW_3 The world is vast, and thus provides unlimited opportunities for humans.	HEP_3 Social and cultural environments are the crucial context for human affairs, and the biophysical environment is largely irrelevant.	NEP_3 Humans live in and are dependent upon a finite biophysical environment which imposes potent physical and biological restraints on human affairs.
Assumptions about constraints on human society:	DWW_4 The history of humanity is one of progress; for every problem there is a solution, and thus progress need never cease.	HEP_4 Culture is cumulative; thus technological and social progress can continue indefinitely, making all social problems ultimately soluble.	NEP_4 Although the inventiveness of humans and the powers derived therefrom may seem for a while to extend carrying capacity limits, ecological laws cannot be repealed.

Figure 2. A comparison of major assumptions in the Dominant Western Worldview, sociology's Human Exemptionalism Paradigm, and the proposed New Ecological Paradigm

constraints. As part of their emphasis on the exceptional characteristics of humans, most sociologists have totally ignored the biophysical environment, as if human societies somehow no longer depend on it for their physical existence and for the means of pursuing the goals they value. These assumptions have predisposed sociologists to accept the optimism inherent in the DWW by naively assuming the possibility of endless growth and progress via continued scientific and technological development.

Given the grounding of our discipline in such a view of the world, it is not surprising that mainstream sociologists were slow in recognizing the significance of environmental problems nor that they continue to lag in recognition of the immense significance of global environmental change (Newby 1991).[7] This perspective, inherently anthropocentric and omniscient in the sense that it assumes that humans will be able to solve whatever problems arise, leads sociologists to seek the causes of social change solely in terms of social phenomena (factors within the realm of human influence) and blinds us to the potential constraints of environmental phenomena such as climate change. It is, we think, the primary answer to the questions posed earlier in this paper as to what accounts for the limited amount of sociological attention to environmental problems.[8]

THE EMERGENCE OF ENVIRONMENTAL SOCIOLOGY (AS VIEWED FROM THE U.S.)[9]

Because of the disciplinary traditions and assumptions just reviewed, sociologists were not in the forefront of scientific inquiry concerning environmental problems when these issues began to receive considerable attention (at least in several industrialized nations, especially the United States) in the 1960s and early 1970s. However, spurred by increased societal attention to urban decay, pollution, overpopulation, resource shortages, etc., a small number of sociologists did begin to examine environmental issues. Typically their studies were largely confined to the application of traditional sociological perspectives to such issues. There were, for example, studies of public attitudes toward environmental issues, members of environmentalist organizations, problems faced by resource management agencies and so forth. We have termed the application of sociological concepts and theories to environmental issues the "sociology of environmental issues," and have previously reviewed such work at length (Dunlap & Catton 1979b, pp. 246-49). Work on these topics, especially on environmentalism as a social movement and public opinion, continues to receive considerable attention from environmental sociologists in the U.S. (see, e.g., Buttel 1987; Dunlap & Mertig 1992) and also in Europe (Lowe & Rudig 1986; Galtung 1986; Newby 1991).

As the sociology of environmental issues began to receive more attention, some sociologists were beginning to examine a topic that went beyond the application of traditional sociological perspectives: they were examining the relationships between human societies and their physical environments (see, e.g., Burch 1971; Michelson 1970). Such inquiries, which inevitably broke disciplinary taboos, were given impetus by the 1973-74 "energy crisis" and the general societal concern with the "limits to growth." Regardless of the degree to which oil shortages had political and economic causes, the sudden scarcity of a fundamental resource whose availability had simply been taken for granted highlighted the dependence of industrialized societies on fossil fuels—and, by extension, other natural resources. Not only did this experience lead to a large amount of sociological work on energy (Rosa, Machlis & Keating 1988), but it helped some sociologists to shed the blinders imposed by the HEP and begin to think explicitly about the need for an alternative ecological perspective for studying modern industrial societies. The industrialized world's experience with the energy crisis thereby directly contributed to the emergence of a self-consciously defined specialty of "environmental sociology," defined as the "study of societal-environmental interactions" (Catton & Dunlap 1978a; Dunlap & Catton 1979a, 1979b).[10]

While many environmental sociologists focused on the potential social impacts of shortages of energy and other natural resources (Catton 1980), some paid more attention to the environmental impacts of social conditions such as economic growth (e.g., Anderson 1976). The latter thus joined the debate over the basic "causes" of environmental problems, stressing that biological ecologists such as Ehrlich (who emphasized population) and Commoner (who emphasized technology) failed to fully appreciate the role of the economy (see, in particular, Schnaiberg 1980). Regardless of whether they focused primary attention on social impacts or on environmental impacts, these sociologists were examining societal-environmental interactions (see Dunlap & Catton 1979b for a review of this work). This work gave legitimacy to the field of environmental sociology, and the field experienced considerable success in terms of institutionalizing itself within the U.S. By the mid-1970s all three of the United States' national sociological associations (American Sociological Association, Rural Sociological Society and the Society for the Study of Social Problems) had developed organizational units devoted to environmental sociology (see Dunlap & Catton 1979b, pp. 245-246).

In this enthusiastic period of growth, some environmental sociologists explicitly recognized that their concern with understanding the interrelations between society and the physical environment was, in fact, a major departure from disciplinary traditions.[11] Such recognition—stimulated by the work of Burch (1970) and other sociologists as well as by the work of biological ecologists—led the authors to argue that implicit within the emergence of environmental sociology was a rejection of the exemptionalist orientation of the larger discipline. It further led us to formulate an alternative to the HEP, termed the "New Ecological Paradigm"[12] (NEP), in an effort to stimulate additional sociological recognition of the significance of ecological conditions for modern industrial societies. The assumptions that constitute the NEP are listed in Figure 2, where they stand in stark contrast to those of the HEP (and DWW). In general, they are designed to overcome the anthropocentrism and hubris of the HEP by stressing the fact that, despite our special abilities, our species cannot evade the ecological principles that govern all biological life on Earth. In a nutshell, they represent an effort to get sociologists to shed the blinders imposed by the HEP and to adopt an "ecological" perspective on human societies and behavior.[13]

Were we at all successful in this endeavor? The answer would seem to be an obvious "no." Besides failing to convert the larger discipline to our ecological perspective (an accomplishment we did not expect to achieve), we were also unable to develop more than a superficial sense of cohesion among environmental sociologists. Not only do scholars interested in the built environment continue to have little interaction with those interested in the natural environment, but many practitioners think of their specialties as "social impact assessment," "energy," "natural hazards," "risk assessment," or "housing," rather than primarily identifying themselves as "environmental sociologists." More significantly, at least in the U.S., the field of environmental sociology experienced a major loss of momentum during the early and mid-1980s. The anti-ecological mood of the Reagan Era, coupled with the Administration's hostility toward social science, made it difficult to sustain interest in this new field. This was obvious from the decline in the number of papers presented at meetings and journal articles on environmental topics, as well as the fact that the two most widely used textbooks in the field (Humphrey & Buttel 1982 and Schnaiberg 1980) went out of print.

Buttel (1987, p. 466) has characterized this first decade or so of environmental sociology as follows:

> During the early years of the ASA Section on Environmental Sociology [formed in 1975], there was a vibrant *esprit de corps* that a new sociology was being nurtured—one that recognized the role of physical-biological factors in shaping social structures and behaviors, that was aware of the impacts of social organization and social change on the natural environment. Environmental sociologists sought nothing less than the reorientation of sociology toward a more holistic perspective that would conceptualize social processes within the context of the biosphere. . . . These lofty intentions, however, have largely failed to come to fruition. The discipline at large has handily withstood the challenges to its theoretical assumptions posed by environmental sociologists. Environmental sociology has become routinized and is now viewed—by both its practitioners and other sociologists—less as a scholarly "cause" or movement than as just another sociological specialization.

While we would not strongly contest Buttel's appraisal, we think it was a bit overly pessimistic.[14] We should note that it was written in 1986, when the situation was particularly gloomy for environmental sociology in the U.S., and just before a major upturn in societal concern about environmental problems. Problems such as toxic wastes, ozone depletion and global warming revitalized environmental concern because they pose direct threats to human health and welfare (including that of future generations) at both the local and global levels (on this upturn see Dunlap & Mertig 1992). This resurgence of societal interest in environmental problems, and a national administration (Bush's) that was at least not openly hostile to environmental concerns and research, appeared to stimulate renewed interest in environmental sociology in the U.S. by the end of the 1980s.

The Emergence of International Interest in Environmental Sociology

Ironically, while environmental sociology was losing momentum in the U.S., it seemed to have been gaining momentum in much of the rest of the world. Just as the 1980s saw the U.S. lose its position of leadership in environmental protection, so—on an obviously far less consequential scale— it also seems to have lost its leadership in environmental sociology in the last half of the 1980s. While our perceptions may be colored somewhat by lack of detailed knowledge concerning earlier developments in other nations, it appears to us that in most of Europe there was little evidence of a self-consciously defined field of environmental sociology until recent years (see, e.g., Martinelli 1989 on the situation in Italy). However, this interest appears to be growing rapidly, not only in Europe but in Japan, the Soviet Union, Australia and New Zealand as well as in the less economically developed nations. This is reflected in the recent establishment of a Working Group on "Environment and Society" within the International Sociological Association.[15] Thus, Buttel's grim assessment of the state of the field, particularly as an international concern, appears to be in need of major revision.

We have not yet formed a clear perception of the state of environmental sociology on an international level, and our observations must therefore be tentative. However, it does appear that particularly in Europe a large portion of early work on environmental issues dealt with "environmentalism" (both in terms of examining the nature and sources of public support for environmental protection as well as in analyzing environmentalist organizations [see especially Lowe & Rudig 1986]). No doubt stimulated by the emergence of the "Greens" as a political force, this work would clearly qualify as the "sociology of environmental issues" tradition. However, just as occurred in the U.S., it appears that such work has stimulated some sociologists to begin to examine the ecological condition of modern societies.

In the United Kingdom, in particular, there is evidence of considerable interest in environmental sociology, particularly its theoretical dimensions. In some instances a familiarity with environmentalist critiques of industrialism has led to a fundamental reassessment of modern societies and, more specifically, of contemporary sociology (Jones 1987). In other cases environmental problems are seen as but one of several theoretical issues prompting a reassessment of our antipathy toward "reductionism" (Benton 1991). Also contributing to the growing interest is a concern that our discipline is failing to contribute (and thereby missing funding opportunities) to an understanding of the impacts of global environmental change (Newby 1991). Not surprisingly, given the European emphasis on theoretical relative to empirical scholarship (compared to the U.S.), this work reveals a level of theoretical sophistication that has been largely absent in U.S. environmental sociology, particularly in *applying (and adapting) classical sociological theory to changing ecological conditions* (see Benton 1989 and Jones 1990 for prime examples). What is particularly notable to us is that these British scholars are almost unanimous in calling for a fundamental reorientation of our basic disciplinary assumptions about the presumed irrelevance of the biophysical environment (see Benton 1991; Dickens 1990; Jones 1987, 1990; and Newby 1991), a position that echoes our call for the replacement of the HEP with the NEP.[16]

THE FUTURE OF ENVIRONMENTAL SOCIOLOGY: MOVING TOWARD ECOLOGICAL SOCIOLOGY

A point that emerges from the foregoing is the degree to which sociological attention to environmental and ecological problems waxed and—at least temporarily in the U.S.—waned with the level of societal concern over such problems. While understandable, and probably typical of many areas of sociological study (especially social problems), this dependence on societal "definitions of the situation" ought to be reduced if our discipline is to provide insight into the increasingly problematic relations between human societies and the environment (ranging from local to global ecosystems). The growing recognition of the seriousness of human-induced "global environmental change" suggests that this may be less of a problem in the future, for it is unlikely that industrialized nations will ever again be able to divert their attention away from ecological problems to the degree that was done in the U.S. during the 1980s.

Global Environmental Change (GEC)

Over the past quarter century a seemingly endless number of environmental problems have emerged throughout the world, especially in the highly industrialized nations. New problems involving the quality of our air, water and land are continually being discovered, but several major trends stand out: (a) humans are having an increasingly negative impact on the physical environment; (b) these impacts are occurring at ever-larger geographical scales; and (c) the resulting degradation of the environment poses major threats to the health and welfare of human beings (EPA Science Advisory Board 1990). Indeed, it is widely recognized that human activities are disrupting the functioning of ecosystems to the point of possibly causing irreversible damage, not only at local levels but all the way to the global level (Silver with DeFries 1990). The consequences for our species could be profound.

Although it is true that throughout history various populations of *Homo sapiens* have modified their physical surroundings to the point that they in turn experienced negative impacts from the resultant environmental change, it is now recognized that the scope and magnitude of human-induced change have reached unprecedented levels. As Frank Press, the President of the prestigious U.S. National Academy of Sciences (NAS), stated recently:

> Human activities are transforming the global environment, and these global changes have many faces: ozone depletion, tropical deforestation, acid deposition, and increased atmospheric concentrations of gases that trap heat and may warm the global climate. For many of these troubling transformations, data and analyses are fragmentary, scientific understanding is incomplete, and long-term implications are unknown. Yet, even against a continuing background of uncertainty, it is abundantly clear that human activities now match or even surpass natural processes as agents of change in the planetary environment. (In Silver with DeFries 1990, p. iii)

In other words, our species has become so dominant in the global ecosystem that we have begun to disturb such fundamental processes as the Earth's climate, something heretofore done by natural processes such as volcano eruptions.

While the above quote calls attention to the impact of humans on the planetary environment, or the role of modern societies in creating global environmental change, the rapidly growing interest in GEC stems from realization that human-induced (or "anthropogenic") alterations of the natural environment will have significant impacts on human societies. A modest change in the Earth's temperature, for example, could have unpredictable effects on agricultural production and fisheries, and might induce major changes in energy needs and migration patterns. In the extreme, a melting of the polar ice caps could raise the oceans' levels enough to flood many coastal areas (Stern, Young & Druckman 1992). Thus, the study of global environmental change inevitably involves the examination of societal-environmental interactions, or the effects of human activities on the environment and the impacts of the resulting environmental changes on human societies. Since such interactions represent the basic subject matter of environmental sociology (see, e.g., Dunlap & Catton 1979a, 1979b; Freudenburg & Gramling 1989), widespread scientific and societal interest in GEC offers a unique opportunity for reinvigorating the field. Indeed, GEC provides an opportunity for environmental sociology to play a more central role in the larger discipline.

More generally, the growing recognition of the unprecedented scale and potentially enormous consequences of anthropocentric GEC represents an incredible opportunity, as well as challenge, to sociology and all of social science (Miller 1991).[17] Natural scientists and policy makers are quickly coming to the realization that understanding the sources of GEC inherently involves examining human behavior and societies (see Stern, Young & Druckman 1992). As the previously cited NAS report states:

> This awareness that humanity is an intrinsic part of the earth system is causing a fundamental shift in the way science is pursued. No longer is it sufficient to explore only the physical dynamics of the earth system. This effort, daunting in itself, may be dwarfed by the effort to decipher the confounding behavior of *Homo sapiens*, the planet's most powerful inhabitant. . . . So potent is the human impact on the earth system that knowledge of physical processes ruling terrestrial or atmospheric change will be incomplete until scientists better understand the human dimensions of that change. (Silver with DeFries 1990, pp. 46-47)

As avowed experts on human behavior, it clearly behooves sociologists, and other social scientists, to take up this challenge seriously and not leave study of the "human dimensions" of GEC to the natural scientists (see Newby 1991). For a good start in this direction, see Stern, Young & Druckman (1992).

The Need for an Ecological Sociology

We believe that sociology is unlikely to make significant contributions to an understanding of global (or even local, for that matter) environmental change until we shed the exemptionalist blinders inherited from our founding fathers. There is a growing awareness in the natural sciences, and in society at large, that humanity is indeed "an intrinsic part of the earth system" (see, e.g., Oates 1989). Not only is our species having an unprecedented impact on the global ecosystem, but the resultant ecological disruptions may lead to profoundly serious consequences for the quality of human (as well as non-human) life. Acknowledging this ecosystem-dependence of modern, industrial societies entails rejecting the exemptionalist assumption that modern technologies have freed us from ecological constraints, an assumption that remains prominent in mainstream sociology.

If our discipline is going to make substantial contributions to understanding the social causes and consequences of global environmental change, we must adopt a truly ecological perspective that sensitizes us to the role that our species plays in the global ecosystem. Reinvigorating environmental sociology, or the study of societal-environmental relations, is not enough: we must develop a full-blown "ecological sociology" that studies the complex interdependencies between human societies and the ecosystems (from local to global) in which we live. Such an ecological sociology will rest on the types of assumptions listed in the NEP, but will require a great deal of conceptual, theoretical and methodological retooling. It will be inherently interdisciplinary, and have to repudiate the separation from bioecology that has become conventional among contemporary sociologists who call themselves "human ecologists" but who embrace human exemptionalism as strongly as the rest of the discipline (Catton 1992).[18]

Elsewhere we have made a very modest beginning toward developing an ecological sociology by clarifying the multi-faceted nature of the relationship between *Homo sapiens* and the natural environments that we inhabit. In particular, we noted that the environment (or, more technically, ecosystems) serves three necessary and often competing functions for our species (as it does for all other species). It serves as our supply depot, our waste repository and our living space (Dunlap & Catton 1983; Catton & Dunlap 1989). In the 1970s energy shortages highlighted potential constraints in resource supplies, and the "limits to growth" debate was couched primarily in terms of the supply depot function. But since the 1980s the environment's inability to absorb the waste products of modern industrialized societies, from the local level (e.g., toxic contamination) to the global level (e.g., ozone depletion), indicates that the more salient limit may be nature's finite ability to serve as our waste repository (see, e.g., Meadows, Meadows & Randers 1992).

Furthermore, it is evident that these three functions compete with one another, and that human use of an ecosystem for one function may interfere with its ability to fulfill one or both of the others. For example, when an area is used as a waste site, whether for a garbage landfill or chemical waste dump, it becomes unattractive as living space. Likewise, should hazardous materials escape from a waste site and contaminate the soil and water, the area can no longer serve as a supply depot for healthy water or food. Finally, converting agricultural or forest land into housing subdivisions creates more living space for people, but means that the area no longer functions as a supply depot for food or lumber. At the global level, use of the Earth's atmosphere as a dumping ground for a range of pollutants (from CFCs, which destroy ozone, to CO_2, which helps trap the sun's heat to produce the "Greenhouse effect") may affect its ability to provide us with natural resources (as agricultural systems and food chains are disrupted) and make it less suitable for living space (as ozone depletion leads to an increase in dangerous ultraviolet radiation reaching the Earth).

We can no longer think of limits to growth as simply a matter of natural resource availability; rather, ecological limits refers to the full ensemble of constraints imposed upon humankind by the environment's finite ability to fulfill all three functions simultaneously.[19] Problems such as ozone depletion, acid rain and global climate change, for example, indicate that there are clearly limits to the Earth's ability to serve as our waste dump and still provide us with the living space and natural resources required for a high quality of life. At a minimum, an ecological sociology must acknowledge this fundamental ecosystem-dependence of human life, and reject the exemptionalist notion that our species (unique though it may be) has freed itself from the constraints of nature.

CONCLUSION

Our discipline was slow in reacting to mounting evidence of the seriousness of environmental problems, in part because our disciplinary traditions suggested that the physical environment was unimportant, but the field of environmental sociology eventually emerged in North America in the late 1970s. Although the field lost momentum in the U.S. during the Reagan Era, it was simultaneously attracting adherents in numerous other nations and has recently been stimulated both in the U.S. and internationally by interest in global environmental change. The recognition of GEC, including its human origins and especially its potential impacts on society, clearly challenges the human exemptionalist orientation of mainstream sociology, and suggests the need for a full-blown ecological sociology. While many environmental sociologists will likely join in this endeavor, the enormity of developing an understanding of the "human dimensions of global environmental change" calls for more widespread sociological involvement. The challenge posed to our discipline by GEC is great, but the cost of ignoring it is even greater.

Notes

[1]The rest of this section draws heavily from Catton and Dunlap (1980) and Dunlap and Catton (1983), both of which contain more extensive citations.

[2]These assumptions appear to be shared by all of the social sciences (see Dunlap 1980), and are particularly obvious in social science perspectives on "modernization" (Orr 1979).

[3]This section draws heavily on Dunlap and Catton (1983, pp. 116-18).

[4]Following Lewthwaite (1966, p. 22), we think "determinism" should be applied only in instances where a *single* factor is purported to be the primary factor influencing human affairs. It does not seem deterministic to us to assert that people's biological characteristics or their physical surroundings may have *some* influence on their behavior.

[5]Given our discipline's resistance to any but socio-cultural explanations for social phenomena (Benton 1991), it is surprising that we are not charged more frequently with being guilty of socio-cultural determinism.

[6]This section draws heavily from Catton and Dunlap (1980, pp. 23-26).

[7]A good indication of the strength of the HEP in blinding sociologists to environmental problems is the fact that from 1970 to 1990 not a single article explicitly analyzing these problems appeared in either the *American Sociological Review* or the *American Journal of Sociology*. An outsider relying upon mainstream sociology journals for information about the world would have little reason to suspect that environmental problems have become significant social issues over the past two decades.

[8]Recently several other sociologists have come to similar conclusions (see, e.g., Benton 1991; Dickens 1990; Newby 1991).

[9]This section is based primarily on the United States, given the authors' limited knowledge of situations in other nations.

[10]It should be noted, however, that environmental sociologists concerned with the "built" environment had already clearly begun to study societal-environmental interactions (see, e.g., Michelson 1970). For a discussion of the "built-natural" cleavage within environmental sociology, see Dunlap and Catton (1983).

[11]There were, of course, a few pioneering sociologists who had called attention to the importance of environmental conditions before environmental quality became a major societal concern, but seldom with any discernible impact (see the brief review in Dunlap & Catton 1979b, p. 245 and the extensive review of early sociological work on natural resources, primarily by rural sociologists, in Field & Burch 1988).

[12]We originally labelled it the "New *Environmental* Paradigm" (Catton & Dunlap 1978a), but quickly substituted "ecological" for environmental (Dunlap & Catton 1979b).

[13]Ironically, our argument was criticized by Buttel (1978), who acknowledged the reality of the HEP/NEP cleavage but argued that it paled in comparison to traditional theoretical cleavages within our field (such as the conflict-order cleavage) and also criticized it for being so abstract as to have no theoretical implications (Buttel 1987). Our responses (Catton & Dunlap 1978b, 1980) noted that we did not intend to dismiss the reality of traditional theoretical cleavages, but reasserted the importance of the HEP/NEP distinction. We also pointed out that part of the debate stemmed from Buttel's usage of a much narrower conception of "paradigm" than we were using. While there was merit in Buttel's criticism, as we benefitted from it (Catton & Dunlap 1980), we must note that elsewhere he has found it useful to employ the HEP/NEP distinction (see Humphrey & Buttel 1982).

[14]For a somewhat less pessimistic appraisal, but one focused much more narrowly on our work, see Freudenburg and Gramling (1989).

[15]In 1992, the ISA group achieved "research committee" status by merging with the already existing Research Committee on Social Ecology (RC 24). The resultant group is now the Research Committee on Environment and Society, and both its membership and leadership include more environmental sociologists than sociological human ecologists (the traditional membership base of RC 24).

[16]In contrast, Yearley (1991) analyzes environmental problems via mainstream disciplinary perspectives such as social problems' and social movements' theory and the sociology of science, and does not suggest the

need for paradigmatic change. His analyses nicely reveal the insights yielded by the "sociology of environmental issues."

[17]It should be noted that Miller (1991) does not see paradigmatic revision within the social sciences as necessary for contributing to an understanding of GEC. For a sharply divergent view, one that is critical of the efforts that "mainstream" social science has thus far launched in the study of GEC, see Orr (1992).

[18]We have previously (Dunlap & Catton 1979a, 1983) described in some detail how most sociological human ecologists share the larger discipline's exemptionalist orientation and have shown little interest in environmental problems. Thus, our plea for an ecological sociology should not be interpreted as a call for greater use of what currently passes for "human ecology" within our discipline.

[19]There is a tendency to think of "natural resources" as materials that can be harvested or harnessed for human use, such as oil, lumber, water and various metals. We are now recognizing that less obvious factors, such as clean air and predictable climate, are also natural resources. Indeed, all of the basic functions that the environment serves for humans represent natural resources. While technology has thus far helped us cope with shortages of specific materials, it is less likely that it will enable us to restore the natural cycles that cleanse our air and water and regulate the planet's climate.

References

Anderson, Charles H. 1976. *The Sociology of Survival: Social Problems of Growth.* Homewood, Ill.: Dorsey Press.

Benton, Ted. 1989. "Marxism and Natural Limits: An Ecological Critique and Reconstruction." *New Left Review* 178:51-86.

Benton, Ted. 1991. "Biology and Social Science: Why the Return of the Repressed Should Be Given a (Cautious) Welcome." *Sociology* 25:1-29.

Burch, William R., Jr. 1970. "Resources and Social Structure: Some Conditions of Stability and Change." *Annals of the American Academy of Political and Social Science* 389:27-34.

Burch, William R., Jr. 1971. *Daydreams and Nightmares: A Sociological Essay on the American Environment.* New York: Harper & Row.

Buttel, Frederick H. 1978. "Environmental Sociology: A New Paradigm?" *The American Sociologist* 13:252-56.

Buttel, Frederick H. 1987. "New Directions in Environmental Sociology." *Annual Review of Sociology* 13:465-88.

Catton, William R., Jr. 1980. *Overshoot: The Ecological Basis of Revolutionary Change.* Urbana: University of Illinois Press.

Catton, William R., Jr. 1992. "Separation Versus Unification in Sociological Human Ecology." Pp. 65-99 in *Advances in Human Ecology*, Vol. 1, edited by Lee Freese. Greenwich, Conn.: JAI Press.

Catton, William R., Jr. and Riley E. Dunlap. 1978a. "Environmental Sociology: A New Paradigm." *The American Sociologist* 13:41-49.

Catton, William R., Jr. and Riley E. Dunlap. 1978b. "Paradigms, Theories, and the Primacy of the HEP-NEP Distinction." *The American Sociologist* 13:256-59.

Catton, William R., Jr. and Riley E. Dunlap. 1980. "A New Ecological Paradigm for Post-Exuberant Sociology." *American Behavioral Scientist* 24:15-47.

Catton, William R., Jr. and Riley E. Dunlap. 1989. "Competing Functions of the Environment: Living Space, Supply Depot, and Waste Repository." Paper presented at the Conference on Environmental Constraints and Opportunities in the Social Organization of Space, University of Udine, Italy, June.

Choldin, Harvey M. 1978. "Social Life and the Physical Environment." Pp. 91-113 in *Handbook of Contemporary Urban Life*, edited by David

Street. San Francisco: Jossey-Bass.

Crosby, Alfred W. 1986. *Ecological Imperialism: The Biological Expansion of Europe, 900-1900.* New York: Cambridge University Press.

Dickens, Peter. 1990. "Science, Social Science and Environmental Issues." Paper presented to the British Association for the Advancement of Science, University of Swansea, August.

Dunlap, Riley E. 1980. "Paradigmatic Change in Social Science: From Human Exemptionalism to an Ecological Paradigm." *American Behavioral Scientist* 24:5-14.

Dunlap, Riley E. and William R. Catton, Jr. 1979a. "Environmental Sociology: A Framework for Analysis." Pp. 57-85 in *Progress in Resource Management and Environmental Planning*, Vol. 1, edited by Timothy O'Riordan and Ralph C. d'Arge. Chichester, England: John Wiley & Sons.

Dunlap, Riley E. and William R. Catton, Jr. 1979b. "Environmental Sociology." *Annual Review of Sociology* 5:243-73.

Dunlap, Riley E. and William R. Catton, Jr. 1983. "What Environmental Sociologists Have in Common (Whether Concerned with 'Built' or 'Natural' Environments)." *Sociological Inquiry* 53:113-35.

Dunlap, Riley E. and Angela G. Mertig, eds. 1992. *American Environmentalism: The U.S. Environmental Movement, 1970-1990.* Washington, D.C.: Taylor and Francis.

Durkheim, Emile. 1950. *The Rules of the Sociological Method*, 8th ed. New York: Free Press.

EPA Science Advisory Board. 1990. *Reducing Risk: Setting Priorities and Strategies for Environmental Protection.* Washington, D.C.: U.S. Environmental Protection Agency.

Field, Ronald R. and William R. Burch, Jr. 1988. *Rural Sociology and the Environment.* Westport, Conn.: Greenwood Press.

Franck, Karen A. 1984. "Exorcising the Ghost of Physical Determinism." *Environment and Behavior* 16:411-35.

Freudenburg, William R. and Robert Gramling. 1989. "The Emergence of Environmental Sociology." *Sociological Inquiry* 59:439-52.

Galtung, Johan. 1986. "The Green Movement: A Socio-Historical Exploration." *International Sociology* 1:75-90.

Humphrey, Craig R. and Frederick H. Buttel. 1982. *Environment, Energy, and Society.* Belmont, Calif.: Wadsworth.

Jones, Alwyn. 1987. "The Violence of Materialism in Advanced Industrial Society: An Eco-sociological Approach." *The Sociological Review* 35:19-47.

Jones, Alwyn. 1990. "Social Symbiosis: A Gaian Critique of Contemporary Social Theory." *The Ecologist* 20:108-13.

Klausner, Samuel Z. 1971. *On Man in His Environment.* San Francisco: Jossey-Bass.

Lewthwaite, Gordon R. 1966. "Environmentalism and Determinism: A Search for Clarification." *Annals of the Association of American Geographers* 56:1-23.

Lowe, Philip D. and Wolfgang Rudig. 1986. "Political Ecology and the Social Sciences—The State of the Art." *British Journal of Political Science* 16:513-50.

Martinelli, Franco, ed. 1989. *I Sociologi E L'Ambiente.* Rome: Bulzoni.

Meadows, Donella H., Dennis L. Meadows and Jorgen Randers. 1992. *Beyond the Limits.* New York: Chelsea Green.

Michelson, William H. 1970. *Man and His Urban Environment.* Reading, Mass.: Addison-Wesley.

Miller, Roberta Balstad. 1991. "Social Science and the Challenge of Global Environmental Change." *International Social Science Journal* 130: 609-17.

Newby, Howard. 1991. "One World, Two Cultures: Sociology and the Environment." *Network (Newsletter of the British Sociological Association)* 50(May):1-8.

Oates, David. 1989. *Earth Rising: Ecological Belief in an Age of Science.* Corvallis: Oregon State University.

Orr, David W. 1979. "Modernization and the Ecological Perspective." Pp. 75-89 in *The Global Predicament,* edited by David W. Orr and Marvin S. Soroos. Chapel Hill: University of North Carolina Press.

Orr, David W. 1992. *Ecological Literacy: Education and the Transition to a Postmodern World.* Albany: State University of New York Press.

Ritzer, George. 1975. *Sociology: A Multiple Paradigm Science.* Boston: Allyn & Bacon.

Rosa, Eugene A., Gary E. Machlis and Kenneth M. Keating. 1988. "Energy and Society." *Annual Review of Sociology* 14:149-72.

Schnaiberg, Allan. 1980. *The Environment: From Surplus to Scarcity.* New York: Oxford University Press.

Silver, Cheryl Simon with Ruth S. DeFries. 1990. *One Earth/One Future: Our Changing Global Environment.* Washington, D.C.: National Academy Press.

Stern, Paul C., Oran R. Young and Daniel Druckman, eds. 1992. *Global Environmental Change: Understanding the Human Dimensions.* Washington, D.C.: National Academy Press.

Yearley, Steven. 1991. *The Green Case: A Sociology of Environmental Issues, Arguments and Politics.* London: Harper-Collins.

Chapter 3

SOCIOLOGY AND THE REALITY OF THE PRESS ON ENVIRONMENTAL RESOURCES

Edgar F. Borgatta

University of Washington, Seattle

In the post World War II period there has been a growing concern with issues associated with a modern version of the Malthusian formulation. The Malthusian formulation was relatively simple. It emphasized the fact that reproduction of humans could outrun the ability to increase food production, creating a situation of food scarcity and dire consequences. The proponents of such a view and the nay-sayers have elaborated the formulation, pointing to the fact that neither human reproduction nor food production are simple variables, and that both are within bounds subject to human control. The amount of cultivable land and other bases for food resources are limited in the world, and forces such as weather and its consequences can influence food production and produce both abundance and prosperity but also disasters. At the same time, the human factor in the production process has become of enormous consequence through agricultural and related technology. And, obviously the resources that are used in the industrial technologies and the consumption patterns associated with the products are also of enormous consequence.

The modernization of the Malthusian formulation has introduced the fact that there are other resources that may potentially be as important as food, including such obvious examples as fresh potable water, energy resources, non-toxic air, and even viable life-sustaining temperatures.

An additional aspect has been added to the Malthusian formulation in the more modern approaches to conservation. That is, the issue of ability to support human life on the planet must be modified from a naive notion that the focus is on how many can exist, literally, to a question of how many can exist with a desirable level of living. In addition, planning must include leaving room for a margin of error and for reserves both for the existing population and future generations.

WHAT ARE THE PRESSURES ON THE RESOURCES?

Any discussion of the pressures on world resources and the consequences for quality of life in the world have to be considered with some historical and situational perspectives.

A United Nations Population Fund publication (*Seattle Times*, May 13, 1991) reported the world's population at 5.4 billion persons, and indicated that "Instead of a stable total of 10.2 billion in 2085, the world may well reach 10 billion by about 2050, and significant growth will continue for another hundred years after that." World population projections, of course, depend on the assumptions that are made about fertility and mortality, and these can vary substantially. Projections with regard to future population growth are a bit like weather forecasting, and we have many humbling experiences of error in the past, especially when the projections are into the distant future. By way of example, however, it is appropriate to note that during the depression of the 1930s in the United States, prognosticators suggested a permanent trend to a stable or even declining population. The post-World War II baby boom, of course, suggested that such prognostications could be fallible.

Because of the unpredictability of the underlying conditions, projections are commonly made with low, medium, and high assumptions, with the middle presumably the most reasonable and viable assumptions.

The projections reported above were not surprising, and in another context, I computed projections using other United Nations data which involved more detail, and came up with the following scenario. The data are based on a publication of the United Nations (1985). To provide a basis for perspective, in 1960 the total world population was estimated to be about three billion persons. The recent estimate noted above for 1991 was for a population of about five and a half billion persons. For the year 2000 the estimated population is about six billion persons, so the doubling of the population since 1960 will have taken about forty years. By the year 2025 it is projected that the world population will exceed eight billion persons, suggesting a somewhat slower rate than the immediate past. This is an increase in population of about a third in the 25-year period, so the assumptions that underlie these projections are inclined to be optimistic about fertility control (i.e., expect fertility rates to decline), or are allowing for substantially high death rates. That the latter is not the case is clear from the fact that the projected life expectancy for the less developed regions in the year 2025 is sixty-nine years of age, which incidentally was about the life expectancy in the more developed regions in 1960. Examining the projections for the more developed regions, it is seen that the increase from 1960 to 2025 was about by half, while the increase of the less developed regions was by three and a half times, or almost doubling twice. By simple extension, with the less developed regions having about the same life expectancy in 2025 as the more developed regions did in 1960, in the subsequent half-century or so the expected increase of the world population would be to about eleven or twelve billion.

It is not useful to argue about whether the projections are high or low for the year 2025 or 2050 because it is clear that major increases in population will happen, and accuracy within one or two billion people more or less is not the issue. Given current world conditions, it is not conceivable that the population increases will not accelerate the pressure on the environment. The more obvious implications are seen in the following question: If the life expectancy in the less developed regions in the year 2025 is the same as it was for the more developed regions in 1960, will the less developed regions also be at the same stage of consumption of resources in 2025 as the more developed regions were in 1960?

WILL THE POPULATION INCREASE PROJECTED ACTUALLY OCCUR?

In the Malthusian tradition, one can ask if there will be interventions that will occur to forestall the population increase projected. It is possible, but the real alternatives do not appear to be attractive. For example, world war and massive use of nuclear weapons could intervene to bring about a radical change, possibly even eliminating all human life, but in fact if such warfare should develop it is unlikely to involve the less developed regions where most of the population increase is expected to occur. Only with the most catastrophic scenario for such a war would the projection of world population growth be substantially attenuated. It is with some relief, however, that chroniclers of current history tell us that while there are small wars going on in many places in the world, the threat of a super war by super powers has receded, so that possibly this alternative should have lesser attention.

It is possible that some other "natural" disaster could intervene. For example, the 7th International AIDS Conference of 1991 in Florence, Italy brought out the fact that the spread of the AIDS disease has accelerated greatly in less developed regions, and in the absence of major investments of medical and other resources, the diffusion will continue. However, even such a scourge as AIDS and the worst case scenario would only slightly attenuate the projected increase in population in the less developed regions.

It is said that at the first World Food Conference after WW II the cynical conclusion was voiced that the more developed regions would simply have to proceed as they have, and the less developed regions would have to go on their own, presumably on to disaster. The presence of famines and disasters in less developed areas where there has already been growth of populations, places such as the arid regions of Africa and in Bangladesh, provide hints of the types of situations the cynics anticipate for the less developed regions. A very recent example of the kind of recurring pattern for the less developed regions is the report on the U.N. Africa recovery program, which the Secretary General Javier Perez de Cuellar called a failure, with the economic crisis of Africa deepening in the five-year period, and: "The average African continued to get poorer and to suffer persistent fall in an already meager standard of living" (Seattle Times, August 28, 1991). Interestingly, Perez de Cuellar's suggested remedies emphasized external canceling of the massive African debts and infusion of funds for technical development, but totally ignored population increase, education, and other issues.

From the point of view of most of the world, there is no reason to anticipate that radical changes will occur so that the less developed areas will reduce fertility and bring population growth under control. There is the example of China which is often noted as the example of a nation taking its destiny into its own hands with regard to fertility control. The one child per family policy appears to have been effectively instituted in many areas, but revisions of appraisals of both the effectiveness of the policy and the consequences in population growth have become conservative, acknowledging the difficulty of implementing the policy generally, particularly in the rural and less centrally controlled areas. However, it must be noted that the example of China is one of an enormous nation with a highly centralized government in which education and expectations of behavior were diffused and imposed in a way that is not possible in many parts of the world.

DOES THE TECHNICAL BASIS FOR FERTILITY CONTROL EXIST?

From the point of view of fertility control, some have noted that the knowledge necessary to reduce fertility performance has long existed and has been effectively utilized at various times and places. Abstinence, of course, has always been a possibility, but more realistic and practical methods of control, including coitus interruptus, sponges, douches, etc., have been known and used, and the more hygienic modern devices and chemical/biological controls have been advances for an endeavor that has been of more than casual concern in history. However, it must be noted that in this history much of the initiative had to come from interested parties at the individual level, and impact in changes of trends in fertility has largely been a matter of changing culture and expectations. The question of culture change, obviously, is a major consideration that must be addressed.

Thus, while it can be acknowledged that if individual motivations and the available knowledge base and resources are there, fertility control can be effectively carried out. Until recently dissemination of fertility control in less developed regions has required education and procedures that have been seen as a barrier to easy acceptance, aside from the more general cost and the cultural issues. This is seen as a problem even within the more developed regions, where lack of education and motivation within some segments of society is considered to result in unwanted pregnancies and difficult personal situations. Thus, at this point in time effective fertility control programs depend on the ability to motivate people who themselves need to develop reasons why they may wish to limit fertility, rather than having to teach them how to achieve fertility control by devices, procedures, or pills, or surgical procedures such as tube-tying or vasectomies.

The newer long-term contraceptives, such as NORPLANT®, require a very minor surgical procedure to properly install and can be administered broadly. Estimates of the "cost" of such a procedure when available on a massive scale are low, possibly as little as five or ten U.S. dollars per person, and the effective period is usually reported as four years. Without going through a scenario of how such contraceptives could be dispensed, if it were used by one billion women, the total cost would be in the range of five to ten billion dollars. In United States terms, we are talking about two to five percent of the U.S. military budget for one year in comparison to the cost for a period covering four years of contraception for a billion women. Even if the estimate were wildly wrong, and the usual political and bureaucratic inefficiencies made the cost five times the five dollars per unit, we are talking about less than the U.S. annual military budget for four years of contraception for a billion women. The technology is now available and the cost factor in this modern world is truly a trivial matter. Of course, if there is failure in contraceptive procedures, aborting unwanted pregnancies is no longer the medical problem it was in the past. The development of the abortion pill, RU 486®, which is now getting more general acceptance in the modern world, provides an additional option for terminating unwanted pregnancies, with a "cost" that is also in the five dollar per person or trivial range.

To answer the question with which this section began, from a technological point of view (and not considering the cultural, religious, and political barriers), effective birth control is available for the world at a trivial cost considering the current gross national product of any large modern nation. So, technology and cost cannot be the issues in looking at the world projections on population and noting that the increases to levels like ten or twelve billion people may create situations that press on the environmental resources of the world. Thus, clearly the issues that are involved are cultural in the broad sense, and this will be discussed.

HOW DOES POPULATION INCREASE
PRESS ON ENVIRONMENTAL RESOURCES?

One of the common responses to the concern that environmental resources may be coming into short supply is that many resources are as yet untapped. While this may be true, it does not contradict the argument that more resources are used when there are more people, and that existing resources can quickly reach a condition of overuse. There are myriad examples of how this may happen, and here we will mention only a few.

With regard to sanitation, for example, in early times in the United States it was not uncommon for a household to be established near a stream, and to use the stream as a source of running fresh water from upstream, and then to use the stream, downstream, to carry away sewage. As soon as another household is established on the stream near the first household, the stream begins to become limited as a resource. One household does not want the sewage of another above it in its fresh water from upstream. Alternatives of privies may come into use, but eventually privies start to press on the availability of fresh water, etc. What can be done to preserve the fresh water supply in any case may involve innovations and introduction of procedures that have different levels of efficiency, and different consequences. However, the limitations of fresh water supplies are not trivial and difficult situations already exist in many parts of the world.

SITUATIONS IN MORE DEVELOPED REGIONS

The focus will be on an external description of conditions. The question of availability of fresh water arises in many guises, the most obvious of which is the occurrence of droughts. Droughts do not occur only in less developed regions, and in a place often thought of in terms of economic opulence, such as the state of California in the United States, maintenance of a consistent sufficient source of fresh water has been considered a serious problem. All things are relative, however, and there fresh water for personal use represents only a small percentage of total use, agriculture and industry taking the major share. Still, by the standards of that area, water shortages are envisioned and rationing that the population has considered limiting has occurred. Shortages of water are seen to limit persons' lovely green lawns and gardens, the swimming pools, the long showers, etc. On the agricultural side the growing of the rich crops for which California is known is threatened, and on the industrial side expansion is seen as limited. So, even in a place known for its riches some limits are noted, and as the population of California increases (largely by immigration) the problem is viewed as potentially severe.

But California is also known to have other problems of an environmental nature, with air pollution of many areas. Los Angeles and surrounding areas are a major concern. The air pollution is caused in large part by automobile emissions, and California probably has the highest standards of technical control on automobile emissions in the world. However, there is no control of use or ownership of automobiles, so the concentration of users creates the concentration of pollution even with standards of automobile technology that many feel are demanding.

To continue the story in lands of riches like California, waste disposal has become a massive concern in general, with special problems. Where is the waste to go from major urban centers if there is to be limitation of dumping into the oceans and into land fills, and if incinerators are banned because they create air pollution? A recent news story (*Seattle Times*, July 15, 1991) reports that the "clean-up" of accumulated dump sites associated with military installations in the state of Washington alone will cost as much as 200 billion dollars, suggesting that nationwide a concept of merely cleaning up the dump sites of the military will involve trillions of dollars, without even considering the industrial and urban dump sites.

What is noted so far is only the tip of the iceberg with regard to actual and potential environmental problems in the United States. The aquifer that has supplied so much of the underground water for the western plains down to Texas is rapidly depleting. The Great Lakes have been long-time dumping locations for industrial and other waste materials, and only after many years of investment in controls is Lake Erie no longer thought of as permanently a "dead" lake. Further, disasters occur in many forms, including besides droughts the opposite situation, too much water too fast, leading to broad regional floods such as the extraordinary case for the summer of 1993 in the midwest of the United States. The point is that the United States, rich and developed as it is, encounters problems of limits of environmental resources in a multitude of ways. But what is true in the United States is no less true in other developed regions.

Industrialization all over the world has been accompanied by the production of waste materials that have cumulatively created vast pollution problems. The sources of fresh drinking water in many locations, especially in some of the east European nations, are said to be threatened and currently of very dubious quality. And, patterns of consumption creating pollution appear to continue to increase much faster than controls on maintaining necessary resources such as breathable air and potable water. The rise of the large cities with democratization of consumption patterns involving the automobile is the obvious example. In nations like Japan and Germany the per capita ratio of private automobiles is over 0.4, and in the United States the ratio is over 0.55! For these three nations one has to think in terms of yearly consumption of hundreds of billions of gallons of fuel and output of billions of tons of waste including carbon dioxide. (*Seattle Times*, November

13, 1990, estimates yearly over 200 billion gallons and over 6 billion tons.)

The values associated with increased production of consumption goods and the consequences on the environment require more intensive study in modern societies. There are both rational and emotional bases for values, and sorting these out is a task for which the sociologist should be particularly qualified. The task is not easy, as can be illustrated by a simple example. Suppose an area is increasing in productive capacity and corresponding labor force needs, and so there is a determination that is generally accepted that more electric power will need to be generated for the area. There will be proponents and opponents to any proposed solution, to nuclear power, to coal- or oil-fired power plants, and to new hydroelectric plants. Some will oppose all new investments in power production, suggesting the development go elsewhere or that the problem be solved by more efficient use and conservation. At another level, for example, the issue of hydroelectric power may involve confrontation between preservationists and conservationists, the former insisting that the "natural" environment should not be disturbed, and the latter suggesting that in addition to hydroelectric power, a new dam will create a great new lake and all its resources. The sociologist presumably can focus on identification of the competing values and relate these to the consequences both in terms of short- and long-term environmental objectives, but also in terms of broad social and cultural objectives and expectations.

What needs to be noted here is often neglected in the concerns with the press on environmental resources. The press increases because of increasing population, but it also increases by changes in the rates of consumption. Population growth in the developed areas on a per unit basis is much more significant from the point of view of consumption of energy and other resources than in less developed areas. So, there are current thrusts of pressure on environmental resources, and then there are those that will be generated as development proceeds in the less developed areas.

SITUATIONS IN THE LESS DEVELOPED REGIONS

Attention often focuses on less developed regions because of the disasters that occur, which are frequently seen as results of natural phenomena such as droughts, floods, and similar causes of human devastation, sometimes accelerated in consequences by the social and political circumstances. The recent history of Somalia is a highly publicized example which has attracted the intervention of the United Nations and other political entities. And, of course, governments and groups in more developed regions may also express concern with the less developed regions as resources for maintaining the wildlife, the rain forests, and other settings are depleted.

Dealing with issues of the press on environment in the less developed regions also implies the need for considering the perspectives taken. If

India, with one-sixth of the population of the world, uses about three percent of the energy resources, with what orientation should it consider problems of environmental resources in dealing with nations from the more developed regions? And, of course, the nations from the more developed regions do not approach some of these issues without moral constraints. For example, the United States policy on providing assistance to nations during the Reagan and Bush periods prohibited providing contraceptive assistance in foreign aid programs.

What can be said in general is that whether the more or the less developed regions are considered, there is no technical reason why the press on the environmental resources must continue to increase due to population increases. It is also abundantly clear that the press will increase unless there are major policy shifts in much of the world.

SOCIOLOGY AND THE PRESS ON ENVIRONMENTAL RESOURCES

There is an apparent consensus that there needs to be more attention in the world to the conservation of the ecological resources. This has become defined quite generally as a social problem of major importance, and thus it is an area to which sociologists should attend. Sociologists are particularly well qualified to study values and social behavior and its consequences on environmental resources. Two directions can be identified that are of particular importance. One is in the analysis of values and value systems in societies and in a broader world perspective. On this score there are myriad questions that can be examined. Obviously, values seen as desirable by persons concerned with maintaining a viable environment in the future are not shared or are not given the same priorities by others, and indeed by entire cultures and even by major religious orientations. At what level and how do these values conflict with the presumed values of maintaining the environment? More to the point, how should sociologists present the facts of their analyses? Looking back historically, it appears that sociologists have largely avoided making statements that could offend or embarrass governments, religions, or particular groups.

The second is in modeling social structures to examine the consequences of implementing values within societies given alternative ordering of priorities of values. Sociologists have, in general, taken their task in dealing with social problems as passive objective observers, evaluating the consequences of given policies. Given statements of priorities of values, sociologists should be moving in the direction of making their science useful by suggesting the alternatives that will accomplish the objectives, even when these conflict with politically convenient solutions proposed. In this sense, sociologists should become proactive in their approach to social problems.

E. Borgatta

Reference

United Nations. 1985. *Periodical on Aging*, Vol. 1, No. 1, 1984. New York: United Nations.

Chapter 4

ECOLOGY AND THE QUALITY OF SOCIAL LIFE

Paolo Ammassari

University of Rome

THE QUALITY OF LIFE

When, at the beginning of the Sixties, the expression "quality of life" made its appearance, it stood for a critical view of aimless economic growth and of ever-increasing material well-being. In this sense it was used, for the first time, by J. K. Galbraith in his 1963 speech to the *American Association for the Advancement of Science*. It soon became the antonym of high level of living, based on the consumption and disposal of material goods. The expression became the banner of the groups who questioned the affluent society and it spread out of the academic community into intellectual settings. The crucial image was Los Angeles, with its very high standard of material life and its ideology of job success, while scarcely livable because of physical pollution and deterioration of social life.

And yet, within a few years, thanks to the intense empirical social indicators research, the term quality of life was divested of its original meaning and it ended up overlapping with terms like level of living, way of life, conditions of life (Szalai 1980, p. 9). In the effort to operationalize the concept in terms of quantifiable indicators, quality of life was subsumed under the concept of life-satisfaction and considered one of its dimensions. Nobody considered it paradoxical that some of the indicators used to compare quality of life across countries included now per capita GNP, private cars per population, TV sets per population, measured not as negative indexes, but on the contrary as positive indicators of a high quality of life (Scheer 1980, pp. 151-55). The measurement of the quality of life was obviously not paralleled by an adequate conceptualization. Some sociologists tried to distinguish a collective from an individual life-quality by means of objective and subjective indicators, the latter anchored to material as well as psychological needs and wants. In some cases, the levels of satisfaction with distribution of goods and services referred also to cleanness of water and air and pointed to a global well-being of the individual and of society in terms of a very wide spectrum of conditions of life, which included, among other aspects, life-satisfaction as experienced by the individuals themselves (Solomon et al. 1980, pp. 228-32). Nonetheless, it is hardly understandable that some researchers used work-satisfaction items, in terms of work chances and success, forgetting the old anti-work ethic debate.

Yet, some sociologists, referring to its original meaning, have begun to recognize the evaluative aspects of the concept of quality of life. The concept itself has been recognized as culture-bound and understandable only in terms of cultural values. Recently, the concept of quality of life regained its value dimension, although unfortunately only with reference to aspects that are merely desirable or undesirable. Indeed, very few scholars seem able to understand the intrinsic prescriptive nature of the concept, which stems from its moral roots. In fact, the quality of life has been one of the few value-laden concepts admitted within sociological theorizing and research. Moreover, in comparison with other value-laden concepts such as progress, civilization and the like, the concept of quality of life is more ethically pregnant. In fact, it is not only evaluative in character like those concepts, but it is also prescriptive of an intrinsically good state of affairs. Such a value-laden concept could not but be resisted by sociologists of different varieties (from positivists to Weberians, from Durkheimians to Paretians). The reduction of the concept of quality of life to a mere dimension of a social indicators system of material and psychological well-being was, for the discipline, a necessary operation in order to divest the concept of its value-content.

The proposal of the new concept of quality of *social* life" for the scientific attention and sociological discussion by the Program Committee of this 30th Congress of the IIS represents, in my opinion, an opportunity to reconsider the entire issue of "quality of life." Indeed, particularly with reference to its original meaning, the "life" with quality sought by those who questioned the affluent and mass-consumer society was, above all, a *social* life.

Now, it is my opinion that an acceptable, or better, a desirable, *social life* means essentially nothing else but good *social relationships*. In other words, from my point of view, social life is made of social relationships and the quality of the former depends on the quality of the latter. But when is a social relationship of "quality"? To answer this question, let me introduce some concepts and distinctions.

THE MORAL AND ETHICAL DIMENSIONS OF SOCIAL RELATIONSHIPS

For the last decade, I have repeatedly brought to the attention of my Italian colleagues the necessity, in analyzing social relationships, to take into consideration a fundamental distinction between two kinds of cognition.

That is, the distinction between knowledge-of-acquaintance and knowledge-about; in the Italian language, between *sapere* and *conoscenza*, in French, *savoir* and *connaissance*, in German, *wissen* and *erkennen*. The distinction was already introduced in 1720 by an Italian philosopher whom I consider the first sociologist ever, Giovanni Battista Vico. The distinction between two kinds of cognition is now incorporated not only into philosophical thinking but it is also part of common sense. Knowledge-of-acquaintance is knowledge by direct experience; it is mostly produced "out-of-awareness" and bears on intuition and imagination; it is subjective and, for a large part, not communicable. When communicated, it relies on the contextual meaning of social relationship. On the other side, knowledge-about is generally linguistically coded, reasoned elaboration of experiences, denotative in its nature. Therefore, it is inter-subjective, mostly conventional, more social and predominantly societal in character.

Now, it seems important to introduce another, although connected, distinction in regard to the fundamental nature of social relationships. That is, the distinction between two kinds of normative facets: the moral and the ethical dimensions. From a structural point of view, these normative dimensions grow out of the cognitive ones. In fact, knowledge-of-acquaintance is a cognition which implies feeling, preferring and evaluating. Also, knowledge-about often mingles together facts and evaluations (Putnam 1981, Ch. 9). However, the two major aspects of social relationships, that is, the cognitive and the normative, are largely autonomous. The distinction between cognitive and normative dimensions of social relationships is, in a certain sense, similar to the distinction between "knowledge" and "virtue" made by the Japanese philosopher Yukichi Fukuzawa ([1875] 1973, Ch. 6). However, his further distinction between private and public virtues is of a different nature with respect to the distinction between moral and ethical normative dimensions, which I am here proposing.

This latter distinction is based on the different types of obligation that the person takes up in the course of a social relationship. The terminology of "moral" versus "ethic" is taken from Hegel ([1820] 1968-74, par. 106 and ff.), who meant the former as being self-oriented and subjective, while the latter as being collectivity-oriented and definitely social in character. Morality is an inner-disposition; ethics refers to socio-cultural standards of conduct. Let me stress right away that the distinction between moral and ethical dimensions of the normative pattern of social relationship is more fundamental than any other. It is neither overlapping with Toennies's distinction between "community" and "societal" relationships nor with Durkheim's distinction between "mechanic" and "organic" solidarity. Like the two cognitive dimensions of knowledge-by-acquaintance and knowledge-about, moral versus ethical obligations are much more basic than any types of solidarity in social relationships. These types of obligations are deeply rooted in the fundamental experiences of the person and they concur, although in a different manner, to build up his sense of identity as a person.

Moral obligations lie in the innermost core of a person's make-up. They are neither communicable nor articulated in rules or norms. They are not necessarily rooted in human biology, although they emerge as experiences out of the biological and psychological aspects of the person in the natural as well as social context. Both biology and sociability concur to shape these basic and tacit moral obligations. On the other hand, ethical obligations are, like knowledge-about, learned and internalized through rules which are linguistically structured and communicated. Ethical obligations can refer to the normative patterns of role-expectations and may be distinguished in terms of Toennies's and/or of Durkheim's typologies.

In other words, moral obligations refer to the person's deep feelings of responsibility toward him/herself, while the binding bond of ethical obligations resides in the sense of duty towards the outside world. Moral obligations are the core of a person's moral conscience; ethical obligations are the value-standards by which the person meets outward expectations. If failure to keep up with moral obligations will foster a sense of guilt, the incapacity to meet ethical obligations will produce a sense of shame.

ECOLOGY AND THE QUALITY OF SOCIAL RELATIONSHIPS

Let me hasten to add that there are not, as Ruth Benedict proposed, cultures of guilt and cultures of shame. Although it might be that some cultures put a greater stress on inner moral obligations while others might focus more on ethical, collectively-oriented obligations, nonetheless both types of obligations characterize any social relationship and both are present in all societies and cultures. In particular, ethical obligations are predominantly typical of mass consumer society, with its other-directed orientations (Riesman 1950) and its focus on performance and achievement.

This brings us to the link between ecology and the quality of social relationships. The quality of social life is largely assured by the quality of the predominant social relationships. I think I do not need to delve into the desirability and the quality of social relationships based on moral obligations. It is not a matter of primary, direct or personal relations. At this basic level, the presence of a "community" instead of a "societal" type of sociability is not relevant; nor is the absence of instrumentality typical of organic solidarity important. What really matters is the fact that in responding to *moral* obligations, the person receives a deep gratification which is fundamentally different from and is much more rewarding than the satisfaction of having responded to *ethical* obligations and of having met social expectations.

The dominance of social relationships based on ethical obligations has developed together with the expansion of the acquisitive, achievement-oriented, mass consumer society and, consequently, with the corresponding over-exploitation of the biosphere ecosystem. As long as this type of social relationship will be prevalent, the deterioration of both the natural environment and the quality of social life will continue and increase.

Environmental sociology (Dunlap & Catton 1979; Buttel 1987) seems more interested in tracing the effects of society on the physical environment than in assessing the impact of natural environments on social life. The new human ecology is studying the effects on social organizations of the basic societal prerequisites derived from their relationship with the biosphere. However, little is known about the impact of scarce natural resources and of polluted and deteriorated ecological systems on societies and social life. The theme of this congress brings also attention to this aspect. The ecological issue is not only, as Luhmann (1986) maintains, a question of how society, as a system, can meet the environmental challenge. The ecological issue cannot be approached through "ecological communication." We need to know, instead, how degraded environment and resource depletion influence social life.

It certainly is an open question, but let me present some working hypotheses toward an understanding of the dynamics of the society-nature ecosystem. It might be that one of the major processes by which the natural environment affects social life is the tendency to make intermediate social groups almost disappear. This process will have relevant effects on the nature of prevalent social relationships in society and culture, because moral obligations develop out of personal experiences in a variety of primary and close groups (family, peer groups, informal groups at work and leisure). It could also be hypothesized that these social experiences are more gratifying when they are contextually framed in natural environments. At least, this was the normal condition in the traditional societies which were, not only because of their agrarian character, strictly dependent on the natural environment. The traditional society was part of a unique society-nature ecological system. However, it would be a mistake to think that today, thanks to contemporary technology, social life has been freed from environmental constraints. My hypothesis is that now these constraints and effects are even stronger, particularly in the direction from nature towards society.

If we pose the question of what to do to confront the dramatic situation of the degradation of our biosphere, I think that realistically there is no easy answer. No national social or economic policy could make any advance in resolving a worldwide problem. This is a major difficulty. Additionally, it is doubtful that any intentional policy could have an effective impact even on a few elements of a general ecosystem. Moreover, there is a vicious cycle at work. The deterioration of the natural environment and the depletion of its resources tend to foster social relationships based on ethical obligations;

these will foster achievement attitudes and performance orientations which will reinforce the societal tendency to dominate and over-exploit the natural environment. Moreover, the dissatisfaction with a social life based on collectively-oriented social relationships will increase the search for surrogate gratifications in intensive consuming, with an additional amplification of the tendency to exhaust natural resources and to degrade the environment.

Some authors think that the root of the problem lies in the ideology of the "human exceptionalism paradigm;" that is, the anthropocentric paradigm which maintains that the unique nature of human beings and their capacity for culture (and hence for technology) give them the right to dominate and exploit without limits the natural environment (Buttel 1987). There can be no doubt that human beings have acted so far on the premise that their manipulation of the natural environment was an unbounded right. Yet, I think it would be an opposite excess to discard the anthropological centrality. Human beings are still unique and central to our natural world. It is not this anthropological humanism which has to be questioned. What has to be questioned and challenged is the right of human beings to dominate, manipulate and exploit nature without any reasonable constraint. Human beings and nature are linked in a reciprocal relationship which is made of moral obligations. Unfortunately, personal experiences within a natural framework are getting rarer and rarer in urban, industrialized society. However, without these inner moral obligations toward natural and social worlds, the deterioration neither of the natural environment nor of social life can be brought to an end.

References

Buttel, Frederick H. 1987. "New Directions in Environmental Sociology." *Annual Review of Sociology* 13:465-88.

Dunlap, Riley E. and William R. Catton. 1979. "Environmental Sociology." *Annual Review of Sociology* 5:243-73.

Fukuzawa, Yukichi. (1875) 1973. *An Outline of a Theory of Civilization*. Tokyo: Sophia University.

Hegel, Georg W. F. (1820) 1968-74. *Grundlinien der Philosophie des Rechts*. In *Gesammelte Werke*. Hamburg.

Luhmann, Niklas. 1986. *Ökologishe Kommunikation. Kann die moderne Gesellschaft sich auf ökologische Gefährdungen einstellen?* Opladen: Westdeutscher Verlag.

Putnam, Hilary. 1981. *Reason, Truth and History*. Cambridge: Cambridge University Press.

Riesman, David. 1950. *The Lonely Crowd: A Study of the Changing American Character*. New Haven: Yale University Press.

Scheer, Lore. 1980. "Experience with Quality of Life Comparisons." In *The Quality of Life: Comparative Studies*, edited by Alexander Szalai and Frank M. Andrews. London: Sage, 1980.

Schuessler, Karl F. and G. A. Fisher. 1985. "Quality of Life Research and Sociology." *Annual Review of Sociology* 11:129-49.

Solomon, Erwin S. et al. 1980. "Unesco's Policy—Relevant Quality of Life Research Program." In *The Quality of Life: Comparative Studies*, edited by Alexander Szalai and Frank M. Andrews. London: Sage, 1980.

Szalai, Alexander. 1980. In *The Quality of Life: Comparative Studies*, edited by Alexander Szalai and Frank M. Andrews. London: Sage, 1980.

Szalai, Alexander and Frank M. Andrews, eds. 1980. *The Quality of Life: Comparative Studies*. London: Sage, 1980.

Chapter 5

INDUSTRIALIZATION, MODERNIZATION AND THE QUALITY OF LIFE

Alex Inkeles

Hoover Institution, Stanford University

Effectively to discuss the relationship of industrialization, modernization and the quality of life we must have some common understanding of the
meaning of those terms, including, indeed, the term "relation" itself.

In the narrowest technical sense, industrialization refers to the process
of increasingly shifting the composition of all goods produced by any society
in two major respects: first, the share of all products resulting from manufac-
ture rather than from agriculture increases markedly; and second, there is a
major shift in the share of all fabrication which is undertaken not by craft
hand-labor but by machine processes, especially as they are driven by inani-
mate sources of energy. Evidently inherent in this second shift is a propensity vastly to increase the total volume of all goods produced.[1] Looking to
England as the first industrializer, we note that the share of agriculture in the
national income fell from an estimated 45 percent in 1770 to a mere 15
percent by 1870, and over the next hundred years this proportion was driven
down to a mere 3 percent (Cipolla 1962, p. 74). In that same century the
United States, coming later to industrialization, reduced the proportion of the
labor force engaged in agriculture from close to 50 percent to less than 5
percent as machines replaced horses and mules and then, in turn, men and
women (United States Census I, p. 240).

The shift out of agriculture, however, was by no means into manufacturing alone, nor indeed into industry more broadly conceived. Thus, the
century which saw such precipitous decline in the importance of agriculture
in the United States witnessed an increase in the weight of manufacturing
personnel as part of the total labor force from about 18 percent to only about
25 percent (United States Census I, p. 240). This was due to the fact that
people moved more and more into services, and of these the most significant
in their implications for development were education, science, and engineering. Profound changes in the mode and capacity of transportation and

communication followed, often in a prodigious surge. Thus, the railroad network of Europe was increased by 70 times in the half century from 1850 to 1890, and in one decade in the United States, from 1870 to 1880, the number of railroad miles was almost doubled (Rostow 1978, III-21, p. 152).

No less important were changes in the character of the population's education and residence. In 1870, no one in the United States lived in a city of a million population, but by 1970 almost 19 million people lived in such metropolitan conglomerates (United States Census I, Series A, pp. 57-72). In education, Canada moved from spending only approximately one percent of its GNP for schooling in 1867 to allocating more than seven percent of its national income for this particular form of investment in human capital by 1967 (Rostow 1978, N-7). Even countries which started from a relatively high level of education linked their industrialization to increasing education for the population. Thus, Japan, although already educating some 30 percent of the 5 to 19 age group by 1880, nevertheless more than doubled that percentage by 1915 (Rostow 1978, N-32, p. 786).

For such reasons it is much too restrictive to limit oneself to measures of industrialization only, and much more appropriate to speak of modernization, a broad process of technological, economic and social change in which even countries which continued to draw more heavily for their production on agriculture or extraction could and did participate. Argentina, for example, expanded its railway network from a mere 15 miles in 1860 to almost 6,000 miles by 1890 (Rostow 1978, Table III-21).

The potential indicators of a nation's industrialization and modernization are numerous, but they are also highly consistent. A set of those elements subjected to factor analysis will yield a strong principal component explaining a large amount of variance and characterized by factor loadings for the participant elements in the 0.8 and 0.9 range. So tightly structured is this syndrome that a simple index based on a set of some ten indicators chosen to be representative of different realms will stand in quite well for the 100 or so measures various scholars might nominate. Indeed, it is often quite serviceable to use a single, readily available number, namely the per capita GNP of a nation, as an indicator of industrialization and modernization.[2]

THE MEANING OF QUALITY OF LIFE

To judge the quality of life we have several alternative modes available. The first critical choice is between subjective and objective measures. Within each of these sets, a second set of choices can be made, providing us with four basic types of potential indicators.

Objective Indicators

Objective measures are those which can be ascertained and rated by an outside observer without reference to the inner states of the persons presumably affected by the conditions observed. The objective measures are themselves divided into those for which there is a clear physical or material referent, such as how many square feet of housing each person enjoys, and those which reflect a social or political condition, such as the legal right to join any church or organization.

Among the physical and material factors that are commonly identified and measured, we can identify at least nine categories of goods and services which are of actual or potential concern to the typical individual. These include: food; housing and associated amenities such as piped water and sewage; medicine and health; education; communications and information; time available, as for leisure; physical security of the person; the social security of the person, usually represented by the flow of welfare expenditures; and, increasingly, environmental and ecological conditions. Each of these categories can and often is represented by a subset of specific indicators. Health, for example, is often assessed by considering infant mortality rates and doctor-to-patient ratios; physical security by rates of victimization from various crimes such as armed assault or robbery; and communications conditions by newspapers published per capita.[3]

Governments and international agencies have a long-standing interest in measures of this type, and they have been systematically and assiduously collected for most nations over decades. From this experience we know that most of these diverse indicators tend to be closely related to each other and to form a syndrome readily summed up in a general index of the physical quality of life for any population.[4]

Objective measures of the *socio-cultural and socio-political* variety can be established by studying laws and their implementation, but also by systematic observation of social behavior. In either case, the measurement does not involve asking people how they feel about an issue. I propose six broad categories: **freedom of movement**, as in moving from the countryside to the city or from one job to another; **freedom of belief**, as in choosing your religion or political ideology; **freedom of association**, as expressed in the right to form and join organizations of common interest; **freedom of political determination**, as expressed in the right to choose your political leaders in meaningfully contested elections; **economic freedom**, as expressed in the employee's freedom to work at a job of his or her own choosing, the consumer's choice of what to buy, and the saver's choice of what to do with savings; and **freedom from discrimination and denigration**, as when black children in the United States are no longer forced to use segregated schools, or, looking to India, when low-caste persons are allowed to draw water from the same well as high-caste persons. Under each of these six major headings, of course, numerous sub-categories can be suggested.

Objective indicators of socio-cultural and socio-political conditions have been less systematically collected than have the physical and material variety, partly because they are less easy to measure, but possibly because many governments find that they raise sensitive and even embarrassing issues. Private organizations have, however, been quite active in this realm. Perhaps best known are the Freedom House ratings, developed by Raymond Gastil and annually applied to all countries worldwide since 1973. By considering the status of some 11 political rights and 12 civil liberties they develop a summary "freedom rating" for each country on a scale from 1 to 14.[5]

Subjective Indicators

Subjective indicators, as the term suggests, are accessible to us only by asking people to express an evaluation, judgment, opinion or belief about their own condition, or the condition of others and the world around them. The main indicators which have been worked with extensively are expressions of personal satisfaction with one or another realm of life. Typically the interviewer confronts the individual with the question: "Now, considering your job, are you very satisfied, only somewhat satisfied, or not satisfied at all?" The same sort of question is regularly put with regard to one or more additional realms of life such as: marriage, family life, one's education, friendships, health, finances, housing, leisure time, community, and nation.

It will be apparent that this list closely approximates the categories dealt with by the objective measures, only in this case it is not the facts which are at issue but rather the perception of them and the feelings such perceptions elicit. Clearly the same approach could be and is taken with regard to the subjective evaluation of the more or less objective measures of socio-political conditions. Thus, while the objective measures will tell us whether individuals have the legal freedom to select their place of residence, the subjective evaluation will tell us how far people feel they really are free to move from one place to another.

For many purposes one would obviously wish to focus on a measure of satisfaction limited to one particular realm, such as housing or the job.[6] And indeed, such specialized lines of analysis, as for example on the quality of urban living, are well developed.[7] Nevertheless, it is the case, as with other measures we have examined, that the set of subjective satisfaction measures tends to be well, although not tightly, correlated, and to constitute a syndrome, so that when satisfaction is expressed in one realm it is likely to be expressed in other realms as well.[8] As a result, it generally proves meaningful to develop a summary index by adding the scores for satisfaction felt in each of several different realms. As with the objective measures it is also possible, and indeed quite practical, to rely on the subject himself or herself to provide a summary judgment, as in response to the question: "Now, taking life as a whole, would you say that you are very satisfied, only somewhat satisfied, or not at all satisfied?"[9]   Asking about whether the person is happy or not provides a similar and equally serviceable summary judgment.[10]

There is a second category of subjective measures of the quality of life whose theoretical status is less well established, but which deserves serious attention. In this category are conditions, states, attributes or qualities of the person; if you like, psycho-social indicators. Perhaps the best example is anxiety. It would seem obvious, for example, that a society which induces the majority of its citizens to be constantly suffering intense anxiety is providing them with a lower quality of life than is one which permits them to enjoy freedom from such noxious feelings.

In this realm there is no agreed upon set of themes or measures, and the research on it has been less systematic and comprehensive. Nevertheless, there have been good studies on a cross-cultural basis of quite a variety of personal properties relevant to evaluations of the quality of life in psycho-social terms. These include measures of trust, personal efficacy and fatalism, self-esteem, cognitive flexibility, a sense of control over one's life, and measures of practical and general knowledge.[11]

RELATING THE QUALITY OF LIFE AND MODERNIZATION

What can we now say about the relations of physical, material, and psychological well-being, on the one hand, and the processes of industrialization, and more broadly of modernization, on the other? The conditions of life can, of course, be the cause of industrialization, driving a people to overcome their lack of natural resources or numbers, and to strive to enhance their power, prestige, or wealth by adopting a highly concentrated program of industrialization. This model has been utilized to explain the rapid industrialization of Japan, and sometimes is also applied to explain the forced industrialization which Stalin pressed upon the Russian and other Soviet peoples. For most of us, however, the more compelling question is likely to involve a different direction in the causal sequence. We want to know whether industrializing and modernizing bring about an improvement or a deterioration in the quality of life.

Getting an answer involves us in some complex analysis because the answer depends in part on which indicators we use; what historical time period we have in mind; and to which groups of the population we pay attention. To anticipate my conclusion, however, let me state my belief that, on the whole, industrialization and modernization, in the overwhelming

majority of the cases where they have been produced, have meant an improved, often vastly improved, quality of life for most people in most places
in most historical periods, including the present. I know this is a statement
which many who read it will challenge; indeed will be prepared to dismiss
out of hand. I am well aware of the complexities of the argument, and to
deal with them with the seriousness they deserve would require a big book.
For now, I request only the courtesy of being allowed to present some of the
evidence on which I base my conclusion.

Contemporary Contrasts

Focusing, initially, on objective indicators of the material and physical
kind, we may seek an answer to our question by contrasting the condition of
people in the so-called advanced countries, those which the World Bank
classifies as "industrial market economies," and those it places in the category of "low income countries." In terms of our critical differentiating criterion, the latter usually have 70 or more percent of their labor force in agriculture; the former typically have only 7 percent so engaged. The World Bank,
the UN, the ILO, the WHO and other international organizations offer us
dozens of measures which make it painfully clear how much the physical
and material condition of life in the poorer countries is inferior to the quality
of life of those in the more advanced nations.

For me, the most dramatic and compelling of such contrasts concerns
women dying in childbirth. In the low income countries, for every 100,000
live births the number of women dying is 607, whereas in the so-called
market economies it is 11. In other words, when she enters her labor a
woman in a less developed country is 55 times more likely to lose her life in
the process of giving birth than is a comparable woman in one of the advanced industrial countries (World Bank 1988, Table 33, pp. 286-7).

Many other measures tell a similar story. Infant mortality per 1,000
live births runs 106 for the less developed versus 9 for the advanced; corre-
spondingly, life expectancy in the former is only 52 years, whereas it is 76
years in the latter. Behind these statistics lie other facts. Those in the least
developed countries will get, on average, 1,200 fewer calories per day; they
will suffer many times over the most debilitating and destructive contagious
diseases; and to deal with these conditions they will have to share each
physician with some 17,500 other persons as compared to the advanced
country ratio of 1 physician per 550 persons. Similar contrasts prevail in
most other realms. In education, for example, the chances of getting to a
university for the typical person of college age is 1 in 100 for a resident of
a less developed country, versus 39 in 100 for those living in the industrialized countries. Summing it all up is the contrast in the per capita income
available to average citizens in the two sets of countries, standing at about

$200 for the least advantaged as against some $13,000 for the most advanced, yielding a ratio of 1:65 (World Bank 1988, Table 1, pp. 222-3; Table 23, pp. 278-9; Table 30, pp. 280-1; Table 33, pp. 286-7).[12]

Industrial and Industrializing Countries across Time

It may be objected that the type of analysis just presented does not satisfy our interest because we well know that the rich and the poor live very differently, and in any event there is no guarantee that in the future the currently poor nations, even if they were to industrialize, would attain the same advantages enjoyed by the now advanced countries. The appropriate response to this challenge is to review the experience of the now advanced countries to assess how far they were always advantaged rather than having improved in the quality of physical life over time. In addition, and perhaps even more relevant because it gets us out of the cultural frame of a Eurocentric analysis, would be an examination of the experience of countries which have only recently experienced a surge of industrialization and modernization, such as Taiwan, Korea and Malaysia.

Turning first to the United States as an example of historical development, and selecting medical and health conditions as an appropriate realm to test the effects of economic growth, we may note that despite the seemingly unlimited resources available to the settlers in a virtually virgin land, the conditions of life experienced by the population before the period of industrialization were those of a typically rural, agrarian, and less developed nation. Many diseases were, of course, only brought under control as a result of breakthroughs in the development of new medicines and vaccines, although even these depend on the science and technology which is an integral part of the modernity syndrome. Nevertheless, I have selected for examination those common scourges which had their roots mainly in poor conditions of life; that is, in inadequate diets and lack of sanitation.

The best data are available for the state of Massachusetts, surely not one of the poorest. In 1861, at the start of the greatest industrial expansion, for every 100,000 of Massachusetts' population there were 365 cases of tuberculosis, whereas a hundred years later, after a long-term and steady decline, the number was down to less than 6. In parallel fashion, infant mortality declined in the same hundred years from 143 per thousand live births, a figure comparable to that for the very poorest countries today, to about 22 (United States Census I, Table B 193-200, p. 63 and Table B 148, p. 57).

Comparable data for the United States as a whole do not go so far back, but those available from 1900 on for the diseases most conditioned by limits on diet, shelter, and sanitation tell a similar story. Thus, the rates per 100,000 fell from 1900 to 1970, as follows: for influenza and pneumonia, from 202 to 31; for gastroenteritis and related conditions, from 143 to less than 1; and for malaria, from close to 200 to less than 2 (United States Census I, Table B 149-160, p. 58 and Table B 291-304, p. 77).

Among the late industrializers the case of Japan is most dramatic from an economic point of view. It is especially notable, therefore, that in 1940 the infant mortality rate there was 90 deaths per thousand live births, higher than in most developing countries today, whereas by 1986 it had fallen to 5.5, one of the lowest rates in the world (UNICEF 1988, p. 40). Other nations which started their industrialization and modernization still later in turn showed comparably rapid rates of decline in infant mortality, the shift between 1960 and 1986 of deaths per 1,000 live births being: for Korea from 85 down to 25; for Malaysia from 73 to 27; and for Thailand from 103 to 41. While these countries were generally cutting infant mortality by two-thirds or more, the nations which were failing to advance economically reduced infant mortality much more modestly (UNICEF 1988, Table 1, p. 64).[13]

RELATING LIFE CONDITIONS TO SATISFACTION WITH LIFE

Let us assume that I have established clearly and unambiguously that the physical and material conditions of existence for the average citizen of the economically less developed countries are generally much worse than those in the industrially advanced nations, and that this is so by very wide margins, with the ratios of disparity being typically in the range from 1 to 5 up to 1 to 30.[14] This puts us in position to address the next, and for some the critical, issue of what difference, if any, these objective physical and material contrasts make in how people perceive their condition and how they feel about it. We ask the question: How far are people more satisfied, content, happy when their physical and material condition is of the highest standard, and how far are they more frustrated, anxious, fearful and worried when their condition is the poorest in the world?[15]

To many, I am sure, the answer to this question will seem obvious, allowing no latitude of opinion. To others, the issue will be seen as inherently intractable and the answer inevitably obscure because they make different assumptions about human nature and espouse a different philosophy of living. In their view the Chinese poet Lao Tsu was closest to the truth when he wrote: "As want can reward you, So wealth can bewilder."[16] More contemporaneously, in one of the strongest affirmations of such views, d'Iribarne (1974, p. 34) has argued that "objective indicators as currently constructed rest on implicit assumptions bearing little relationship to reality." Our own experience indicates that this position is too sweeping, for, as we shall see, the data show that at least some subjective assessments closely mirror physical and material conditions and support some rather clear-cut conclusions, which I shall attempt first. But the data also reveal ambiguities, present apparent contradictions, and raise some challenging conundrums, to which I shall turn subsequently.

First, I present, in Table 1, data on the evaluation of a set of life conditions as judged by representative samples from five continental areas studied in what the Gallup organization claimed to be "the first global public opinion survey covering 60 nations with 90 percent of the population of the free world" (Kettering 1979, p. 41).[17]

It is clear from these data that the people in the less advantaged countries recognize that they are deprived, worry much more about managing the demands of everyday living, and in general are much less likely to have a sense of satisfaction with life or to see their life as a happy one. Perhaps most clear are the progressions in the proportion of people who say yes to the question: "Have there been times during the last two years when you did not have enough money to buy food (or medicine, or clothing) for your family?" Typically only some 15 percent of the population in North America and Europe had this experience, whereas it was the norm for 50 or 60 percent in Latin America and the Far East, with a high of 81 percent in Sub-Saharan Africa reporting lack of sufficient resources to clothe their families.[18]

Making more summary judgments of their condition, less than 8 percent in North America were "not too happy," whereas this was true of 28 percent in Latin America, 31 percent in Sub-Saharan Africa, and half the population in the Far East. Forty-four percent of East Asians felt they were at the bottom of the ladder representing "the worst possible life you can imagine," whereas only 6 percent of North Americans saw their situation in such negative terms. This survey provides numerous additional contrasts in the perception by rich and poor peoples of their respective conditions of life, with disparities in the proportions dissatisfied or worried often in the range of 1:5. Taken together these data give grounds for supporting the Gallup study's conclusion that: "Nearly half the people of the world are engaged in an unending struggle for survival. Only in the advanced industrial states of the Western world can the inhabitants engage in anything akin to a 'pursuit of happiness'" (Kettering 1979, p. 56).

Pressing the argument further, that same report concluded that it was "most striking that the gulf which separates the advanced societies from the developing nations in respect to *material well-being* is just as wide in respect to *psychological well-being*" (Kettering 1979, p. 56; italics supplied). This proposition was, however, not specifically tested by them in the way the argument about physical and material conditions was tested. We may then ask: How strong is the association between objective advantage and subjective feelings of deprivation?

Table 1. Regional patterns in evaluations of quality of life
(percent reporting condition)*

	North America	Western Europe	Latin America	Sub-Saharan Africa	Far East
Worry a lot	34	42	61	43	60
Satisfied with health[1]	73	64	62	45	30
Satisfied with housing[1]	67	64	51	23	19
Satisfied with Living Standard[1]	59	53	48	30	44
Not able to meet expenses[2]	26	22	69	69	68
No money for food[2]	14	8	40	71	58
No money for medicine[2]	15	5	40	57	48
Life in general "not too happy"	9	18	28	31	50
Life near worst possible[3]	6	8	13	28	44

*Calculated from tables in Kettering (1979). North America is represented by the United States. Canada is represented in Table 2. See text for explanation.

[1]The figure for those "satisfied" equals the cumulative percent who placed themselves on the top four rungs of a 10-step ladder of satisfaction.

[2]Represents those who said they lacked money for various needs "all the time" or "most of the time."

[3]Proportion placing themselves on lowest four rungs on the ladder of possible life satisfaction.

More than a decade before the Gallup global survey, Hadley Cantril, working with outcome measures very similar to those later used by Gallup, elaborated a "development index"—based on 11 objective measures including GNP per capita—and compared national scores on the index with those on the ladder of life. The rank order correlation between the standing of his 14 national samples on the index of development and where their populations stood in satisfaction on the ladder of life was 0.67 (Cantril 1965, pp. 193-99).[19] Much later, for the period around 1984, Inglehart correlated national average "satisfaction with life scores" with the GNP per capita for 24 countries, mostly in Europe, and obtained a comparable level of association, also with a correlation coefficient of 0.67 (Inglehart 1990, Fig. 1-2, p. 32).[20]

It seems clear from these results that knowing the level of a nation's economic development tells us a good deal about how the population will rate its condition of life. But it is also apparent that the association is very imperfect, since we are predicting only some 45 percent of the variance even with such highly aggregated data. It is time, then, to look to the anomalies, conundrums, and apparent contradictions. We should also enlarge our explanatory scheme to take account of other factors, among which two are critical. First comes the role of cultural traditions which may strongly mute or intensify the expression of satisfactions and discontents. And second, we must take account of the psychology of adjustment, which apparently leads people to bring their aspirations so far into line with the realities of their situation as to greatly diminish the extent to which expressed satisfaction exactly mirrors objective disadvantage.

Cultural Sensitivities and Distinctive National Response Propensities

In his pioneering study of The Pattern of Human Concerns, Hadley Cantril long ago called attention to the fact that countries in generally comparable social and economic conditions nevertheless showed markedly different preoccupations when asked what they were most concerned about. At the same time, one could point to instances in which national populations differing markedly in their economic condition nevertheless expressed certain concerns in equal degree. Thus, when West Germany and the U.S. were paired as two well-developed nations, the latter showed almost twice as many people worried about family life as did the former. And when two very poor countries such as India and Egypt were paired, the Egyptians proved to be worried about ill health twice as often as the Indians. Cantril also noted that "in the 'rich' United States economic aspirations and fears were mentioned almost as frequently as they were in 'poor' India" (Cantril 1965, p. 170).

Similar distinctive national patterns were later reported in the Gallup world poll. The French, for example, were outstanding among developing

Table 2. Quality of life as perceived in different nations (in percent expressing certain views*)

	Canada	United Kingdom	West Germany	France	Italy	European Economic Community	Brazil	Japan
Worry a lot	36	31	31	50	45	39	58	25
Very satisfied with family[1]	47	43	39	37	34	39	57	14
Very satisfied with health[1]	44	40	23	28	28	31	42	42
Very satisfied with housing[1]	37	27	32	24	20	28	37	35
Very satisfied with living standard[2]	24	16	18	7	14	15	22	8
Not able to meet expenses[2]	15	22	10	22	29	19	50	41
No money for food[2]	6	8	7	6	15	8	26	14
No money for medicine[2]	4	1	1	8	9	5	36	5
Generally very happy	36	38	12	22	9	22	36	9
Very satisfied with life in general[1]	18	17	11	8	8	12	14	5

*Calculated from Tables in Kettering (1979).

[1]The very satisfied in these cases represent all those who placed themselves on the top two steps of a 10-step ladder of possible satisfaction.

[2]Percentages represent those who reported lack of sufficient money "all the time" or "most of the time."

countries in the proportion who worry a lot, whereas they were much like the European average in the satisfaction they found in family life, whereas the Japanese were only half as often worried as the French, but they very seldom took pleasure in family life.[21]

Of course, it might be argued that such variation in the sensitivities and satisfactions of national populations will tend to be randomly distributed and thus would cancel themselves out when peoples came to assess their overall condition. But there is strong evidence (assembled in Table 2) to suggest that the response to one's objective condition is strongly influenced by cultural propensities to see most things in either a more positive or negative light. Thus, it is clear (from the data in Table 2) that Brazilians have a strong propensity to see things more positively, expressing much more satisfaction in their health and educational attainments than their objective condition would seem to justify. Indeed, on many dimensions the proportions well satisfied with life conditions in Brazil equals or exceeds that in the most advanced countries of Europe and North America. By contrast, the French, and indeed also the Italians, repeatedly showed markedly smaller proportions satisfied, and larger proportions worried and discontent, than was the case with their comparably advanced European partners.

The pattern observed in the evaluation of the various specific domains of life was manifested in the summary judgments as well. The English-speaking world represented by Canada and the U.K.—but also the U.S. and Australia—is populated by individuals who tend to be well above the European average in the frequency with which they report themselves as happy and as satisfied with life in general. The French and Italians are fairly consistently well below average in this respect. The Brazilians, on the other hand, seem impervious to the reality of their objective situation, and report levels of general satisfaction equal to that found in the most advantaged countries in the world. At the other end of the continuum the Japanese, despite their great economic success, seem remarkably unable to muster any but the smallest number ready to place themselves in the category of the most satisfied and most happy. All this should make it apparent why efforts to relate GNP per capita, or other indexes of economic development, do not yield such strong correlations. It is because national groups display a response propensity, evidently an aspect of their cultural orientation, to see most things in either a positive or a negative light.

Differences *within* Countries

Another great challenge to the idea that objective differences in people's material and physical life situation ought to determine their level of happiness and satisfaction comes from the analyses comparing individuals with differing degrees of objective advantage living within the *same* country.

Logically, if we assume the average person in a poor country will be less satisfied with her life than an average person in a rich country, then it should be true that *within* any country the rich, those with the prestigious jobs, and those who have garnered the most education, would also be more satisfied, and that there would be a regular progression of such satisfaction as one moved up the several different ladders of lifetime achievements.

As it turns out, this proposition does hold, broadly speaking, but the statistical association is so weak as to seem quite counter-intuitive. Thus, in a regression analysis I applied to a joint index of satisfaction and happiness for each of the countries covered by the Eurobarometer, the eight most powerful objective variables—including income, education, and occupation—could explain only an extremely small proportion of the variance, at worst a mere 1.2 percent in the Netherlands and at best 8.5 percent in Italy. In country after country I found the proportion happy and satisfied among the rich versus the poor to be much the same, as it was when I compared those with prestigious jobs and those who do society's dirty work. Moreover, this outcome is not unique to my research nor to the Eurobarometer nations, but rather has been well documented in quite independent investigations in other places.[22]

By contrast with the socio-economic status variables such as income and occupation, entering "country" as a variable into the regression made a much more appreciable difference. Putting all the national samples in the Eurobarometer together in a single pool, and then using eight objective explanatory variables such as income, we found we could explain almost 14 percent of the variance in our summary scale of well-being. Of this total, however, the other seven objective variables together could explain only 2.6 percent of the variance, whereas the country variable explained 9.3 percent, three and a half times the impact of the other variables in the equation combined.[23]

This again provides strong evidence for the relative importance of the cultural factor in explaining differences in expressed well-being. But even though the cultural factor is a much more powerful predictor of satisfaction in life than are the usual socio-economic measures, it too leaves a great deal unexplained. In particular, we are challenged by the implication that whatever governments may do, and however much we may improve objective standards of living, people will be no more satisfied than they were before their economic situation improved. We must therefore turn to such measures as we have available to assess how far changes in the conditions of individuals and communities may be reflected in their perceived and expressed sense of satisfaction and well-being.

The Effect of Changed Conditions

Expressions of well-being are not immutable. On the contrary, there is considerable evidence to support the argument that they are intelligibly responsive to changed circumstance. People who experience an improvement in their financial condition in any year respond by expressing much more satisfaction with their standard of living in the immediately subsequent period.[24] Divorced women express strongly negative assessments of the state of their interpersonal relations almost six times more often than do all married women, and do so thirteen times more often than former widows who have experienced the gratification of being newly remarried (Campbell, Converse & Rodgers 1976, Table 10-5, p. 332).[25] Black men in America show their feelings about being economically disadvantaged and socially discriminated against by reporting themselves "not too happy" twice as often as do whites (Campbell, Converse & Rodgers 1976, p. 447). Unemployed persons, but especially men, have markedly lower scores on indexes of well-being than do those who still have jobs at comparable levels of skill and training (Campbell, Converse & Rodgers 1976, pp. 313-14).[26]

Given such responsiveness of the life satisfaction measures to changed conditions of existence, it would seem reasonable that at the national level we should find rising standards of living—especially of the kind associated with successful industrialization and modernization—to be reflected in increasing proportions of the populations in the more successful nations declaring themselves happy and expressing general satisfaction with life. But this assumption must meet some stiff challenges. Indeed, the predominant opinion, largely shaped by Easterlin's path-breaking study, holds that improving the living standards of a nation does not lead to increases in the sense of well-being in the population (Easterlin 1974).[27]

It is notable that most countries, most of the time, report levels of satisfaction which are remarkably stable over periods of a decade or longer. As I have shown elsewhere, for the ten countries covered in the Eurobarometer the absolute percentages of those reporting themselves as very happy fluctuated very little over the decade from 1976 to 1986, and the relative standing of each country in relation to all the others was remarkably stable (Inkeles 1991, esp. Tables 1 and 2, p. 95).[28] A decade is, of course, a short span of time, but data for longer spans of time suggest the same kind of stability. Thus, Gallup showed 39 percent of the U.S. population claiming to be "very happy" in 1946, and a virtually identical proportion of 40 percent thirty years later.[29] Much the same kind of stability over thirty years was manifested by Canada and Great Britain.[30]

France, however, showed considerable improvement in this thirty-year period; its proportion very happy rising from 8 to 22 percent. In 1946, France was, of course, barely freed from German occupation and was still reeling from the shock of wartime destruction of its economy. The observed change can, therefore, be interpreted as showing that general improvements in a nation's condition, at least in part economic, can produce a considerable increase in the proportion of satisfied or happy individuals. To test this idea we should have data for longer periods of time for more countries which have undergone industrialization and modernization in recent decades. And it would be helpful to have the indicators include scores for satisfaction with life, which might serve our purpose better than the measure of happiness, considered more volatile.

Taiwan, Korea and Thailand, among others, would be ideal candidates, but, at least to date, I have not located the necessary data for these countries, if, in fact, they exist. However, appropriate data are available for five nations whose populations placed themselves on the ladder of life around 1960 and then again some seventeen years later in 1977. All but one enjoyed vigorous economic growth in the period in question,[31] and all but that one showed marked increases in the proportions well satisfied with their lives. The percentage placing themselves on the top four rungs of the ladder of life rose in West Germany from 25 percent to 50 percent; in Brazil, from 22 percent to 42 percent; and in the United States from 52 percent to 75 percent. Cantril also presented data for Japan, although in somewhat different form, and there as well our calculation suggests a strong upward movement in the proportion placing themselves on the top rungs of the ladder, the number rising from 17 percent to 32 percent. India's economy was growing much more slowly in this period, and that seems to have been reflected in a much more modest increase in the proportion of those placing themselves on the top four rungs of the ladder, starting at slightly over 4 percent around 1960 and still at a low 7 percent in 1976.[32]

Our findings must meet the challenge of seemingly contradictory evidence.[33] We must also allow for the real possibility that these results are an artifact of our method.[34] But if they are not such an artifact, then the conclusion seems warranted that as economic conditions improve in particular countries, especially as reflected in per capita income, then the proportions of the population who express satisfaction with the general condition of their lives also increases.[35]

Of course, we must entertain some caveats with regard to this conclusion. First, there must surely be ceiling effects, such that increases in the percentage content with life get harder and harder to achieve as the average proportion satisfied gets into the range of 70 and above. Secondly, regardless of the absolute level of satisfaction, there are probably comparison and "diminishing returns" effects, so that a given economic gain won against a background of economic deprivation will bring larger increments in satisfaction than will a gain of the same magnitude, absolute or proportional, won at higher absolute levels of affluence. Many other constraints on raising the levels of satisfaction in contemporary communities may be suggested, not least among them the fact that increasing affluence, especially that based on industrial expansion, brings with it a host of new discouragements. Roads become choked with cars whose occupants, and others in turn, choke on smog-filled air; people find fish laced with toxic substances and meat larded with chemicals; they boat on, or stroll along, rivers which have been turned into open sewers; they worry that their housing may have been built over hidden poisonous waste dumps; and on vacation they find it harder and harder to locate pristine forests to camp in before all the trees are either lumbered or die of acid rain.

So here we rest. We have some evidence that national levels of expressed well-being may be relatively constant despite rising levels of economic wealth and an increasing flow of goods and services, a constant which could be explained by either deep-seated cultural propensities or by the tendency of the new problems faced and burdens imposed on modern populations to offset the positive effects of material prosperity and social and political freedom. We also have some evidence, more limited and possibly less reliable, which nevertheless supports the reasonable proposition that in countries experiencing marked increases in the standard of living and general economic and social development the population should show increasing proportions satisfied with what their lives bring them from day to day.

To come much closer to a resolution of the disagreement among these positions we must hope to find data for key countries such as Taiwan, Korea, Thailand, Singapore, Hong Kong, and Malaysia over the period of their most vigorous economic growth. If those countries can be shown to have been following the pattern I have suggested may have earlier characterized Brazil, Japan, and West Germany, that will provide less discouraging evidence for policy makers and a more encouraging prospect for those seeking to improve the physical condition they live in, since, in that case, they may assume that the increases in the flow of goods and services which industrialization and modernization bring will also gain for the population a heightened sense of psychological well-being. However, we must also assume from experience that such gains will be constrained by two counter forces. First, cultural propensities seem to determine the general range within which any national population falls in expressing happiness and life satisfaction. And second, we may expect sharp increases in the levels of expressed satisfaction to be followed by a stabilization of each national population at a new level as people become accustomed to their prosperity and new improvements come to have little or no effect on satisfaction because of the continually heightened expectations which develop.

Notes

[1]A simple but striking indicator of the great surge in the production of goods is given by the consumption of cotton in the United Kingdom. In 1750 the consumption of cotton was 1,000 metric tons. By 1850 it had increased by 267 times, and by 1900 by 788 times. Imported for the mills which were a central part of the early growth of manufacturing, the cotton went into a flood of cloth partly consumed in the U.K. and in great part sent off to Europe and other parts of the world. See Mitchell (1976, pp. 427-33).

[2]While the measure of GNP per capita may be serviceable, it is not necessarily preferable as an indicator. GNP may reflect spending on massive construction and defense which contribute little to the flow of goods and services to individuals, which was the pattern in the Communist countries of Eastern Europe. And oil exporting nations may be recorded as having high GNP per capita income even though they are little industrialized and not at all modernized. Per capita income measures also do not describe the inequalities of distribution within a nation. Nevertheless, for many purposes GNP per capita may serve as a useful rough measure of the flow of goods and services to a nation's population, and the general pattern of results obtained using it will be found to be very similar to the pattern obtained with more refined or detailed measures.

[3]Probably the most extensive effort to measure the overall physical and social quality of life for a single country was undertaken in West Germany. Ten different realms were identified, including social mobility, health, and "participation," and 196 specific measures were included. (See Zapf 1980.) This project in West Germany closely followed a model which had been elaborated for the larger community of nations in the Organization for Economic Cooperation and Development through its "Social Indicator Development Program." (See OECD 1976.) The West German project was, however, exceptional in the thoroughness with which the data was collected and evaluations made of progress on different indicators. The OECD (1991) continues to publish a "Compendium of Social Indicators" under eight major headings ranging from health to wealth and including some thirty odd separate measures.

[4]The Physical Quality of Life Index developed by Morris (1979) has become something of a standard in work with less developed countries. It is based on three elements: literacy rate, life expectancy at age one, and infant mortality rate. An alternative Physical Standard of Living Index developed by Williamson (1987) is based on four components: caloric consumption per day per capita, protein consumption per day per capita, infant mortality rate, and life expectancy at birth. Evidence that these elements formed a single coherent syndrome was reflected in the fact that all four showed very strong factor loadings in the range .80 to .91. An effort to measure the physical quality of life using the Morris criteria applied to a wider range of countries, including the advanced, will be found in Cereseto and Waitzkin (1986). This source gives incidental evidence that other measures, such as number of physicians per capita or school enrollments, also form part of the more general syndrome of physical quality of life.

[5]For a succinct summary of the characteristics evaluated and of the scoring procedures for the scale, see Gastil (1990, pp. 25-50).

[6]For example, see the publications of The European Foundation for the Improvement of Living and Working Conditions, especially the annual *Programme of Work*.

[7]For example, see the papers collected by Fried and Hohenberg (1974) on behalf of the Council of European Studies, and in Frick (1986).

[8]This pattern tends to be manifested within any one realm as well as across different realms. For example, in a study specifically focused on the quality of consumption in the Detroit and Baltimore areas of the U.S., Pfaff (1976) found consistent correlations around 0.3 between satisfaction with standard of living and with job, savings, housing, and automobile. Campbell, Converse and Rodgers (1976) cross-correlated seventeen different domains of life in their U.S. study and concluded: "Almost without exception there are positive correlations between all the domain satisfaction measures. People who say they are satisfied with one aspect of life are likely to report relatively high satisfaction where other domains are concerned." They also reported that the experience of the Social Science Research Council of the United Kingdom, working with nine domains, was similar to that of the American researchers (see pp. 68-75).

[9]The reasonableness of using such summary indexes of happiness and satisfaction was definitively established by Campbell, Converse and Rodgers (1976) in their finding that the set of 17 different domain satisfaction scores, taken together, could explain 54 percent of the variance in their general

index of well-being, which was based in good part on responses to the question about overall satisfaction with life (see p. 80).

[10]I make this statement with full awareness that general affirmations of happiness and declarations of satisfaction with life in general are not overpoweringly correlated. Cantril (1965, Table 52, p. 415) reported for his U.S. sample around 1960 the correlation of satisfaction with life and where people placed themselves on the ladder of life to be 0.36. Campbell, Converse and Rodgers (1976), in their 1971 U.S. sample, found the single item general happiness measure and the single item general satisfaction measure to be 0.50. The suggestion that either item can be substituted for the other is based on research experience which indicates the pattern and structure of the interrelations of each of these measures with other measures either of socio-economic background or of attitude and value. For a systematic and nearly exhaustive discussion of the interrelation of various global measures of well-being, see Andrews and Withey (1976). Ruut Veenhoven, of the Erasmus University Rotterdam, maintains a world database on the measurement of happiness and planned to publish in 1991 a catalog of empirical research findings under the title *Correlates of Happiness*.

[11]The U.S. sample in Cantril (1965) was asked to rate itself on self-confidence and respect for oneself. Campbell, Converse and Rodgers (1976) included measures of anxiety and of personal competence in the instruments used in their sample. The Baltimore-Detroit Area Study of 1971-72 included measures of personal control. Using ten psycho-social measures ranging from "trust" to "feeling down," Krebs and Schuessler (1989) developed a Life Feelings Scale for the U.S. and West German populations. Although the combined scales were unidimensional in both samples, the authors were left with some doubt as to "whether the feelings underlying the scales are identical in both populations."

[12]Data for the less developed countries are for 35 countries, excluding China and India, and are weighted by population size. Data for the industrial market economies cover 19 countries and are also weighted for population size. Due to the influence of exchange rates and other difficulties in measuring GNP it might be reasonable, in order to assess actual living standards, to weight the GNP per capita cited for the least developed countries by a factor of 3, which would reduce the ratio indicated to a still resounding 1:32.

[13]One of the benefits of worldwide development is that even countries which are not advancing economically at a rapid rate can, nevertheless, experience considerable improvements on important indicators such as the infant mortality rate. This comes about partly from direct aid, and from

technology transfer from the modern advanced countries. It also results from the stimulation and support by international agencies of local government programs to aid pregnant women and young mothers and their infants. Nevertheless, the countries developing most slowly are much less able to reduce infant mortality than are those which are accelerating industrialization and general economic development. While countries in Asia and Africa which developed rapidly the last three decades had typically brought their infant mortality rate down from 1960 levels to the point where their 1986 rates were only 30 percent of the former, the less rapidly growing nations in the same regions typically had rates in 1986 which were still about 70 percent of the former rate.

[14]There are, of course, many reasons to object to the use of averages, as my presentation does, because they may conceal not only gross disparities in distribution, but also disguise situations in which the average may rise but some major groups suffer actual deterioration of their condition. To deal with this issue requires more space than I have available here. I must limit myself to declaring that the more common pattern is for most, indeed often all, segments of society to benefit from rising levels of national productivity, although certainly not in equal degree nor in all realms. Using income distribution as a rough indicator of what is at issue, we certainly can say that it tends to be more equal in advanced industrial countries than in low income nations. Whether or not most steps along the way from underdevelopment to industrialization and modernization bring a general movement toward greater equality in the material and physical condition of life requires detailed analysis. I offer only my impression that the process does occur. Certainly it is the case that some medical improvements have a totally equalitarian distribution. Today no one in the entire world, no matter how wretchedly poor and neglected, can contract smallpox, once one of the greatest scourges of humankind.

[15]I am thus again brought face to face with a question I first raised more than thirty years ago, when in a paper that was more widely cited than most I raised the question: "Will raising the incomes of all increase the happiness of all, or does it require an unequal gain to bring happiness to some?" See Inkeles (1960, p. 18).

[16]As translated in Bynner (1978), Poem No. 22, p. 359.

[17]In conducting this world poll the Gallup organization was not able to include the countries of North Africa, nor those of the Communist nations of Eastern Europe. Nations from both those areas have, however, been included in other quality of life surveys. Cantril (1965), for example, includ-

ed Cuba, Poland and Yugoslavia in his set of 14 nations. Certainly these nations manifest some distinctive patterns, some of which may have been peculiar either to the kind of Communist country they were or to other national particularities. In general, however, there is little convincing empirical evidence to indicate that either the patterns of response or the levels of satisfaction in socialist countries markedly distinguishes them from other nations at comparable levels of economic development.

[18]In most of its tables the Gallup world poll summary did not give a continent-based average for North America, but rather listed the data for the U.S. and Canadian samples separately. The Canadian results were, however, consistently very close to those for the United States, and given the vastly greater population of the latter any continental average would have mainly reflected the outcomes for that colossus. I have therefore arbitrarily used the figures for the U.S. to represent North America in Table 1. Comparable data for Canada alone are reproduced in Table 2.

[19]Cantril's 14 nations were selected to give wide representation of the world's regions. Their standing on his index of development, based on data for the years 1957-1961 was: U.S. 1.00, West Germany 0.71, Israel 0.67, Japan 0.60, Poland 0.45, Cuba 0.35, Panama 0.31, Yugoslavia 0.19, Philippines 0.17, Dominican Republic 0.16, Brazil 0.16, Egypt 0.14, Nigeria 0.02, and India 0.00.

[20]Each person expressed overall satisfaction with life on a 10-point scale, and the correlation used the mean score for each country to relate to GNP per capita. Intermediate to these periods, the Gallup world poll data for 1976-77 was correlated with GNP, and with an N of 17 yielded a correlation of 0.74. See Veenhoven (1984, p. 149).

[21]Fifty percent of the French worried a lot, well above the average for most industrial countries, whereas only 25 percent of the Japanese gave that response. Being on the highest step of the ladder of satisfaction with family life was true of 18 percent of the French, close to the European average, but that condition held for only 8 percent of the Japanese. (Kettering 1979, pp. 137-38 and 177-78)

[22]For example, in their exhaustive analysis of the measures of general life satisfaction reported by a representative sample of the United States' population, Campbell, Converse and Rodgers (1976) found that a larger set of objective circumstances, including even race, could explain no more than some seven percent of the variance in their index of well-being, and the subset of family income, education, and personal income explained only 2.5

percent of the variance (see p. 368). A large Canadian sample showed income and age to be among the strongest predictors of a measure of general life satisfaction, but together they accounted for only 2.4 percent of the variance (see Blishen & Atkinson 1980, p. 30).

[23]The country variable was entered in the regression as a "dummy" variable.

[24]Persons who reported that this year they were better off than last year were more likely to express general satisfaction with their standard of living, as described by Pfaff (1976) for the Baltimore-Detroit study of economic well-being. The correlation was 0.29, as reported in Table 8-4. No degrees of improvement were specified in the question used. We may assume that a *sharp* rise in income would produce a much stronger change in the sense of satisfaction.

[25]The results for men were broadly similar.

[26]Campbell, Converse and Rodgers (1976) report that the average score for unemployed men was a full standard deviation lower than that for men with full-time jobs, and the differences remained substantial even with adjustments for lowered income. This finding is particularly notable because on most measures such as income the differences separating the more advantaged from those less favored were generally quite small fractions of a standard deviation. My reanalysis of data from Eurobarometer 9, the only one with a reasonably reliable measure of unemployment, in general confirms the results obtained earlier for the United States. For the Netherlands, for example, when we compared the happiness and life satisfaction of those who had experienced unemployment at some point in the preceding three years and were currently unemployed with those who also had previously experienced being out of work but were now employed, we obtained a gamma of 0.68, significant at the .01 level despite a very small N. In Australia, Feather (1990) collected relatively rare longitudinal data and found considerable differences in life satisfaction among school leavers who had found steady work as compared to those who had failed to find it or who found it and lost it. See especially Tables 8-1 and 8-2, pages 180 and 186.

[27]Easterlin (1974, p. 90) argued that the appropriate conclusion was "skepticism of a positive correlation between output and welfare." He reanalyzed Cantril's data and concluded that Cantril had specified too high a correlation between his index of development and the measures of popular satisfaction. As to the critical issue of whether national levels of satisfaction rise in response to rapid increases in economic development, he presented a

national time series for the United States only. In that case, he found a fluctuating pattern between 1946 and 1970, rather than the long-term increase one might have expected if happiness reports were tracking improvements in income. There is, of course, good reason to expect a stable level of satisfaction in a nation such as the U.S., which reached the stage of a mature industrial society many decades ago. This does not settle the question as to whether marked increases in popular satisfaction might not result from sudden spurts of growth starting from either depressed conditions, such as those of France and Germany after World War II, or from low levels of development in newly industrializing countries such as Taiwan. These specific conditions and the data for evaluating them were not dealt with by Easterlin.

[28]Over the ten surveys, The Netherlands, which always ranked No. 1, reported variation in the percent "very happy" from a low of 38 percent to a high of 49 percent. There was, however, no visible long-term trend. Italy, always in rank 9 of 10, and outstanding in the frequency with which people reported themselves "not too happy," had proportions in that category ranging from 27 percent to 44 percent, with the second half of the decade more likely to reveal negative affect. With reference to Italy it is worth noting that in analyses I presented some thirty years ago, based on data going back as far as 1948-1950, I reported levels of happiness and satisfaction in Italy and France which were substantially lower than those for comparable European countries (see Inkeles 1960).

[29]The stability of the measures for the years cited masks a certain amount of fluctuation from year to year. Thus, Campbell, Converse and Rodgers (1976) describe six studies of the happiness of the U.S. population from 1957 to the fall of 1972, noting fluctuations in the percent claiming to be "very happy" ranging from a high of 35 percent in 1957 to a low of 22 percent in the fall of 1972 (Table 2-1, p. 26). It is not clear how much of this variation was connected with a long-term decline, how much to differences in the study design and sampling, and how much it may have reflected current events at the time the surveys were taken. We now have long enough series of data with questions of this type to make it meaningful to attempt to explain the year-to-year fluctuations on the basis of economic and political events. Thus, the General Social Surveys for the U.S. conducted by the National Opinion Research Center have asked about general happiness every year since 1972. In 1986, the proportion very happy stood at 33 percent.

[30]Data for 1946 are from Cantril (1951); data for 1976 are from Kettering (1979). The percentages "very happy," with 1946 first and 1976 second, were: Canada 32/36; Great Britain 36/38; France 8/22.

[31]Average annual growth in GNP per capita for the years 1960 to 1976 were Brazil 4.6 percent; West Germany 3.4 percent; U.S. 2.3 percent; and India 1.3 percent. For Japan the figure was 5.2 percent (World Bank 1978, Table 1, pp. 76-77).

[32]Ladder ratings for 1976 are from Kettering (1979), obtained by adding the percent on each of the top four steps of the ladder as presented on pp. 129-30. Ratings for 1960 are from Cantril (1965, Table 21, p. 378), weighting male and female scores equally and taking the average. For Japan, Cantril did not have the original data, but relied on information provided by the Central Research Agency. However, Figure IV:8 permits a reasonably accurate calculation of the cumulative percent on the top four steps of the ladder. Data for Cantril did not present the data for Japan in the same form as for the other countries. The precise figure Cantril did report was a mean rating, which stood at 5.2. Applying the standard method of calculating the score to the data for Japan in Kettering yields a 1976 mean of 5.9. The difference of 0.7 is significant well beyond the 0.01 level, and is, by my rough estimate, considerably larger than one standard deviation.

[33]Over roughly the same span of time as our ladder ratings measured, the happiness measure for the U.S. showed a decline rather than a parallel increase. In 1963, 32 percent of Americans reported themselves as very happy, but by the spring of 1972 that proportion was down to 26 percent. In addition to the passage of time, these comparisons saw a shift from a nation-wide quota sample to a nationwide probability sample (see Campbell, Converse & Rodgers 1976, p. 26). By 1977, Gallup showed the proportion of U.S. citizens who were very happy back up to 40 percent, seeming to reverse what had appeared to be a long-term decline in the happiness ratings Americans assigned themselves (see Campbell, Converse & Rodgers 1976, p. 26 and Kettering 1979, pp. 129-30). Such fluctuations might, of course, reflect a number of influences, not merely economic. International conflict and domestic tensions can also play a role. In his analysis of national differences in life satisfaction, Inglehart (1990, pp. 32-33) reached the same conclusion, stating: "economic development is not the only explanatory variable; other historical factors must also be involved."

[34]The question put to the respondents was similar, but was not phrased in exactly the same way in the studies compared. In Cantril's case the stimulus was: "Here is a picture of a ladder. Suppose we say that the top of

the ladder (pointing) represents the best possible life for you and the bottom (pointing) represents the worst possible life for you. Where on the ladder (moving finger rapidly up and down ladder) do you feel you personally stand at the present time?" (Cantril 1965, p. 23). In the Gallup survey the respondent was shown a picture of a mountain rather than a ladder, although one also having ten steps, and was asked the question: "Suppose the top of the mountain represents the best possible life you can imagine, and the bottom step of the mountain represents the worst possible life you can imagine. On which step of the mountain would you feel you personally stand at this time—assuming the higher the step you feel better about your life and the lower the step the worse you feel about it. Just point to the step that comes closest to how you feel." There were also some differences in the size and quality of the samples for particular countries collected in the two studies. Cantril sought for representative probability samples. The Gallup survey for the Kettering Foundation was based on sampling world regions, but to permit reporting on individual nations the national samples of certain countries were augmented to reach a minimum of 300 cases. For the countries discussed, the respective N's, with Cantril cited first, were: Brazil 2739/382, West Germany 480/303, India 2366/354, U.S. 1549/1014.

[35]This assumption is supported by Inglehart (1990). Thus, in comparing the situation of Belgium and Germany he states: "Despite a predominant pattern of stability, life satisfaction in the Belgian public declined, while that of the German public rose slightly, in response to their respective experiences from 1973 to 1987" (p. 31). However, he did not specify what the differences in experience were, and it is clear in the context that this conclusion is quite tentative.

References

Andrews, Frank M. and Stephen B. Withey. 1976. *Social Indicators of Well-Being: Americans' Perceptions of Life Quality.* New York: Plenum Press.

Blishen, Bernard and Tom Atkinson. 1980. "Anglophone and Francophone Differences in Perceptions of the Quality of Life in Canada." Pp. 21-39 in *The Quality of Life: Comparative Studies,* edited by Alexander Szalai and Frank M. Andrews. London: Sage Publications.

Bynner, Witter. 1978. *The Chinese Translations.* New York: Farrar, Straus, Giroux.

Campbell, Angus, Philip E. Converse, and Willard L. Rodgers., eds. 1976. *The Quality of American Life: Perceptions, Evaluations, and Satisfactions.* New York: Sage Publications.

Cantril, Hadley, ed. 1951. Prepared by Mildred Strunk. *Public Opinion, 1935-1946.* Princeton, N.J.: Princeton University Press.

Cantril, Hadley. 1965. *Patterns of Human Concerns.* New Brunswick, N.J.: Rutgers University Press.

Cereseto, Shirley and Howard Waitzkin. 1986. "Capitalism, Socialism, and the Physical Quality of Life." *International Journal of Health Services* 16(4):643-59.

Cipolla, Carlo M. 1962. *The Economic History of World Population.* Harmondsworth, England: Penguin Books Ltd.

d'Iribarne, P. 1974. "The Relationships between Subjective and Objective Well-Being." In *Subjective Elements of Well-Being. Papers Presented at a Seminar of the Organization for Economic Cooperation and Development, Paris, May 15-17, 1972,* edited by Burkhard Strumpel. Paris: Organization for Economic Cooperation and Development.

Easterlin, Richard A. 1974. "Does Economic Growth Improve the Human Lot? Some Empirical Evidence." Pp. 89-125 in *Nations and Households in Economic Growth: Essays in Honor of Moses Abramovitz,* edited by Paul A. David and Melvin W. Reder. New York: Academic Press.

European Foundation for the Improvement of Living and Working Conditions. 1990. *Programme of Work for 1990. 1992 and Beyond: New Opportunities for Acting to Improve Living and Working Conditions in Europe.* Luxembourg: Office for Official Publications of the European Communities.

Feather, Norman T. 1990. *The Psychological Impact of Unemployment.* New York: Springer-Verlag.

Frick, Dieter, ed. 1986. *The Quality of Urban Life: Social Psychological and Physical Conditions.* Berlin: Walter de Gruyter.

Fried, Robert C. and Paul M. Hohenberg, eds. for Council of European Studies. 1974. *The Quality of Life in European Cities.* Pittsburgh: University of Pittsburgh.

Gallup, George. 1978. *The Gallup Poll: Public Opinion 1972-1977,* Vol. 1. Wilmington: Scholarly Resources, Inc.

Gastil, Raymond D. 1990. "The Comparative Survey of Freedom: Experiences and Suggestions." Pp. 26-50 in *Studies in Comparative International Development: On Measuring Democracy,* guest editor Alex Inkeles 25 (1).

Inglehart, Ronald. 1990. *Culture Shift in Advanced Industrial Society.* Princeton, N.J.: Princeton University Press.

Inkeles, Alex. 1960. "Industrial Man: The Relation of Status to Experience, Perception, and Value." *American Journal of Sociology* 66(July):1-31.

Inkeles, Alex. 1991. "National Character Revisited." *The Tocqueville Review* 12:83-117.

Kettering, Charles F. Foundation and Gallup International Research Institutes. 1979. *Human Needs and Satisfactions. Summary Volume.* Princeton, N.J.: Gallup International Research Institutes.

Krebs, Dagmar and Karl Schuessler. 1989. "Life Feeling Scales for Use in German and American Samples." *Social Indicators Research* 21:113-131.

Mitchell, B. R. 1975. *European Historical Statistics 1750-1970.* New York: Columbia University Press.

Morris, D. M. 1979. *Measuring the Condition of the World's Poor: The Physical Quality of Life Index.* New York: Pergamon Press.

Organization for Economic Cooperation and Development (OECD). 1976. *Measuring Social Well-Being. A Progress Report on the Development of Social Indicators.* Paris: OECD.

Organization for Economic Cooperation and Development (OECD). 1991. *Historical Statistics 1960-1989.* Paris: OECD.

Pfaff, Anita B. 1976. "The Quality of Consumption." Pp. 187-217 in *Economic Means for Human Needs: Social Indicators of Well-Being and Discontent,* edited by Burkhard Strumpel . Ann Arbor: University of Michigan.

Rostow, Walt W. 1978. *The World Economy: History and Prospect.* Austin: University of Texas Press.

United Nations Children's Fund (UNICEF). 1988. *The State of the World's Children 1988.* Oxford: Oxford University Press.

United States Bureau of the Census, U.S. Department of Commerce. 1975. *Historical Statistics of the United States, Colonial Times to 1970.* Bicentennial Edition. Washington, D.C.: U.S. Government Printing Office.

Veenhoven, Ruut. 1984. *Conditions of Happiness.* Dordrecht, Holland: D. Reidel Publishing Company.

Williamson, John B. 1987. "Social Security and Physical Quality of Life in Developing Nations: A Cross-National Analysis." *Social Indicators Research* 19:205-27.

World Bank. 1978. *World Development Report, 1978.*

World Bank. 1988. *World Development Report 1988.* Oxford: Oxford University Press.

Zapf, Wolfgang. 1980. "The SPES Social Indicators System in Comparative Perspective." Pp. 250-69 in *The Quality of Life: Comparative Studies*, edited by Alexander Szalai and Frank M. Andrews. London: Sage Publications.

Chapter 6

THE PUZZLE OF "QUALITY OF LIFE"

Erwin K. Scheuch

University of Köln

I

The notion of "Quality of Life" is characteristically an expression of cultural doubt at the moment of relative material well-being in a social system. In this way it was articulated at the peak of political success of the Roman Empire. The notion was revived in Western Europe with early industrialization as part of the Romantic protest against economic modernization. Since the 1970s, the quest for quality of life is part of the challenge to the primacy of economic values in contemporary modern societies. At a time of unprecedented material well-being, further economic growth as a goal is challenged by protesting that the Quality of Life is actually being reduced.

The notion of quality of life has thus reached politics. Former French Prime Minister Madame Cresson recently pronounced that the Japanese may earn more than their French counterparts, but their quality of life was immensely lower. According to her, the Japanese live in rabbit hutches, spending endless hours commuting between home and workplace. No money would make up for this. Let us leave aside the correctness of such a description, and let us consider the innocence with which a dilemma is resolved by Madame Cresson that is central to all quality of life debates: the need to decide a trade-off between value dimensions—here between housing standards and income levels. Weighing dimensions is necessary whenever the notion of quality of life is used for comparisons with the aim of evaluation. Theoretically that problem is insoluble but in practice, as research shows, approximate solutions can be developed.

An antecedent of the current debate was the concern of classical economists with welfare—with individual welfare and the welfare of nations. As expressed in the words of Bentham, the goal of the economy was to be the greatest happiness for the largest number. This is quite an indeterminate formulation as it refers to both individual happiness and the state of a collectivity. With the classics, the concern was really the welfare of the collectivity, and within a collectivity in the state of relative happiness one assumed that this condition implied the greatest individual happiness as well.

Subsequently, the relation between welfare as individual benefit and collective welfare was problematized. In economics and politics one used the measure Gross National Product (GNP)—certainly a very problematic measure, even for the monetized economies, and much more so for developing countries. The GNP, even when used as a yardstick for the performance of the economy and not the society at large, ignores the distributive side of the economy. The GNP is a defensible yardstick for modern economies if it is only the overall volume of the economy that counts. It is wanting if attention shifts to the individuals in an economy. It is here that the so-called "welfare economics" of Marshall or Pigou demanded to judge the performance of the economy by aggregating the amounts of individual welfare to an overall welfare measure.

This proved to be an impossibility, however, as Kenneth Arrow showed. Whenever the individual curves for saturation, the so-called welfare functions of the individuals, did not coincide, aggregation is highly problematical. In a highly differentiated society such as ours, the problem of aggregation cannot be solved. This is of great but forgotten relevance for measuring the quality of life. That is, in theory; in practice, one may agree to approximations.

II

The social indicator movement is on the one hand a descendant of welfare economics, and in addition a descendant of big technology, such as space research. In the United States, big technology led to the movement of so-called "technology assessment" early in the 1960s. One may even trace this back to the Eisenhower years. Technology assessment tries to give an answer to the misgivings, even fears, that accompany new technology, such as atomic energy or new telecommunications techniques. Theoretically, technology assessment is a hopeless attempt, as it is, mostly by implication, a social prediction. We know that social predictions are very often widely off, predicting developments that never occur, and worse, missing changes that are of major importance. The upheavals in the former communist empire are a case in point. However, predictions are necessary not only in public but also in our private life, and in our private life we are ready to revise predictions as life goes on. Technology assessment pretended initially to be more than conjectures, but rather statements with the authority of a scientific diagnosis. As a social monitoring of technological change, rather than as a binding assessment, technology assessment is becoming a routine.

Some of the undertakings of technology assessment fused with the activities of the welfare economists to become the "social indicator movement." In its early stages in the 1970s, the proponents of social indicators aimed at aggregating the indicators to a comprehensive measure of success in directing social change. The movement was part of the then prevalent hope to initiate a new round of social engineering, as was tried earlier in the Roosevelt days. The social indicator was conceived as an objective and therefore binding measure of the success of such social engineering. In the 1960s, there were several attempts in the U.S. to provide a scientific base for the selection and processing of social indicators. The 1968 report for the Russell Sage Foundation is the most important example here.

However, an objective procedure to select and process indicators presupposes a universally accepted theory of society, and this does not exist and probably never will. Therefore social indicators have to be rethought as a convention, as a result of political deliberations inspired by social science knowledge. The relation of the sets of indicators to the notion quality of life has weakened in this process. Such indicators are now in Germany part of societal monitoring, having shed the pretense of providing a binding measure of the success of a socio-political order.

III

The quality of life movement developed in the U.S. as part of cultural criticism. Thus it took a very different route than the movements I have so far mentioned. Unlike the condition for cultural criticism in Europe, in the U.S. cultural criticism required numbers in order to become effective. The quality of life figures in the U.S. aimed at complementing and even contradicting the purely economic measures that were prevalent.

The first landmark in this development was the publication by the Survey Research Center in 1971 of *The Quality of American Life* (for an overview of studies in the U.S., see Converse, et al. 1980, Appendix B). Already by then it had become obvious that there would not be a binding figure, such as the way the GNP is treated. I use the phrase "the GNP is treated" because the GNP also, of course, reflects a political deliberation and is not a purely objective number. We have the convention to treat the GNP as though it measured as a thermometer measures temperature in Centigrades. This is the way in which it is hoped in the U.S. to ultimately develop quality of life measures.

Quality of life measurement is but a new and more comprehensive round in bouts at social monitoring. In carrying development further, it becomes quite clear that we would not have at the same time a number that expresses the collective quality of life and a number that reflects the individual appraisal of the quality of life.

E. Scheuch

Table 1. Correlations of yearly fluctuations in GNP with fluctuations in happiness in the EC countries between 1976 and 1986

Country	Same Time	One-Year Lag
Belgium	-.29	+.88
Denmark	-.31	+.52
Germany	+.28	-.04
Great Britain	-.73	+.42
France	-.13	+.47
Ireland	-.06	-.34
Italy	-.28	+.70
Luxembourg	-.18	-.12
Netherlands	+.12	+.40
EC as a whole	-.12	+.56

SOURCE: Veenhoven 1988a.

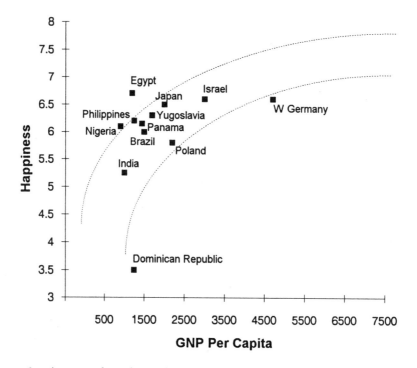

Figure 1. Average happiness in countries of different wealth in 1960
(SOURCE: Veenhoven 1988a).

In the last decade empirical research has shifted away from the measurement of the collective quality of life—which is still continued as the social indicator movement—to the measurement of individualistic qualities of life. Here the emphasis is on the subjective feelings about life conditions. And if we measure quality of life in order to have a number for individual happiness, why not ask the people (Strack, et al. 1991)? In this way, quality of life indices are being developed not only for research but also for a variety of practical applications (Schuessler & Fisher 1985).

IV

"Why bother" with measures that can only be approximations of doubtful theoretical standing? Why don't we stay with the GNP? Can't we assume that, after all, material welfare is at the bottom of all feelings of well-being? Table 1 and Figure 1 depict the results of an international survey in which the dependent variable was happiness and the other variable was the GNP per capita.

Here we observe two things. First, the GNP at a given moment influences happiness with a delay. If I use figures for the same year, the correlation is quite low. If I use figures for one- or two-year lags, the correlation is sometimes in the 50s to 70s. But overall the correlations are so imperfect that it would be perilous to use the GNP as a substitute for an index of the quality of life.

Secondly, there is also a ceiling effect. The very poor countries and the very rich countries show lower correlations between GNP and happiness, and the countries in between that are moving forward, a stronger one.

Of course, one may object that a dependent variable "happiness" is a black box, and that the happiness of a country as a collectivity cannot be gauged by aggregating individual happiness. We shall leave both questions to be answered later. Let it suffice to say here that a blanket response to a general question on happiness is a better indicator than aggregated scores to many specific happiness questions.

If you are very well off, you don't bother about material well-being and can indulge in the luxuries of post-materialism. The saturation effect for richer countries makes it necessary to include further indicators beyond the GNP for the quality of life.

For the richer countries, where economic well-being does not determine happiness of life that much, there is the additional problem that the dependent variable, "happiness," is an extremely fickle, nervous measurement. This can be seen in the time-series for Germany from 1957 into the 1980s (Figure 2).

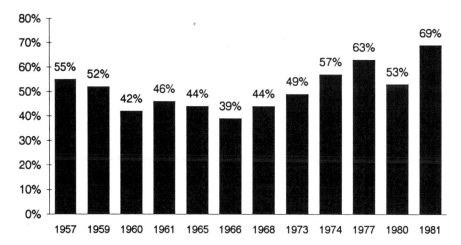

Figure 2. Question: "Thinking of the future: Will life in general become
ever more easier or increasingly harder?" (SOURCE: Secondary analysis of the
B.A.T. Freizeit-Forschungs-Institut, Data from: Allensbach, Hamburg 1983.)

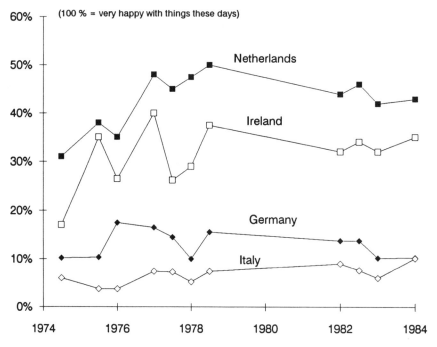

Figure 3. Question: "Taking all things together, how would you say things
are these days—would you say you are very happy, fairly happy, or not
too happy these days?" (SOURCE: *Public Opinion*, April/May 1985)

Among other information, Figure 2 shows two things: (a) considerable nervousness, and (b) from 1955 to 1968, a tendency to become less happy, even though economic well-being increased. It is very difficult to compare happiness figures across all countries and all times. One is on safer ground when one stays within areas and within a period.

Referring to Table 2, with the exception of Luxembourg—but here the sample is small—ranks for happiness and for satisfaction coincide within one unit. Obviously the two questions refer to pretty much the same thing. Satisfaction/happiness within Western Europe tends to decline with size of country; the only small country with a low level of satisfaction is Greece. We may be observing here another instance of the curvilinear relation between material well-being and general satisfaction. Greece is the only very poor country among those covered in this survey. All the others are reasonably well off, and then other factors determine happiness—where small size of country may mean less bureaucratization and alienation.

Figure 3 depicts the happiness ratings during the time span from 1975 to 1984 in four different countries. There are two relatively unhappy countries, Italy and Germany, and two rather happy countries, Ireland and The Netherlands. There are absolutely no economic reasons for the Irish to be happy, nor is there a good reason for the Germans to be unhappy. With all the instability over time, it becomes clear that there are different cultural standards which have to be considered if one wants to interpret a social change. If one goes across continents, one is in deep water. But, on the other hand, if, over time, the countries retain their relative distance from each other in terms of subjective happiness—we after all are measuring something, we are not just measuring words but properties of countries—then the result here suggests that there is verity in the slogan "small is beautiful"; in this case, "small is happy."

Figure 4 represents East and West Germany as of the beginning of the summer of 1990, when the standards of living between both parts of the country were drastically different, East Germany having at best about 40 percent of the standard of living of West Germany. And yet, one can see in Figure 4 that the relative ranking of domains, with one important difference, is about the same in West and East Germany. And there is obviously something like a general happiness that extends across the various domains. The one obvious exception is the supply of goods, but otherwise we see that there is a spill-over of a general feeling of satisfaction into specific domains.

V

Measuring individual satisfaction by domain is more problematical, of great practical relevance, and very instructive. The main problem is aggregating domain scores.

Table 2. Average percent of high and low levels of happiness
and satisfaction in 10 EEC countries: 1975-1985

Country	Happiness		Satisfaction		Rank	
	very happy	not too happy	very satisfied	not at all satisfied	happiness	satisfaction
Netherlands	43	6	42	1	1	2
Denmark	35	12	55	1	2	1
Ireland	32	11	36	4	3	3.5
Belgium	29	11	34	3	4	5
Great Britain	26	14	31	4	5	6
Luxembourg	24	10	36	2	6	3.5
France	15	22	12	7	7	8
Germany	14	15	19	2	8	7
Greece	11	30	8	7	9	10
Italy	8	33	11	10	10	9

NOTE: The question wording for Happiness was "Taking all things together, how would you say you are these days—would you say you're very happy, fairly happy or not too happy these days?" The question wording for Satisfaction was "On the whole, are you very satisfied, fairly satisfied, not very satisfied, or not at all satisfied with the life you lead?" Figures for Japan tend to coincide with the results for western Germany.

SOURCE: Inkeles 1988.

Measuring quality of life by domains has special importance in the field of medicine, and here is where it is especially problematic (see Table 3). Physicians used to define their task as being a technician of the body that in turn was seen as a machine in repair condition. The newer perspective is that of a person who is supposed to make the patient happy. He needs to broaden his criteria in deciding how to act. Especially in research on cancer, this is obvious. When should you operate on someone? This old problem is now no longer decided on purely medical grounds, but also based on a prediction about the quality of life that the patient would enjoy after surgery. British medicine has a bureaucratically standardized measure for determining the quality of life of patients, called "LAZA." LAZA is used for the decision of doctors whether to perform surgery or not. As a routine tool—it is not the only one, there are other measures in Great Britain such as

FLIC (Functional Living Index Cancer; Schipper, et al. 1984)—it is also used to decide how to allocate resources for medical research. In distributing public funds, priority is given to fields of research where the improvement of the quality of life of patients is most likely and greatest.

Some in the medical profession would like to use the numbers for quality of life, like a pulse beat or the measurement of body temperature. A sociologist, however, has to warn here that such usage of a test score violates nearly everything that we teach students when they learn measurement and scale construction: we do not know whether the dimensions have the same kind of metric; we do not know the weight of the factors; we do not know whether a dimension is represented by several measurements and thus given undue weight; we cannot aggregate scores of individual items, as done here; and so on. Anything one can do wrong in constructing a scale is being committed here by the medical profession in England. But methodological qualms do not matter when a convention is desired. Not every doctor wants to decide by himself, and the LAZA relieves him from the responsibility for a decision whether to perform surgery or not. After all, the GNP is not that hot a measure, either, and it is nevertheless used universally. Thus one could argue that a bad measure is better than no measure at all—except that there is a sham degree of precision suggested!

The latest case of the desire to escape personal responsibility by using sham scales is a formula proposed by a certain Mr. Shaw. He defined the measurement of "Quality of Life" (ql) as the "product of the patient's natural endowment (e) and the efforts made on his behalf by his family (h) and society (s); that is, $ql = e \times (h + s)$." Of course, none of the terms that are given here as part of a mathematical formula can be defined precisely, and the operators between terms are arbitrary. This whole movement in British medicine is developing in the wrong direction, and there is a chance that other countries may follow suit.

VI

While measurement by domain of satisfaction as a first step towards a summary score may raise quite a number of issues that are difficult to deal with, these measurements afford instructive insights into the psychic/social climate of modern societies. In measurement of subjective well-being in this substantive way and looked at domain by domain there are no major measurement problems.

To begin, the measurement by domain can be informative about the importance that people attach to various aspects of their life. The most interesting of these studies uses a "critical incidence" technique. Critical incidents are defined as those that affect one's quality of life adversely or positively. A total of 6,500 incidents were reported (experience especially

E. Scheuch

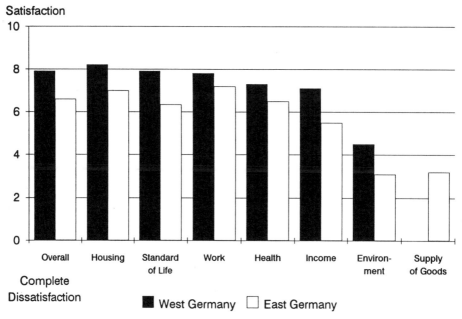

Figure 4. Satisfaction by domain (West and East Germany) (SOURCE:
Wohlfahrtsurvey for West Germany, Summer 1990 in East Germany)

Table 3. Routinization of measurement: individual quality of life—
Linear Analog Assessment (LAZA)

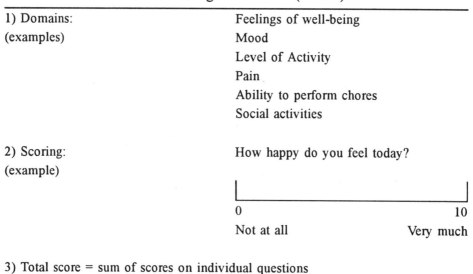

SOURCE: Priestman and Baum 1976.

gratifying, or conversely as cases where one could not do what one very much wanted to do). Judges then grouped the incidents into fifteen "factors." One thousand persons for each age grade (30, 50 and 70 years) were then asked to rate the importance of these factors (see Table 4).

This can be summarized as follows (Flanagan 1982, p. 58):

1. Material comfort
2. Work experienced as rewarding
3. Health and personal safety
4. Active recreation
5. Learning; acquiring new knowledge
6. Relationship with spouse/other person of opposite sex
7. Socializing, participating in social organizations
8. Expressing oneself; being creative.

This hierarchy is quite different from the image that dominates the current discussion of the presumed value change in Western societies. The desire to express oneself, to realize one's individuality, may be central to the intellectuals of our time but is of secondary importance to the vast majority of the population. The satisfaction derived from the immediate environment is dominant.

Satisfaction with the immediate environment is much greater than the valuation for the more distant conditions: public safety, the churches, the environment.

This is the characteristic mood in Western societies now at a high level of material well-being: a positive, warm feeling in the world of firsthand experience, and troubles with the world as it is experienced via the media. The positive personal experiences are no longer generalized as the basis for evaluating conditions at large. An extreme example is the state of public opinion in East Germany—the former GDR. The majority reports that their life conditions improved, while at the same time a majority complains that conditions in East Germany worsened. All areas where one's judgment is based on personal experience receive stable judgments, while the areas where judgment is based on media reports show highly unstable ratings.

The data from the "critical incidence study" (Table 5) must be read with Table 4 in mind. In Table 5, satisfaction is reported as relative to the importance of the factor. The overall finding is that of a negative correlation between the importance of a factor and satisfaction. Thus, health and personal safety are rated highest in importance but lowest in satisfaction for males and females at age 30. Participating in governmental and local affairs is the least important factor among the 30-year-olds but it is the same factor where needs of this age group are best met. Read as relative satisfaction we infer that age is generally a stronger factor than gender. For males the age

Table 4. Percentages reporting each of the 15 components as important or
very important to their quality of life

Component	Male			Female		
	30 years	50 years	70 years	30 years	50 years	70 years
Physical and material well-being						
A—Material comforts: desirable home, food, conveniences, security	80	87	87	75	84	84
B—Health and personal safety	98	96	95	98	97	96
Relations with other people						
C—Relationships with relatives	68	64	62	83	76	79
D—Having and rearing children	84	84	82	93	92	87
E—Close relationships with spouse or member of opposite sex	90	91	84	94	81	42
F—Close friends: sharing views, interests, activities	71	77	75	79	81	89
Social, community, civic activities						
G—Helping and encouraging others	60	72	67	71	77	81
H—Participating in governmental and local affairs	47	63	67	42	59	59
Personal development and fulfillment						
I—Learning, attending school, improving, understanding	87	68	52	81	68	60
J—Understanding yourself and knowing your assets and limitations	84	84	80	92	90	88
K—Work that is interesting, rewarding, worthwhile	91	90	56	89	86	60
L—Expressing yourself in creative manner	48	42	39	53	56	58
Recreation						
M—Socializing with others	48	47	55	53	50	63
N—Reading, listening to music, watching sports, other entertainment	56	46	54	53	56	65
O—Participation in active recreation	59	55	50	50	53	52

NOTE: Question: "At this time in your life, how important is _____?"

SOURCE: Flanagan 1982.

grade 50 appears to be quite favorable, while women show much more positive values at the age of 70.

Data from Germany on levels of satisfaction come closer to our expectations (see Table 6). The dominant impression is one of high levels of satisfaction. Dissatisfaction is concentrated on just three areas: religious institutions, environment and public safety. More important than specific results is the overall message: in six areas (of sixteen) there was a statistically significant decline between 1978 and 1984. This coincides with a general souring of the public mood in Germany during the 1980s, even though this was a decade of steady increases in material well-being. This is another confirmation that material well-being and satisfaction with life are two—although correlated—dimensions.

While there is a remarkable similarity in the patterns of change across domains, one area stands out: in the span of just six years, satisfaction with the state of the environment is nearly halved! No environment can deteriorate so fast as to justify such a change in the evaluation as describing real conditions. The only reasonable explanation is to view the change as a consequence of agenda-setting by the media.

Time series data from surveys show an increase of the difference between "quality of life" as immediately experienced and the quality of life as perceived via the media. Thus, at least for medium-term judgments there is a divorce of media reality from the aggregated reality of individual experiences, and this in turn suggests that a great deal of contextual knowledge is needed in dealing with such "feeling data" (Schuessler 1982; also Krebs & Schuessler 1987).

In contemporary cultural criticism it is usual to portray the world of work as the prime source of alienation. Quality of life data show that this is erroneous. Especially in the (relatively) booming countries, Germany, The Netherlands and Switzerland, satisfaction with the work situation is very high, and dissatisfaction is limited to wages (see Table 7).

Even in Italy, which among the developed countries of Western Europe leads in level of complaints, we find high satisfaction with social relations at the workplace!

While the economies of developed countries constantly rationalize, social critics bemoan a presumed inhuman intensity of work. Again we find that this evaluation from the outside does not coincide with the world of immediate experience (see Figure 5). Yes, work is demanding, but not constantly so, and this is true regardless of the level of efficiency in a country. The structure of judgments in countries with very different economies coincides. From this one can infer that most people in developed countries adjust their valuation to average conditions—whatever the average in a country is.

E. Scheuch

Table 5. Satisfaction by domain

Component	Male			Female		
	30 years	50 years	70 years	30 years	50 years	70 years
Physical and material well-being						
A—Material comforts: desirable home, food, conveniences, security	26	28	23	24	32	27
B—Health and personal safety	14	16	16	14	18	21
Relations with other people						
C—Relationships with relatives	19	29	29	19	29	32
D—Having and rearing children	20	16	18	17	13	16
E—Close relationships with spouse or member of opposite sex	16	18	14	19	28	31
F—Close friends: sharing views, interests, activities	19	19	18	18	21	23
Social, community, civic activities						
G—Helping and encouraging others	39	28	28	38	27	27
H—Participating in governmental and local affairs	46	40	37	46	39	40
Personal development and fulfillment						
I—Learning, attending school, improving, understanding	42	36	28	50	44	36
J—Understanding yourself and knowing your assets and limitations	26	25	24	29	26	22
K—Work that is interesting, rewarding, worthwhile	21	24	24	21	32	22
L—Expressing yourself in creative manner	40	32	27	43	32	31
Recreation						
M—Socializing with others	27	26	26	26	30	28
N—Reading, listening to music, watching sports, other entertainment	29	28	20	30	25	20
O—Participation in active recreation	36	40	34	37	41	37

NOTE: For the 50- and 70-year-olds, the question read, "How well are your needs and wants being met in this regard?" For the 30-year-olds, the question read, "How satisfied are you with your status in this respect?"

SOURCE: Schipper, et al. 1984.

Table 6. Satisfaction by domain (scores: 0 to 10, dissatisfied to satisfied)

	Rather Satisfied		Rather Dissatisfied		Average Scores	
	1978	1984	1978	1984	1978	1984
1. Marriage/Partner	97.4	95.1	0.8	2.4	9.0	8.8**
2. Family life	95.7	93.4	2.0	1.8	8.7	8.4*
3. Management of household	93.6	93.9	1.9	2.8	8.5	8.6
4. Workplace	89.2	90.4	5.1	2.6	7.6	7.9*
5. Household chores	86.9	85.1	5.1	7.6	7.9	7.9
6. Division of labor	85.6	85.4	6.9	8.4	7.9	7.9
7. Housing	83.2	85.4	6.8	5.6	7.8	8.0**
8. Leisure	82.7	81.5	10.4	9.6	7.6	7.7
9. Standard of life	84.6	80.8	6.6	9.5	7.4	7.4
10. Health	79.0	74.1	11.6	14.9	7.3	7.1
11. Income	82.2	74.1	10.0	14.5	7.2	6.9**
12. Social security	76.6	74.2	13.6	13.7	7.0	6.8
13. Education	70.9	72.2	17.1	15.5	6.7	7.0**
14. Church	56.8	54.8	24.6	25.1	5.9	5.8
15. Environment	40.4	22.2	38.7	58.3	5.0	3.8**
16. Public safety	43.7	46.5	40.0	31.4	5.0	5.2**

*Significant change at level 0.01
**Significant change at level 0.001

SOURCE: Zapf, et al. 1987, p. 53.

The most important of the factors that influence the feeling of well-being is the combination of demographic and labor market situations (see Table 8). The least satisfied are the unemployed, and the old are the most satisfied. The latter is quite surprising and may be restricted to old people who live with the benefits of the retirement system of the Federal Republic.

The most important message of the secondary analysis in Table 8 is the low level of dissatisfaction. There is no group where one finds a glaringly different level of dissatisfaction. The increase in structural differentiation and divergence of lifestyles thus coincides with the greater homogeneity of well-being. We shall return to this point!

One of the characteristics of modern society is supposed as that it makes people lonely (see Table 9). Do not believe so; it is just one of the prevalent myths.

Table 7. Conditions at the workplace

| | Satisfaction with . . . | | | |
	"Perks"	Management	Social Relations	Wages
Federal Republic of Germany	76	64	81	55
The Netherlands	74	62	81	61
Switzerland	70	60	77	53
Great Britain	64	59	78	50
Belgium	58	45	67	50
France	59	47	66	48
Italy	36	42	60	37

SOURCE: International Survey Research Limited, Deutscher Instituts-Verlag 13/1988.

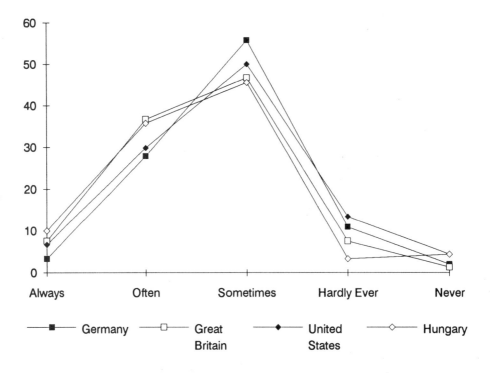

Figure 5. Question: "How often does it happen that you come home exhausted from work?"
(SOURCE: Zentralarchiv für empirische Sozialforschung, ISSP Poll 1989)

However, there are some situations where loneliness is more frequent. Social isolation is most frequent if one lives alone, and especially if one is unmarried. The message of Table 9 is that it is good to be married and have children. These effects are of course intensified by age. One can do nothing worse for oneself than stay alone. This shows especially after age 60.

Table 8. Satisfaction with life one leads
(scale: 0-most dissatisfied to 10-most satisfied)

	Not satisfied	Rather satisfied	Completely satisfied	N
Unemployed	28.6	60.5	10.9	248
Incomplete family	15.3	73.4	11.3	124
Divorced	13.4	73.8	12.8	336
Handicapped	16.8	67.3	15.9	791
Laborer	13.2	71.8	15.0	227
Farmers	6.7	88.3	5.0	60
The old	9.5	65.1	25.4	1,307
Young families	4.7	75.5	19.6	387
Large families	5.5	78.2	16.3	418
Germans	7.1	73.6	19.3	8,830
Foreigners	10.6	68.3	21.1	2,989

SOURCE: Sozio-ökonomisches Panel 1984.

A variety of ways to express the well-being by domain using data from different countries gives a cohesive picture. The formula for personal happiness is: get a good job, marry well, stay healthy, and have kids. The world of firsthand knowledge (the "Lebenswelt" of the phenomenologists) is experienced as mostly satisfying, but the world at large is problematical. By now this dark perception is affecting the appraisal of the "Lebenswelt," too. The world of work is rewarding, especially in international relations, and thus the loss of work increases isolation in general. Nevertheless the overall satisfaction with the life one leads is high, and the ratings of different domains correspond to each other.

Thus, summarizing subjective quality of life is defensible on substantive grounds, provided one treats these numbers as indicating a very rough rank order. Comparisons over time and across cultures using such summary measures are very problematical. A summary self-rating by respondents ("How happy do you feel these days...") is probably a better indicator, provided one aims at comparing groups within countries rather than countries.

Table 9. Social isolation by type of household

Type of household	No regular contact with relative	No close friends	Neither relatives nor friends	No contact with neighbors	Feels lonesome
18-30 years					
Alone	21	10	1	54	22
With spouse	11	13	2	43	18
With spouse & child	14	25	2	34	14
31-59 years					
Alone	32	32	11	41	40
With spouse	24	29	5	42	12
With spouse & child	21	33	7	28	10
60 and older					
Alone	32	44	13	23	46
With spouse without children	68	43	33	25	18
With spouse-empty nest	14	9	9	25	11

SOURCES: Wohlfahrtssurvey 1984; and Statistisches Bundesamt, ed., 1989, *Datenreport* (Wiesbaden).

VII

The view of the world derived from social surveys is completely divorced from the world of non-quantitative social science texts. Since the early 1970s, however, a theory based on quantitative data has become dominant in social science debates that shares with conventional cultural criticism the valuation that the world as just sketched here is a non-rewarding place—but about to disappear. It is a 68-type message in the cloak of quantitative research.

Ronald Inglehart is the author of the theory, that there has been a silent revolution of value change. A new value type, the "Post-Materialists," will replace the old-fashioned materialists and realize a new quality of life. Post-materialists have as a central goal self-realization instead of seeking conventional rewards.

The theoretical base for this claim is a combination of two existing theories. Theory number one is a level theory of personality, as formulated by Maslow. Actually this is nothing else but a restatement of Spranger. The level theory states that once the elementary needs of a person are satisfied, his higher needs then come to the fore. Higher and lower is defined in terms of materialism, with materialism being "low." I personally have a different notion. I do not understand why a refined dinner is not more elevating than a lousy play in the theater.

In addition to the level theory of personality, there is the theory of political socialization as it is prevalent in Ann Arbor; namely, that one receives one's formative impressions about public life and one's values how to respond to this, during teenage years. Inglehart argues that the generation that is now in their early forties in America, and in their early thirties in Europe, grew up at a time of relative affluence. Thus, this generation takes material rewards for granted, and on this basis strives for self-realization.

Figure 6 depicts a one-dimensional factor solution for the various indicators that Inglehart has been using.

A post-materialist person is a person who believes that it is ideas that matter. At the bottom of the figure a "materialist" is characterized as someone who has as priority items "fight inflation," "combat crime" and "encourage economic growth." These materialists are about to be discontinued and give way to post-materialism.

What is the greatest tragedy in science? A beautiful theory slain by an ugly fact. We now have figures for a period of eighteen years for Western Europe combined, about the prevalence of post-materialists. Inglehart has convinced the High Commission in Europe that post-materialism is the wave of the future, and therefore the Eurobarometer's yearly surveys of 14,000 people in Europe include his indicators. Rarely could we wallow in data as in this case.

The majority of people are neither materialists nor post-materialists! We factor analyzed Inglehart's data and found that the majority of Western Europeans are security-minded. The relative importance of various needs is as follows: (1) social security, (2) economic growth, (3) self-realization. Who should be surprised?

From Figure 7, if the saturation-socialization thesis would have been correct, we should have had a curve like A for a constant increase of post-materialists. However, the empirical distribution, B, is one which lends credence to the interpretation that whatever Inglehart has measured is predominantly an age plus education effect.

E. Scheuch

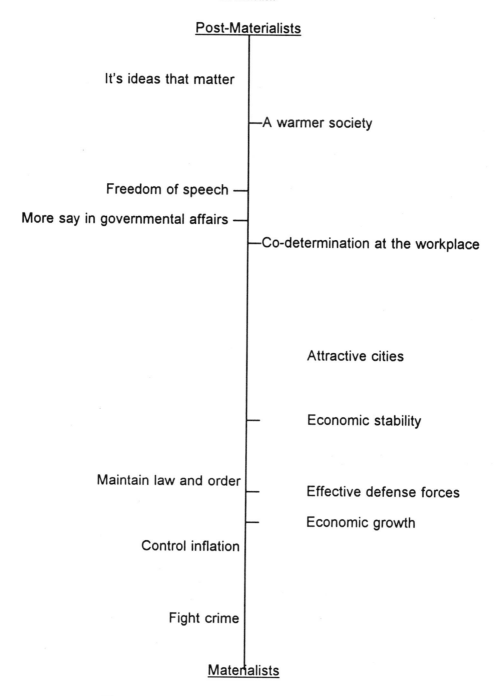

Figure 6. MDS-scaling of value orientation—
projection onto the main dimension (cf. Inglehart 1977)

"Post-materialism" is a transitory phase in the growing up of young people with above-average education from affluent homes. But even among the young, we could not find a change in the frequency of post-materialists (see Figure 8).

Table 10. Distribution of materialists and post-materialists in the Federal Republic of Germany, 1970-1982 (percentages)

	1970	1973	1976	1979	1980	1982
Materialists	43	42	41	37	42	38
Mixed	47*	50*	48*	52*	47	48
Post-materialists	10	8	11	11	11	14

*Not published by Inglehart but calculated by us.

SOURCE: 1970-1979 values, Inglehart 1980; 1980 values, Wildenmann 1980. Data for 1982 are taken from the ALLBUS surveys, which are available in the Zentralarchiv, Cologne.

There is value change in Western Europe and in the United States, but it is dominantly not in the direction of post-materialism. The major change occurs in other areas. It is above all the leveling of differences between the sexes. The females acquire many of the characteristics of males, the males adopt a smaller share of the characteristics of females, such as female standards of bodily cleanliness (never were European males as clean as they are now). Furthermore, the percentage of university graduates increases rapidly, and with that the importance of communication and symbolic politics. Thirdly, there are more options available to people, and that means, of course, there is the possibility to lead one's life in more ways than one.

VIII

The real issue is not post-materialism replacing the materialistic world, but the consequences of a situation where many options are open to people. This leads to a proliferation in the ways in which people organize their lives.

There is widespread agreement in the European social sciences community that the range of choices in organizing one's life is by now quite large, but some disagreement in looking for ways in which range is utilized. In Germany for a long time the notion "individualization of life careers" prevailed. Ulrich Beck as the principal proponent argues that an important expression of these new opportunities is not only the way in which people live at a given moment, but the sequence of choices in the course of life (Beck 1986). The consequence of the individualization is a loss of orientation in a society that has become opaque. Individualization has the parallel

E. Scheuch

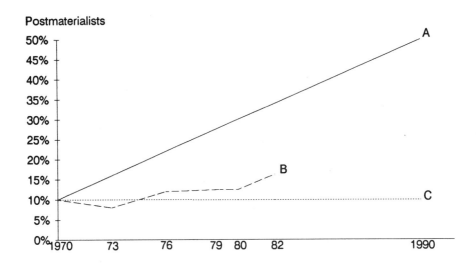

A: generation-socialization hypothesis
B: empirical distribution 1970-1982
C: life-cycle-effect hypothesis

Figure 7. Post-materialism (SOURCE: Bürklin 1984)

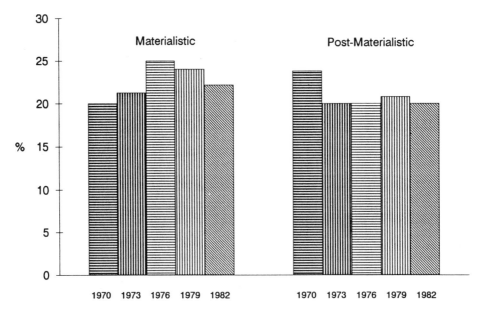

Figure 8. Distribution of materialistic and post-materialistic values among 15-24 year-olds (SOURCE: Secondary analysis from Inglehart data in the Zentralarchiv)

consequence that institutions are liquified—something which Beck likes to demonstrate with alternatives to the conventional family. By now Beck has become the sociologist for alternative lifestyles (Beck 1988, 1991).

The prevailing perspective is the search for lifestyle groups. The world of marketing is credited with first identifying lifestyles. This occurred in reaction to the declining importance of the usual demographic variables in explaining variations in behavior. Especially social class does not "explain" very much in current Western Europe in accounting for variations in behavior. In voting research, too, the milieus (social environments) no longer stabilized behavior, and the percentages of floating vote (Stanford Research Institute 1981) went up. Lifestyle was to be the successor to social class/milieu in understanding individual behavior as being influenced by groups.

Lifestyle is the joint occurrence of choices in goods or actions or people that are being treated as belonging to a family of emotional associations. In a specific lifestyle group, proper behavior calls for choosing the correct automobile, the newspapers fit to be read in this brand of car, the acceptable dress, and friends that fit. Actually, the realization that people do not choose each article by itself, but that choices come as proper packages is not that new. Proper behavior is the core of Max Weber's notion of "standesgemäßes Verhalten"—behavior fit for one's estate.

Important for the social scientists in the U.S. was a study for the Stanford Research Institute (SRI) of Western European populations. The SRI applied a typology developed in the U.S. to samples in France, Italy, Germany, Britain and Sweden. The indicators had been selected with the assumption underlying the "symbolic politics" orientation: behavior is not determined primarily by economic or technological considerations, but by "soft" factors such as aspirations and beliefs. This approach was in turn influenced by the notions of David Riesman and the theories of Maslow (which in turn had inspired Ronald Inglehart). Accordingly, the population of the five countries was sorted into nine "lifestyle groups" as shown in Table 11.

These groups are fitted into an evolutionary scheme ranging from the "need driven" to the "integrated." There are two roads to the top: via achievement or by self-actualization (see Figure 9).

Of course, the differences between countries do not make any sense at all. And the highly ideological character of the classification should be equally obvious. But that appears to be the price for a theoretically grounded lifestyle measurement.

Equally theoretically grounded but less bizarre than the U.S. approach is Bourdieu's (1984). Here, too, material factors have less importance now, while cultural factors alone dominate. With our standard of living, distinction in tastes takes the place of distinctions by buying power. Man succeeds by building up "cultural capital" via befriending the right people by choosing the right things.   The description of behavior in the report by Bourdieu shows the actors on the lookout for the correct things to say and use in order to be with the right people and avoid the wrong ones.   There is some criticism that Bourdieu is not an analyst of contemporary French society but the ethnologist of sophisticated Paris—or for that matter New York's East Side. Using the indicators of Bourdieu but finding culturally equivalent expressions for them we repeated the Paris study in Cologne (see Table 12).

Table 11. Lifestyle groups

	France	Italy	Sweden	U.K.	Germany	U.S.
Need driven						
Survivors (poor)	0	0	4	9	11	4
Sustainers (near poor)	18	20	15	14	40	7
Outer-directeds						
Belongers (traditionalists)	33	25	30	32	11	35
Emulators (upwardly mobile)	12	11	16	16	7	10
Achievers	20	15	22	0	17	22
Inner-directeds						
I-am-me (anti-materialists)	10	9	1	0	13	5
Experiential (post-materialists)	5	0	3	12	0	7
Societally conscious	0	18	7	14	0	8
Integrated (wise)	2	2	2	3	1	2

SOURCE: Stanford Research Institute 1981.

We then factor analyzed the data by means of a non-parametric measure-correspondence analysis (see Figure 10). The first axis can be interpreted as an education axis; indeed, education is ever-increasing as a determining factor for behavior. It is replacing income as an explanation, and it begins to be more important than occupation. Education also allows one to develop one's taste. The second factor can be seen as qualification in the working world; those with qualification stick with familiar things. This finding again points to the centrality of work for the life of modern man, in addition to marriage with children and a good income (Blasius & Winkler 1989).

In contrast to the followers of Bourdieu—Bourdieu is more balanced—we can identify several milieus that are characterized by both demographic variables and taste variables. Thus, objective factors and preferences that can be interpreted as lifestyles are related, as in the notion of Standesgemäße Lebensführung (lifestyle befitting one's estate). But there are also some groupings of preference-styles that are pure lifestyle.

With our data from Cologne, we find that there is definitely still a working class milieu where interest in consumer goods coincides with lack of art appreciation and a liking of Johnny Cash type music. This is different from the behavior patterns of those who are not part of the work force. Here, traditional art, attention to solid food, and bodily care are preferred as a package. Close together in space is the cluster of white collar occupations (employees, professions, owners) where "great art" is appreciated. Fourthly, there is a cluster of those in positions of authority over others, where 20th century art is preferred. Then we can identify two age related groupings: a "young cluster," where rock music and modern painting is liked, and an "old cluster," which is related to a preference for antiques, classical art, and refined living. The indicators selected by Bourdieu proved to be quite informative, but the theory less so, as the behavior that we identify can hardly be viewed as the attempt to amass cultural capital.

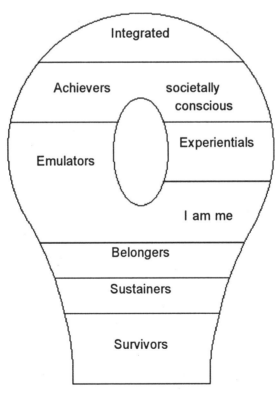

Figure 9. SRI typology of lifestyle

Table 12. The heterogeneity of taste

Correspondence Analysis in Reaction to Bourdieu:
"Distinction—Critique Social du Jugement"

I.   Independent variable:
     a. Respondent's occupational status
     b. Father's occupation
     c. Father's education

II. Dependent variable:
     a. Types of museums preferred
     b. Preferences in pop music
          1. Rudolf Schock (traditional opera and folk songs)
          2. Peter Maffay (rock and pop)
          3. Udo Lindenberg (aggressive, political rock)
          4. BAP (hard rock)
          5. Konstantin Wecker (pop music, contemporary music)
          6. Peter Alexander (traditional pop music)
          7. Roland Kaiser (traditional pop and folk)
          8. Freddy Quinn (lower class pop)
          9. Milva (chanson)
     c. Preferences for painters
          1. Brueghel
          2. Rubens
          3. Rembrandt
          4. Dürer
          5. Renoir
          6. Impressionists
          7. Kokoschka
          8. Kandinsky
          9. Eastern art
          10. Beckmann
          11. Chagall
          12. Picasso
          13. Dali
          14. Abstract painters
     d. Types of stores preferred
     e. Preferred living conditions

SOURCE: Blasius and Winkler 1989.

Most lifestyle investigations are completely unrelated to any theory, and the purpose is the definition of descriptive categories. The routine of such studies is to collect a wide array of preferences, beliefs and behavior, use factor analysis or cluster analysis to group the data—usually unjustifiably so as the level of measurement is at best only ordinal—and find names for the groupings. Usually around seven to ten such groups are calculated, and that is more than is possible given the stability of the numbers. The fickleness of the groupings becomes evident as one finds very different lifestyle taxonomies in preparing for a political campaign, in the marketing of automobiles or in selling prepared food.

A quite typical case of lifestyle groupings as it is used in analyzing involvement in public affairs is that shown in Figure 11.

If lifestyle research is stripped of some of its pretenses, it is useful in characterizing diversity of behavior in modern societies. Only four decades ago the image of the future was mass society. The current fantasy is individualization, fractionization. Lifestyle research helps us to understand that neither of these fantasies is correct. The reality is characterized by something we might call "ordered diversity."

IX

Given the diversity of aspirations, social locations and differences in behavior, which has become so obvious in research on lifestyles and on value change, it is not feasible to come up with a single score that does all the things that those using "quality of life" wanted it to do. Nowhere in modern Western societies is a new consensus in sight that as a result of value change would result in at least an official agreement on values.

If one is interested in social politics, and needs a yardstick to express success and failure, one cannot be satisfied with using percentages of people proclaiming to be happy. Happiness and even more so satisfaction or contentment express to a large degree the successful adjustment of individuals to conditions over which they mostly have no influence. In addition, due to the ceiling effect that follows from the high level of happiness in modern societies, it is quite hopeless to relate statements of happiness to measures of social policy. There is no way forward unless it is accepted that the measurement of conditions and the measurement of feelings are two different things.

In measuring conditions for well-being and/or the state of the collectivity there is no other way than to define what the measure is to express. This has been the preference in Europe, and the work of the OECD is a prime example of this approach (UNESCO 1978). The latest example is the "Human Development Report" that characterizes countries by the conditions they offer for human development (United Nations Development Programme

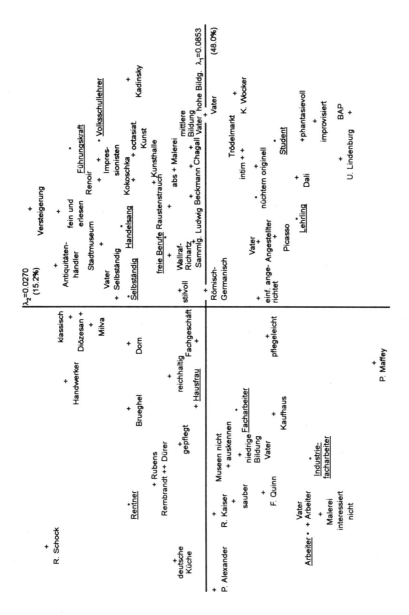

Figure 10. Non-parametric measure-correspondence analysis (Cf. Blasius & Winkler 1989)

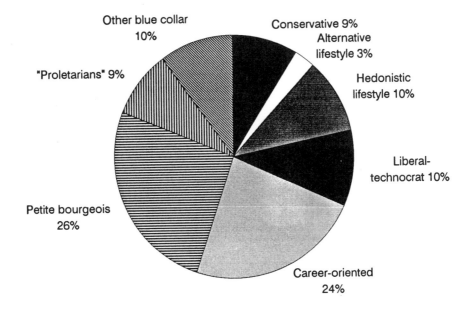

Figure 11. Lifestyle groups
(SOURCE: Prepared for Spiegel Publishing House, Hamburg 1986)

1992). Development is conceived as a process towards more choices for people. The "Human Development Index" is a weighted average of life expectancy, adult literacy, years of schooling, GNP per capita. Of course, one could argue that other factors should have been included, such as crime rates, but this would probably not change the placing of the five best rated countries: Canada, Japan, Norway, Switzerland and Sweden. Other measures in the same report are the Human Freedom Index and the Profile of Human Development for the developing countries. The latter includes such criteria as access to safe water or caloric supply that have no meaning for modern societies.

The Americans have preferred measures of individual, subjective well-being, with a special emphasis on happiness research (see Converse, et al. 1980). This research has done much to increase our understanding for the way in which people cope with their life conditions (see Burt, et al. 1978), but it is quite difficult to use happiness scores in comparisons between countries. To a considerable degree this is made difficult by a gift that people have: to adjust their aspirations as long as it is possible to the situations in which they live (Veenhoven 1988a; also 1988b).

There is an important substantive message following from this diverse research: quality of life in modern societies is experienced by the large majorities as quite good along very traditional dimensions.

References

Beck, Ulrich. 1986. *Risikogesellschaft—auf dem Weg in eine andere Moderne.* Frankfurt: Suhrkamp.

Beck, Ulrich. 1988. *Gegengifte—die organisierte Unverantwortlichkeit.* Frankfurt: Suhrkamp.

Beck, Ulrich, ed. 1991. *Politik in der Risikogesellschaft.* Frankfurt: Suhrkamp.

Blasius, Jörg and Joachim Winkler. 1989. "Gibt es die feinen Unterschiede?" *Zeitschrift für Soziologie und Sozialpsychologie* 41:72-94.

Bourdieu, Pierre. 1984. *La distinction: critique sociale du jugement.* Paris.

Bürklin, Wilhelm. 1984. *Grüne Politik: Ideolog. Zyklen, Wähler und Parteiensystem.* Opladen: Westdeutscher Verlag. [Beiträge zur sozialwissenschaftlichen Forschung Bd. 64]

Burt, Ronald S. et al. 1978. "Structure of Well-Being: Form, Content, and Stability over Time." *Sociological Methods and Research* 6(3):365-407.

Converse, Philip E., et al. 1980. *American Social Attitudes Data Sourcebook: 1947-1978.* Cambridge, Mass.: Harvard University Press.

Flanagan, John C. 1982. "Measurement of Quality of Life: Current State of the Art." *Archives of Physical Medicine and Rehabilitation* 63:56-9.

Inglehart, Ronald. 1977. *The Silent Revolution: Changing Values and Political Styles among Western Publics.* Princeton: Princeton University Press.

Inkeles, Alex. 1988. "National Character Revisited." *Wissenschaftszentrum Berlin* December, pp. 89-103.

Krebs, Dagmar and Karl F. Schuessler. 1987. *Soziale Empfindungen.* New York: Campus; Frankfurt: Main.

Priestman, T. J. and M. Baum. 1976. "Evaluation of Quality of Life in Patients Receiving Treatment for Advanced Breast Cancer." *The Lancet* 1:899-901.

Schipper, H., et al. 1984. "Measuring the Quality of Life of Cancer Patients." *Journal of Clinical Oncology* 2:472-83.

Schuessler, Karl F. 1982. *Measuring Social Life Feelings.* San Francisco: Jossey-Bass.

Schuessler, Karl F. and G. A. Fisher. 1985. "Quality of Life Research and Sociology." *Annual Review of Sociology* 11:129-49.

Stanford Research Institute (SRI). 1981. *Values and Lifestyles in Western Europe.* Stanford: Stanford University Press.

Strack, Fritz, et al., eds. 1991. *Subjective Well-Being.* Oxford: Pergamon Press.

UNESCO, ed. 1978. "Indicators of Environmental Quality and Quality of Life." *UNESCO Reports and Papers in the Social Sciences,* No. 38.

United Nations Development Programme (UNDP). 1992. *Human Development Report 1992.* New York: United Nations.

Veenhoven, Ruut. 1988a. *The Happiness Revenues of Economic Wealth and Growth.* Arbeitspapier Nr. 263 des Sonderforschungsbereichs 3. der J. W. Goethe Universität Frankfurt und Universität Mannheim.

Veenhoven, Ruut. 1988b. "The Utility of Happiness." *Social Indicators Research* 20:333-54.

Zapf, Wolfgang et al. 1987. *Individualisierung und Sicherheit.* München.

Chapter 7

NEW SOCIAL MOVEMENTS AND ALTERNATIVE MODES OF DEVELOPMENT

S. N. Eisenstadt

The Hebrew University of Jerusalem

In our discussion of development we have to take into account that the contemporary world is a world in which modernity and modernization, modern technology, different patterns of economic development and institutions, modern political ideologies, and modes of political protest and participation constitute central characteristics. But the more these and other aspects of modernization, which originated in the West, have spread throughout the world, the more difficult and problematic it has become to define exactly what is meant by modernization, and especially to define how and to what degree different contemporary modern societies move in the same direction or directions, or become more and more similar.

Contrary to the suppositions of some of the earlier theories of development, it has become more and more apparent that there has been continuously developing a far-reaching reformulation of the vision of modernization, of modern civilizations.

Instead of looking at the process of modernization as the ultimate endpoint of the evolution of all known societies—which brings out the evolutionary potential common to all of them and of which the European experience was the most important and succinct manifestation and paradigm—modernization, modernity, has to be seen as one specific type of civilization which has originated in Europe and which has spread, in its economic, political and ideological aspects, all over the world, encompassing, especially after the second World War, almost all of it.

Just as was the case with respect to an expansion of all historical civilizations, the civilization of modernity in particular, it challenged the symbolic and institutional premises of those societies that were incorporated into it, calling for responses from within them, opening up new options and possibilities. Out of these responses there developed a great variety of modern or modernizing societies, sharing many common characteristics, but at the same time also evincing great differences among themselves. These differences crystallized out of a selective incorporation and hence also a recrystallization and transformation of the major symbolic premises and institutional formulations of both the original "Western," as well as of their own, civilizations.

It is the continuous interaction or feedback between a great variety of such processes—the basic premises of those civilizations and societies on which the new modern international systems impinged and the points of entry of these societies into these international systems; the types and modes of technology and of economy prevalent in these civilizations; the tradition of response to situations of change; and the traditions of heterodoxy, rebellion and innovation that have developed in the history of these civilizations in particular—that has generated the crystallization of the varying institutional and symbolic contours of modern and modernizing societies, their dynamics, and the different patterns of economic development within them.

It is out of these processes that there have been continuously crystallizing in different societies and civilizations different modes of incorporation and reinterpretation of the premises of modernity; of the different symbolic reactions to it; as well as the development of various modern institutional patterns and dynamics, or conversely, different modes of reinterpretation of the premises and historical traditions of the civilization.

These different symbolic and institutional constellations have developed first of all with respect to the interpretation of the basic symbolic conceptions and premises of different modern civilizations; with respect to the ways in which these basic symbolical premises of modernity are selected and reinterpreted according to the new "modern" traditions; in their conception of themselves and of their past; and with respect to their new symbols and collective identity and their negative or positive attitudes to modernity in general and to the West in particular.

These processes of reinterpretation also apply with respect to the basic concept of economic development. While the emphasis on economic and technological development has certainly become part of each modern or modernizing society or civilization, these still differ greatly with respect to the overall meaning of such development in the context of their overall cultural and social premises. Above all, they vary with respect to the degree to which the emphasis on economic development is connected with an emphasis on the mastery of their respective environments as against an adaptation to it; to the relative importance of economic goals in the panorama of human goals; to conceptions of the social order; to productive as against distributive economic orientations with respect to the type of political regimes—whether authoritarian, pluralist or totalitarian regime: with respect to major modes of political protest and participation; to conceptions of authority, hierarchy, and equality.

Similarly, the crystallization of these different developments has been taking place continuously—in close relation to those on the symbolic level—with respect to the different forms of modern organizations and institutions. While such processes as urbanization, industrialization, and the spread of modern communications are indeed common to all these societies, the concrete institutional answers to these problems still tend to vary greatly, closely related as they are to the basic concepts of social and political order that have developed within them.

But it is not only within the societies beyond the West that developments took place which went beyond the initial model of Western society. At the same time in Western societies themselves there have taken place some far-reaching changes which have greatly transformed this model—pointing out to some new directions which are of interest from the point of view of approaches to development.

One of the most important of such changes has been the development of new types of formal movements which differ greatly from the "classical" ones—the national and socialist ones which were characteristics of the initial vision of modernity.

In the initial stages of the development of modern and industrial society, most movements of social protest revolved around the revolutionary vision of the broadening of the scope of participation and channels of access to the centers, changing or reforming their cultural and social contents, solving the problems of unequal participation in them and finding ways to attenuate or overcome, through the policies of the center, the most important problems arising out of industrialization and the development of capitalist economy. It was the reconstruction of the centers of societies that constituted the major goals of most social and national movements in this period of modernity, and these goals were perceived as embodying the most important charismatic dimension of the modern socio-cultural order. Or, in other words, it was the construction of the socio-political center, or centers, and of national communities, the quest for access to it, and participation in it, in combination with the vision of economic progress, that constituted the major foci of the orientations and movements of protest of modernity. The fullest illustration of such movements of protest has been in the classical "nation-state" and "class struggle" as envisaged by most revolutionary and reformist socialist as well as by the various nationalistic movements.

These centers were viewed as the principal arenas for the implementation of the charismatic orientations through which the modern social and cultural orders are defined and also as the most important reference point for individuals' cultural and collective identities. They were also conceived as being able, through appropriate social policies or through revolutionary change, to restructure those aspects of the modern economy that were regarded as most conducive to alienation and anomie.

The new movements of protest that have developed from the 1960s on, starting from the students' rebellions, and up to the more recent ecological movements—those stressing growing participation in work, different communal orientations, citizen movements, and the like—entailed a different orientation. Instead of conflictual-ideological focus on the center and its reconstitution which characterized the earlier "classical" social movements of modern and industrial societies, the new ones were oriented at what one scholar has defined as the extension of the systemic range of social life and participation.

Perhaps the single simplest manifestation of change in such orientations has been that from the emphasis on the increase in the standard of life which was so characteristic of the 1950s as the epitome of continuous technological-economic progress to that of "quality of life"—a transformation which has been designated in the 1970s as one from materialist to post-materialist values.

These changes in the basic orientations of the movements of protest have been influenced by the changing relations among state, economy and society, which have developed in late industrial societies and have been reinforced by the bureaucratization of the channels of mobility that developed in capitalist and socialist countries alike, as well as by the growing internationalization of economic markets, corporations and government activities. These processes were very closely related to the growing transformation of the overall structure of political economy in Western democratic societies, from an overwhelmingly "liberal market" model to one based on a combination effected by the development of welfare state and Keynesian policies—of market and distributive policies, and of the concomitant, even if paradoxical, weakening of the charismatic importance of the center, and to a restructuring of the social strata which we shall discuss in the next paragraphs.

Very central in the shaping of these developments was the growing importance of education and knowledge as the major bases for occupational advancement. While this growing importance of education—and the extension of universal education—has certainly not abolished class distinction and inequalities, it has yet introduced a very strong element of cultural egalitarianism and of dissociation of the old type of status relations between occupational and cultural arenas. This element has also, of course, been reinforced by the mass media; by the unique combination of homogenization of many of the messages of these media together with the broadening—through these very media—of access to many of the arenas of cultural creativity.

All these tendencies have been connected with a very far-reaching shift from viewing either the technological-economic or the political centers as the basic arenas of the charismatic dimension of the ontological and social visions.

The center, the political center, does still constitute the major arena for the distribution of resources, but it no longer constitutes the major focus of the charismatic dimensions and orientations of various social movements—or of large sectors of the society.

These various processes of change and the development of the revolutionary movements of protest in particular had very far-reaching impact on several crucial aspects of social life in Western societies.

Among the most important of such aspects have been, first, a weakening of the former, relatively rigid, homogeneous definition of life patterns, and hence also of the boundaries of family, community, or of spatial and social organization; second, the development of a strong tendency to the dissolution of most of the major roles from encompassing, society-wide, symbolic, and institutional frameworks. Occupational, family, gender and residential roles have become more and more dissociated from "Stande," class and part-political regional frameworks. Such various roles tended more and more to crystallize into continuously changing clusters, with relatively weak orientations to such broad frameworks in general, to the societal centers in particular.

Third, there has taken place a redefinition of many roles and role clusters—especially the occupational and citizenship roles. Thus, for instance, in the occupational sphere, there has developed, first, the growing inclusion of community or "service" components into purely professional and occupational activities; second, there tends also to develop a growing dissociation between high occupational strata and "conservative" political and social attitudes, creating generations of high executives with political and cultural "leftist views" and with orientation to participation in some of these new "permissive enclaves" or subcultures.

In the political sphere and in the definition of the citizenship role there have developed tendencies to the redefinition of boundaries of collectivities; to growing dissociation between political centers and the social cultural collectivities; and to the development of new nuclei of cultural and social identity which transcend the existing political and cultural boundaries.

Fourth, one of the most important institutional changes connected with those tendencies has been the development of various structural, semi-liminal enclaves within which new cultural orientations, new modes of search for meaning—often couched in transcendental terms—tend to be developed and upheld, partially as counter-cultures, partially as components of new culture.

These enclaves, in which some people may participate fully, others in a more transitory fashion, may serve in some situations as reservoirs of revolutionary activities and groups, but on the whole they tend to serve as loci or starting points of far-reaching changes in roles and cultural orientations.

The combinations of these changes in the symbolic definition of different arenas of social life and of structural changes gave rise to a growing diversification of the process of strata formation, to the development of a very diversified crisscross of political, sectoral and occupational formations.

Thus, instead of the situation characteristic of the "modern" and "industrial" society, in which different strata had relatively separate cultural traditions and focused around some broad common political symbols, there has continuously developed greater dissociation among the occupational, cultural, and political spheres of life.

On the other hand, different strata no longer have separate, totally different "cultures" as before; they tend more and more to participate in common aspects, foci and arenas of culture in general, and mass culture in particular.

These developments have given rise to very complicated differences in styles of life among different status groups and new status sets, and new patterns of status of class conflict and struggles, new types of status or "class" consciousness, to the weakening of any overall, especially "class" or "social" ideological orientations, in the crystallization of such consciousness.

There is an interesting parallelism between these developments in Western societies and the emergence of new patterns of development all over the world. While these are not necessarily similar, yet they point to rather similar or parallel trends, namely that of creation of new spaces in place of a homogeneous approach to the structuration of social life in which alternative social and cultural activities are tied.

Chapter 8

SOCIAL MOVEMENTS AND SOCIAL POLICIES: A MISPLACED POLARITY IN SOCIAL RESEARCH

T. K. Oommen

Jawaharlal Nehru University

I propose to argue in this paper that (a) the confluence between social movements and social policies is continuously increasing, viewed in terms of the goals pursued by them, (b) the changing conceptualization of the State has played an important role in bringing about this confluence, and (c) sociology could not play a creative role in this context because of the limited empirical base from which it tended to conceptualize and theorize social reality.

Those who did research on social movements and revolutions initially viewed them either as pathological aberrations or anti-systemic eruptions, the conservative band. Their commitment appeared to get the system quickly back to equilibrium while the radicals who did research on this theme constituted themselves into a demolition squad, as it were, to squash the state system. They invariably opted for revolutionary transformation and structural change, rarely realizing that no system ever undergoes total change. But neither the conservatives nor the radicals ever asked themselves what kind of research would be useful to those who lead movements, viewed in terms of the objective of movement activists, namely the reconstruction of society. Reconstruction does not call for total destruction. However, partial destruction, selective retention, judicious borrowing and gradual accretion are all necessary ingredients of authentic reconstruction. To wit, we have a sociology *of* social movements but no sociology *for* social movements (see Rootes 1990).

In contrast, those who did research on social policy thought it to be an instrument of conflict management, which would bridge the conflicts between classes, interest groups, the majority and minority groups as well as a tool investing legitimacy in political, economic and social institutions. Their ultimate commitment was to system stability, although, of course, they were willing to concede some concessions in the form of changes in the system (see Oyen 1986). However, even a cursory acquaintance with the history of successful social policy unfolds its potentials to bring about an incremental revolution leading to the emergence of a society characterized by equity and justice. But social policy researchers have invariably ignored this. That is, we have a sociology *for* social policy and not a sociology *of* social policy (see Sigg 1986).

I suggest that the present predicament of the state of research on social movements and social policies is the result of this ignoring of the historicity of context of these phenomena. I propose to examine the validity of this proposition by tracing the trajectories of social movements and social policies.

THE TRAJECTORY OF SOCIAL MOVEMENTS

Conventional wisdom in sociology views social movements as a united effort on the part of the deprived social categories to bring about social change. In this perspective, movements are defined as oppositional forces against the status quo. This perspective probably had greater validity at a time when the state operated as a mere police state, confining its attention to the protection of the citizens from external aggression and providing them with adequate internal security to facilitate the pursuit of their chosen economic activities. But with the emergence of the notion of welfare and socialist states, what had hitherto been defined as private worries have become public issues (Mills 1959). And in the case of New States, consequent upon their gaining independence at a particular juncture in history, the state had to inspire and institutionalize far-reaching changes (see Worsley 1964; Rex 1974). In this process, the state has had to mobilize its vast masses into collective actions; the state bureaucracy which was hitherto taken to be an agent of the status quo was gradually turned into, at least by definition, an instrument of change and development. This transformation in the functions of the state and the mode of its functioning has tremendous significance for the analysis of social movements in the contemporary world situation, particularly in developing countries. In all the socialist countries the state was the chief and often the only agent of mobilization of people, the most telling example of which was the Cultural Revolution in communist China. But the large-scale mobilization of people to bring about change is not altogether absent in other countries. Thus, India's massive rural reconstruction program was intended to operate more as a movement than a bureaucratic venture. It is not argued here that governmental programs can be easily equated with movements, as is conventionally understood. However, what I am suggesting is that the change in the overall orientation and in the mode of functioning of the state is likely to bring about changes in the nature and types of developmental strategies and the techniques of mobilization employed by it. If this is so, one must take into account this dimension while analyzing social movements.

Viewed in a broad historical perspective, we may identify four major phases in the transformation of political authority structures and the concomitant variations in the nature of social movements. The first is the "prepolitical" or "stateless" phase during which movements of the type we are familiar with since the 16th century did not exist. Most movements of this phase were akin to elementary collective behavior or, if one prefers, spontaneous mobilizations. That is why the description of the activities of movements during this phase is often invoked through notions such as primitive rebellions, tribal outbreaks, slave riots, etc. The principal contenders of power in these contexts were primordial collectivities such as clans and tribes, often led by their hereditary chieftains operating in limited geographical locales.

As the scale of human communities increased, large aggregations and collectivities came to be organized under a limited number of central authority systems—the era of empires, nation-states, and colonies. Gradually, the notion of nation-state assumed wide currency and an increasing number of territorially bound primordial collectivities—religious, linguistic, regional groups—came to claim the status of nation-state. The typical movements of this, that is the second, phase were anti-imperialist and anti-colonial mobilizations.

During the third phase, with the spread of science and technology following the industrial revolution and development of modern capitalism, the antagonism between classes grew and movements of particular class or occupational categories came into vogue—the working class movements and peasant revolutions. They either led to structural change, that is, changed drastically the class character (not class composition) of those who wielded authority, or they facilitated the emergence of new wielders of authority who, at least by definition, identified themselves with the poor, the disadvantaged and the oppressed, exemplified by the political power-holders of the socialist and the welfare states respectively.

The present phase is marked by the consolidation of capitalism and the decline of socialism, on the one hand, and the emergence of a limited number of "post-industrial" societies, on the other. These developments gave birth to the notion of a global division of state-societies based on the type of economy and the level of economic development—First, Second, Third, and now even Fourth, World. This phase has also witnessed a proliferation of international movements for human rights, dignity of women, disarmament, environmental protection, ecological balance, etc.

Admittedly, the above characterization of changes in the structures of authority and of movements cannot be viewed as a sequence for the entire world, given the differing levels of development prevailing in different parts of the world and sometimes within the same state-societies. However, if our characterization is broadly correct, it may safely be asserted that the changing features of the structures of authority alter substantially the nature of social movements. Notwithstanding the fact that a segment of the human population still continues to be pre-political in terms of consciousness and that a minority of humanity has entered the post-industrial phase, almost the entire humanity is today organized into state-societies. In spite of the existence and proliferation of a large number of global organizations and movements and the increasing visibility of international public opinion, the effective authority structures exist only at the level of state-societies.

In terms of the world situation today, we can visualize at least three possible relationships between the state and social movements. First, the authoritarian states run by military juntas, religious fundamentalists, and racist groups which invariably oppress, or attempt to oppress, all social movements which challenge state authority: Second, one-party systems which oppress effective challengers of state authority but sponsor such movements which work to their advantage so as to sustain and nourish state power. Third, the multi-party systems which allow a large number of social movements to originate and proliferate but resort to repression against those movements which pose an explicit threat to the very existence of the state. That is, no state by its very nature permits the operation of movements which undermine its authority, notwithstanding the fact that the elasticity of permissiveness and the limits of tolerance admittedly vary according to the source of its authority.

An increasing number of states in the world today are accepting the welfarist ideology, inspiring and institutionalizing changes in a direction demanded by citizens through the instrument of social policy. The ideology and the mode of functioning of states have undergone substantial changes, which cannot be ignored when an effort at empirically rooted theory-building is attempted. Thus the most fertile empirical setting for understanding the state's response to social movements is provided by a state which combines a 'socialist' or welfarist ideology with a multi-party system.

The following types of social movements may emerge in the kind of empirical setting referred to above: (a) social movements sponsored or supported by the government if a section of the "national" population is perceived as a stumbling block in institutionalizing change in terms of state ideology; (b) social movements against the government by an overwhelming majority of the population either because it deviates from the professed state ideology or because the government perpetuates itself in power through state violence; (c) social movements against the government as well as against a section of the collectivity which supports it, to stem the aberrant tendencies which crept into the mode of functioning of the state. These possibilities prevail because the government in a multi-party system is supported by one or more specific political parties or organizations and the opposition parties and movements are permitted to exist and function.

It should be clear from analysis so far that state response to social movements does not fall into a unilinear pattern; it is dictated by the nature of mobilization attempted by a movement. Conversely, the character of the party in power is a critical variable in determining state response. Armed with this understanding, let us look at the plausible patterns of state response. We can discern at least four empirical possibilities:

1. The ideology and the means of a movement correspond to those of the state. That is, both the state and the movement pursue the same goals, and the means employed by the movement are defined as legitimate by the state. In such a situation, state-sponsored movements come to stay, and in all probability the state-response is one of *facilitation*.

2. The ideology of a movement differs from that of the state but its means correspond to those perceived as legitimate by the state. The typical state response is that of *toleration*.

3. The ideology of a movement corresponds to that of the state but the means differs. That is, the movement and the state compete to attain the same goal but through different routes. The state attempts at *discreditation* of the movement.

4. Both the ideology and means of a movement differ from those of the state. The state would spare no effort at *repression* of such movements.

It may also be stated here that social movement is the weapon of the weak against the strong whether viewed globally or within the confines of state-societies. Movements, therefore, are a mechanism of transfer of power from the entrenched vested interests which project themselves as the legitimate power holders, whether the source of legitimacy is divine or secular, to the hitherto powerless and marginalized. Movements are enterprises which endeavor to move those in the periphery to the center, or which attempt to create new centers of power so that the alienated and marginalized are brought into the orbit of participation which is one of the indices of quality of life (see Oommen 1990).

And yet, not only is the efficiency of social movements as instruments of the poor's welfare doubted, it is even argued that organized social movements do not serve the interests of the poor as they cannot afford to expend voluntary time to maintain movement organizations, a privilege of the middle class and the affluent (see Piven & Cloward 1979). Further, it is argued that the poor achieve the most when they resort to riots and rebellions; that is, when they take to non-legitimate means to pursue their goals. This is said to be so even in the case of large-scale violent mobilization; viz., revolutions (see Sckopol 1979). The implications of this argument for the present purpose are mainly two. First, if the poor want to achieve culturally pre-scribed goals, they should take recourse to socially proscribed means. But in the process the forces of vested interests, often operating through and as the state, would easily oppress the poor: operation successful, patient suc-cumbed. Second, revolutions and movements do not need theorists and activists; they occur in spite of them because of the conjunction of certain structural conditions. Thus the role of human action and agency are not only dispensed with but even disparaged.

However, both these propositions stand controverted in the light of other studies. Let me cite just two of them. Castells (1977) concludes after studying urban riots in Paris that unruly protests are unsuccessful and that orderly collective actions are most productive of desired results. Touraine (1981) accords centrality to social action, sociological knowledge and to human agency. According to him, without bestowing any cognitive privilege to the theorist over the ordinary activists, the researcher can play the role of a committed sociological interventionist, capable of guiding social transfor-mation. It is not possible or even necessary for one to go into the issue of the sustainability of Touraine's assumptions here. Suffice it to say that one can discern a sociology *for* social movements in his writings.

THE EVOLUTION OF SOCIAL POLICY

The parentage of social policy as we understand it today may be traced to industrial urbanism and the ideology of the welfare state. Its major instrument is social legislation and its chief clientele is constituted by materi-ally deprived citizens and vulnerable groups. Social policy is conceived as an instrument of conflict resolution between classes, interest groups and even institutions—market and government (see for example, Titmuss 1958; Mishra 1981; Offe 1984).

I have argued above that concomitant to the changes in the character of the state the nature and types of social movements that would emerge in a state-society may vary. The proposition holds true, albeit in a different way, in the case of social policy too. Analyzing the evolution of social policy historically, Titmuss distinguishes between three different models of social policies—the Residual Model, the Achievement-Performance Model, and the Institutional-Redistributive Model (see Gore 1983).

Under the Residual Model the state accepted very limited responsibili-ty; it provided for the basic minimum needs of only the destitute because the needs of the vulnerable groups were to be attended by family and kin, neighborhood and community, religious organizations and charitable trusts. By the early and mid-20th century the Achievement-Performance Model became popular in the capitalist societies of Western Europe, as the state stepped in to provide for the basic needs of these citizens who belonged to the vulnerable groups. But the individual recipients were required to make a contribution in order to deserve state assistance. In the Institutional-Redistributive Model the state provides the citizens with all the basic needs irrespective of their contribution. This model of social policy, in effect, led to the convergence of the ideologies of the welfare state and the socialist state.

Notwithstanding the differential value-orientations in the three models, two things are common to them. First, the focus of attention in all the three models is the individual, and second, the emphasis is on meeting the material needs. But social policy has undergone profound changes in regard to these dimensions in recent times. The scope of social policy has enlarged to encapsulate the non-material needs and aspirations of the vulnerable groups. The unit of social policy today is as much a group as it is an individual. Presently I propose to trace the trajectory of this transformation.

Though social policy of one type or another is accepted by most contemporary societies, the Western capitalist states in which industrial revolution occurred first did not show any concern for the poor and the needy in the beginning. But thanks to the Fabian Socialists who articulated their concern for distributive justice, the state gradually endorsed the ideology of welfarism. This process was at least partly accelerated because of the centrality given to distributive justice in the emerging socialist state. But within the European context, the populations of state-societies, be they capitalist or socialist, were/are largely homogeneous, consisting of one physical type (race), one religion (Christians/Catholics/Protestants) and speakers of one language, constituted as they were on the maxim one-nation, one-state, barring a few exceptions. The needy citizens—the poor, the destitute, the physically handicapped, the mentally deranged, and the well-off ones, were all drawn from the same people.

The scenario changed drastically when multi-racial, poly-ethnic and/or multi-national states emerged due to large-scale immigration, colonization and conquest. The vulnerable groups in these state-societies were not simply the poor and the physically or mentally handicapped but also the racially distinct (as in the case of the Native Americans and the Blacks in the U.S.), culturally different (as in the case of different nationalities in the U.S.S.R.) or the socially stigmatized (as in the case of the Scheduled Castes and Scheduled Tribes in India). If the vulnerable group, the traditional target of social policy in homogeneous societies, is an aggregate of individuals drawn from the same people, in heterogeneous societies the vulnerable group is an aggregation of organic collectivities. Consequently, the primary source of deprivation, at any rate the cognition about it, shifts from individual biography to collective history. Understandably, the structure of deprivation provides the moment for collective action and the deprived collectivities often resort to it.

On the other hand, the state itself would have to respond to the situation by introducing innovations in social policy. Affirmative action in the U.S., nationalist policy in the U.S.S.R., protective discrimination in India afford examples of social policy to cope with the mobilizations of the deprived. But to the extent distributive justice and participatory development constitute important elements of state ideology, the situation gets further complicated. The people are no more mere targets to be developed through centralized planning, they are not clients of the state bureaucracy but are participants, at least by definition, in the very process of planning and development.

I have referred above to the shift in the unit of social policy from individual to collectivity as one moves from homogeneous to heterogeneous state-societies and have pointed to the concomitant shift in three contexts: (a) in the structure and source of deprivation, (b) in the nature of social policy, and (c) in the possibility of response patterns by the deprived who may resort to collective action. But the state-society still provides the frame of reference for policy formulation. Presently, I propose to show that gradually the definition of deprivation and the distribution of the deprived has shifted from particular state-societies to whole blocks of them. This changed cognition is made possible because of a paradigm shift in social science. There are several elements/steps involved here.

First, the world has come to be conceptualized as one unit, thanks to the omnipresence and omnipotence of the capitalist system, popularized as the World system model (see Wallerstein 1974, 1979). Second, notwithstanding the above, these differences in the levels of development and patterns of culture have led to cognizing the world as different: viz., the First, the Second, the Third, and sometimes even the Fourth Worlds (see Worsley 1984). Third, once the world came to be viewed as one system, a new cognition crystallized: development or underdevelopment of blocks of state-societies was not simply a matter of production but was as much a matter of unequal exchange. The Third World, perching on the precarious periphery, is eternally disadvantaged, and the First World, occupying the center, is perennially advantaged, according to the refrain of dependency theory (see Frank 1969). In this conceptualization, the vulnerable are not simply individuals and groups *within* state-societies but a whole set of state-societies, the Third World.

Even the world system model accounts only for the human world and ignores the non-human environment. The emerging new paradigm of development focuses on participatory and endogenous development which encapsulates the ecological perspective as an alternative to modernization (see

Alechina 1982; Capra 1982). Authentic development implies quality of life and it is possible to achieve this only if development is sustainable, the prerequisites being regulating the consumption of energy, avoiding ecological degradation and environmental pollution. The paradigm of limits to growth, initially enunciated by the Club of Rome and currently articulated in the multiple incarnations of green movements all over the world unfolds a new cognition about the concept of quality of life.

From the perspective of the present discussion then, we may say that invention and indiscriminate application of high technology create two new types of vulnerable groups which are the targets of social policy. First, high technology, due to its labor-displacing orientation, prevents the aspiring young from entry into the employment market while depriving the employed of their current employment. Available evidence suggests that the victims in this context are mainly the less skilled, particularly the women. Second, the application of high technology leads to the dislodging of the peasantry and the tribes from their traditional habitats and, in the absence of appropriate rehabilitation policies, makes them destitute. The burden of my argument is to unfold a dilemma. The ongoing process of development paradoxically increases the size and variety of the deprived and the vulnerable, the objects of social policy.

Even as we take cognizance of this phenomenon we should not be impervious to the importance of consciousness in the emergence of deprived groups. First, there are multiple sources of deprivations and the saliency of the source varies from one category to another. A new source of deprivation may surface because of a new perception by a category.

Second, new consciousness is also a function of changing self-definitions and perceptions. Thus, the erstwhile stigmatized groups—unwed mothers, prostitutes, homosexuals—who voluntarily retreat from the mainstream society and may have remained invisible earlier, demand special considerations from the state and other agencies of social welfare. This in turn necessarily leads to a change in the definition of vulnerable groups by the state, leading to an expansion of the constituency of the deprived.

Third, the contemporary democratic ethos and the collective mobilization which it implies can create subjectively deprived groups such as the rural elites, the new bourgeoisie emerging from the traditionally underprivileged groups or those from the traditional aristocracy but currently experiencing a downward mobility. Given the arithmetic of adult franchise, they can put considerable pressure on a soft state through frequent collective mobilizations.

The point I want to make is that the size, the context and the variety of those who are defined as deprived are constantly bulging, not simply because development is dysfunctional but also because new groups demand attention and consideration from the state. In turn, this often leads to a confluence of state action articulated through social policy measures and through people's action manifested in social movements. And yet, researchers on social policy confine their attention to the nitty gritty of social policy, ignoring the wider issues. That is why we have a sociology *for* social policy and not a sociology *of* social policy.

TOWARDS A BALANCED QUALITY OF LIFE INDEX

Let me finally, and very briefly, deal with the changing content of social policy which points to the emerging notion of quality of life. Essentially, social policy is concerned with two sets of issues: equality and freedom, both of which contribute to human welfare, understood in the broad sense of the term. While it is relatively easy to quantify, measure and define equality as compared with freedom, yet there have been endless squabbles about both conceptualizing and operationalizing even the notion of equality.

The concept of equality has two major elements: equality in regard to the access, possession and ownership of material goods and equality of opportunity. Nobody ever argued in favor of absolute equality in regard to the distribution of material goods, given the premise that human needs vary enormously. But most people endorse equality of opportunity, a device which leads to the social differentiation of individuals based on their competence. To provide equally to everyone, ignoring their differential capacity, inclination to work or contribution to society, it is agreed, would sap individual initiative, dull motivation and erode incentive. However, there is consensus as regards the providing of basic needs to all, irrespective of their capacity or worth or inclination to work.

While basic or minimum needs certainly include provision for nutriment, clothing, housing, health care, etc., it is widely acknowledged that human beings do not live by food alone. Precisely because of this recognition the need to construct an authentic quality of life index, by fusing the needs of food and freedom, is widely accepted. But there is a catch here. While man cannot live by food alone, he cannot live at all without food. That is, to exercise freedom, man must live, to live he must have food. To put it pithily, there is a hierarchy of needs—both material and non-material—and to ignore this is to invite utter confusion. One has to recognize the relative weighting and contextual relevance of different items which go into constituting the quality of life index. What I am suggesting would be evident if we look at the recent document of the United Nations Development Program (UNDP) entitled *Human Development Report for 1991*.

I am not suggesting that indices for development and freedom should not or cannot be fused in order to construct a composite quality of life index but I am insisting that this should be done with great care so that it is rendered authentic. The freedom index of UNDP has some forty indicators and the toppers in the list are the small homogeneous state-societies of Western Europe. They also figure among the development toppers led by Japan. Why is it so? As I have tried to indicate earlier, in multi-national, multi-racial and/or poly-ethnic state-societies a wide variety of interest groups emerge and demand "freedoms" which may endanger the very existence of that society. Serious conflicts can ensue between the parts and the whole in such systems. The state may have to, and often it does, intervene to moderate such conflicts which invariably would mean infringement on freedom. This may be illustrated with an example.

The United States of America, the classic land of free enterprise and individual freedom, ranks thirteenth among the freedom rankers. That is, constitutional intention cannot always be put into practice unless the existential reality makes it possible. The fact that the U.S. is a multi-racial and poly-ethnic society necessarily breeds a wide variety of inter-group conflicts and the state has to manage conflicts often by limiting freedom.

Another difficulty arises out of giving equal weightings to all freedoms. The UNDP document gives equal weightings to the restriction put by the state on travel abroad and the torture meted out to criminals, militants and secessionists by the state! It is well-known that the new states which emerged following nearly two centuries of colonial rule are yet to consolidate themselves as "nations." The state in these societies has no option but to take appropriate action to contain and control elements which attempt destabilization, often abetted and sponsored by outside agencies. On the other hand, if a substantial proportion of the highly qualified, competent and trained manpower from developing countries opts to migrate to affluent countries, after having availed themselves of liberal state subsidies for training, in search of better pastures, the state would be constrained to intervene and restrict it in the "national interest."

Thirdly, the UNDP document defines freedom mechanically. It recognizes the "right to determine the number of one's children" as a personal freedom. But one can have a dozen children and abdicate one's moral responsibility to rear them, which can be catastrophic from the societal point of view in an underdeveloped and over-populated country. On the other hand, one can abstain from the process of human reproduction even when one has adequate material resources to support a couple of children. In a society in which the population is fast declining this would have adverse consequences. The point of all this is that (a) freedom cannot be understood independently from responsibility, and (b) freedom will have to be evaluated contextually.

The notion of "quality of life" as a universal concept needs to be demystified; to be meaningful it should be concretized in terms of the historicity of context to which it is being applied. To evolve authentic indices of quality of life, social research should abandon its traditional inhibitions. I suggest that in order to construct an authentic index of the quality of social life the following factors should be taken into account. First, the changing role of the state and its harnessing social movements as an instrument of social transformation. The notion that the state and social movements are eternally locked in an inimical relationship is contrary to facts, particularly in multi-party democratic societies. Second, the evolution of social policy from a system-maintaining to a change-inducing tool, particularly in socialist and welfare states, ought to be recognized. Social policy is capable of bringing about an incremental revolution, if formulated and implemented properly. Third, pursuant to one and two above, it is imperative to recognize that both social movements and social policies contribute to quality of life, although they traverse different routes. Finally, the conceptualization of quality of life calls for a judicious mutation of the indices of food and freedom, taking into account the historicity of context.

References

Alechina, I. 1982. "The Contribution of the United Nations System to For-
mulating Development Concepts." Pp. 9-68 in *Different Theories and
Practices of Development*. Paris: UNESCO.

Capra, F. 1982. *The Turning Point*. New York: Simon & Schuster.

Castells, Manuel. 1977. *The Urban Question*. London: Edward Arnold.

Frank, A. G. 1969. *Latin America: Underdevelopment or Revolution*. New
York: Monthly Review Press.

Gore, M.S. 1983. "Social Policy and the Sociologist." *Sociological Bulle-
tin* 32(1):1-13.

Mills, C. W. 1959. *The Sociological Imagination*. New York: Oxford
University Press.

Mishra, R. 1981. *Society and Social Policy: Theories and Practice of Welfare*. London: Macmillan.

Offe, C. 1984. *Contradictions of the Welfare State*. London: Hutchinson.

Oommen, T. K. 1990. *Protest and Change: Studies in Social Movements*.
New Delhi, London, Newbury Park: Sage Publications.

Oyen, Else. 1986. "The Muffling Effect of Social Policy: A Comparison of
Social Security Systems and Their Conflict Potential in Australia, the
United States and Norway." *International Sociology* 1(3):271-81.

Piven, F. F. and R. Cloward. 1979. *The Poor People's Movements*. New
York: Vintage.

Rex, John. 1974. *Sociology and the Demystification of the Modern World*.
London: Routledge & Kegan Paul.

Rootes, C. A. 1990. "Theory of Social Movements: Theory for Social
Movements?" *Philosophy and Social Action* 16(4):5-17.

Sckopol, Theda. 1979. *States and Social Revolutions*. Cambridge: Cambridge University Press.

Sigg, Roland. 1986. "The Contribution of Sociology for Social Security."
International Sociology 1(3):283-95.

Titmuss, R. M. 1958. *Essays on the Welfare State*. London: Allen & Un-
win.

Touraine, Alain. 1981. *The Voice and the Eye*. Cambridge: Cambridge
University Press.

Wallerstein, I. 1974. *The Modern World-System*. 2 Vols. New York and
London: Academic Press.

Wallerstein, I. 1979. *The Capitalist World Economy.* Cambridge: Cambridge University Press.

Worsley, P. 1964. *The Third World.* London: Weidenfeld & Nicholson.

Worsley, P. 1984. *The Three Worlds: Culture and Development.* London: Weidenfeld & Nicholson.

Chapter 9

QUALITY OF LIFE, DEVELOPMENT POLICIES AND FEMALE CHILDREN AND ADOLESCENTS

France Govaerts

Free University of Brussels

INDICATORS OF THE QUALITY OF LIFE

Access to health, nutrition, education, and conditions to exercise with dignity social-human and economic roles, training to survive and to earn income, as well as activities which make time more valuable to individuals and communities, all these can be considered primary indicators of quality of life.

With equal opportunities for women and men and girls and boys, these indicators reflect the dimensions of the social-human development of a society, which can also be measured in terms that include the life expectancy and literacy rates achieved by various population groups. It is insufficient to rely on national averages. These dimensions are reflected in the distribution and structure of the means of living which vary among social groups. Such variations reveal the discrimination which keeps some of those groups out of the mainstream of participatory development policies.

These groups include mothers, married working women, the elderly and girls (defined as between 0 and 19 years of age). Statistics on the quality of life or social-human development provide quantitative indicators on the social process which affects such groups, a process characterized by "totalization" and "exclusion."

With regard to "totalization," a concept derived from the sociology of knowledge, identity is denied to specific population categories. Girls, for instance, are often amalgamated with boys under the concept of children. Inadequate access to quality of life opportunities for girls often signifies their "exclusion" from certain fundamental roles, the end result of a discriminatory marginalization process. The totalization process from which girls suffer when they are referred to only as children consists in integrating contradictory elements (i.e., girls vs. boys) into one single simplified unit: children.

Diversity is simplified by progressively excluding or by marginalizing the least relevant traits of the totalization. Discrimination is at work in this operation which is in itself an integral part of a social process of hierarchies creation and regroupings by which a society produces itself. However, the resulting discrimination can be corrected by economic and social-human development policies.

During the childhood phase of a woman's life, discrimination is evidenced by fewer opportunities than those open to men and boys. In terms of a development policy, it means that quality of life must be enhanced through measures focused on improving living conditions for mothers, married working women, the elderly and girls from 0 to 19 years old. Our purpose is to sensitize sociologists to the issue of discrimination against female children so that, by examining and identifying the problems, they may help improve the lives of female children. Our aim, in sociological terms, is to help them attain a better quality of life in the context of social-human development policies. The goal is inscribed in the Convention on the Rights of the Child and is underlined explicitly, as far as female children are concerned, in the World Declaration on the Survival, Protection and Development of Children and the corresponding Plan of Action to implement the World Declaration approved at the World Summit of Heads of State and Government held in New York at the United Nations on September 29-30, 1990 [1,2].

It is, however, in Asia, that this new awareness of discrimination against female children has been growing in the course of the past three years.

The seven Heads of State of the South Asian Association for Regional Cooperation (SAARC), meeting in Islamabad, Pakistan in June 1990, declared 1991-2000 the "SAARC Decade on the Girl Child." This declaration by Bangladesh, Bhutan, India, the Maldives, Nepal, Pakistan and Sri Lanka—the SAARC countries—sought to focus attention on the inferior status of girls in their respective societies and the need to upgrade their status [3 to 14].

From a sociological perspective the issue of status is of primary importance, because status characterizes a person, a group, roles and activities. Quality of life is closely linked with status.

Over the last few years, quality of life has become a sufficiently significant concept to warrant the use of social indicators, roughly the same as those taken into account by the *Human Development Report 1991* of the United Nations Development Programme (UNDP) [15]. But what are we really talking about?

WHAT IS MEANT BY SOCIAL INDICATORS?

Like social statistics, social indicators are a means of quantifying social situations. Like economic indicators, they must provide a way of assessing trends in the overall context of a society's development. Similarly, in the case of social-human development, these indicators must provide a way to assess trends in their multiple dimensions in such a manner as to account for the quality of life. Their objective is to measure and quantify qualitative elements into accessible and understandable figures and terms.

Social indicators are constructed on the basis of a model of social processes. In order to measure something, there must first be a hypothesis leading to the development of the appropriate instrument of measurement.

For instance, in the case of female children, the model would be an hypothesis of early gender discrimination based on different values associated with the status of boys and girls. The differences can be measured, but only if statistics for girls and boys are disaggregated instead of being amalgamated (as is currently the case in most instances), as a result of the very totalization which leads to discriminatory marginalization.

As far as quality of life for girls is concerned, indicators should be chosen in relation to the totalization-exclusion process, a process that becomes apparent through measuring observable differences. With the exception of some specific studies, gender-disaggregated data on children are usually not reflected in official statistics other than those for school enrollment. Infant and child mortality rates, for example, are usually not disaggregated by gender, in national and international statistics.

To stimulate research and action in this domain, official statistics are needed both at the international and national levels. Political will and administrative decisions are required at national and international levels to expand social indicators in order to measure discriminatory practices and in order to eliminate them.

This holds as true for indicators of resources as it does for indicators of results. Indicators of resources provide statistical information on costs and available resources. They should be gender disaggregating if one wants to eliminate discrimination against girls.

In eliminating discrimination against female children, the problematics require data relevant to the intervention. When the intervention aims to improve the quality of life through social-human development programs, the social problematics of the concerned group must be taken into account. From the outset, this has to be done systematically when elaborating the construct of the indicators of both resources and results. What is needed are indicators of disparities which constitute the basis of the problematics. As to the problematics of female children, we all realize that the appropriate statistical systems have not yet been established which would adequately reflect the disparities on a large scale.

We want to pave the way for the scientific research and political awareness necessary to realize the social-human indicators needed to measure the quality of life for girls. Therefore, we will stress facts about observable differences between girls and boys, especially in developing countries. Furthermore, we will relate some recommendations for development policies.

SOCIAL-HUMAN CONCERNS AND DEVELOPMENT POLICIES

Development policies need statistical information to measure social-human concerns. These concerns are expressed through recommendations presented to the planning authorities in each country or at the international level. Preliminary studies are necessary to formulate recommendations and to establish the appropriate statistical information systems. In practical terms, the problem is an important one for the future of those groups denied access to the mainstream leading to quality of life. We are referring here to women and girls who are excluded from the power structures, and particularly to those who belong to the poorest groups.

Social-human concerns relating to quality of life should be analyzed in such a way that discrimination against girls and women is recognized as a major obstacle to improving their quality of life and is recognized also as an active inhibiter of social-human and economic development.

Development policies should eliminate those obstacles, especially in the case of the most disadvantaged, those women and girls whose inferior roles and grinding poverty are often taken for granted. It should be noted that some groups of men and boys are also in that situation.

Discrimination against women is a social fact long identified in sociology but only now gaining recognition in terms of its impact on female children. To ignore such facts among social-human concerns and quality of life indicators amounts to a distortion of development values. From the point of view of methodological analysis, it would lead to a sociology reflecting a built-in bias in its approach to the social reality which it is meant to study.

Let us take an example. Leisure time and leisure activities are important dimensions of the quality of life. The amount of free time and its use are affected by the various roles assigned to girls and boys, to women and men, as a framework for their activities. Through such roles and their normative influence, day-to-day activities are transformed into social performances in response to social and human needs. Social structures do not offer everyone the same free-time opportunities. Girls in developing countries often have less free time than boys for playing. They miss an important aspect of their childhood, due to the fact that they must fulfill roles assigned them based on family priorities and work responsibilities. In practice, such recreational opportunities are determined by the status associated with the roles. When less positive value is given to the girl than to the boy, her status is inferior, which, in turn, has an impact on her access to survival, health and nutrition, her literacy, her school enrollment. Indeed, the economic productivity of girls is less valued than that of boys. The inferior status of female children has an impact on their share of work and leisure, their age of marriage, their childbearing, even on their life expectancy.

By defining rights and duties, status determines the ranking of role in the social and family structure. In patrilineal structures, where the civil code is still influenced by patriarchy, the status of women is inferior to that of men from the time of their birth and even before. All the more reason why social-human concerns and quality of life indicators should take status into account. There is a need for monitoring correlations between gender status and the basic dimensions of development policies.

Beyond specific ideologies or opinions which affect access to quality of life, there are common values for measuring and evaluating progress towards that goal. These include: improved welfare, better health and nutrition, more education, literacy, longer life spans, delayed marriage and childbearing, decreased fertility, equality of income and greater happiness. Similarly, setbacks or deterrents to progress can also be accounted for. The absence of security and social protection has measurable impact on the welfare of a particular social group. Depreciation of girls' and women's work lowers their income potential; poverty reduces their opportunities for development and happiness in a safe physical environment. All of these combine to deny the world's marginalized women, its grown-up female children, a normal life span. Equality of opportunity and treatment is a key word for development policies based on social-human concerns. It finds its meaning in the concepts of democracy and cannot be ignored if girls are to no longer face deprivation in the framework of human well-being and people's increased capabilities.

HUMAN RIGHTS AND FEMALE CHILDREN

The Convention on the Elimination of All Forms of Discrimination Against Women of 1979 is a very important part of the human rights instruments of the United Nations. It deals with all kinds of rights: civil and political, economic, social and cultural. It also covers women's needs in terms of health, education and employment; equal rights in the legal and social security systems; protection against exploitation and prostitution; and assures equality in the family.

Ratified by more than 100 countries, the main legal obligations of this Convention are:

1. removal of discriminatory laws and barriers to equality;

2. promotion of equality by affirmative action;
3. elimination of attitudes, conduct, prejudices and practices which are based on inferiority or superiority of gender.

New possibilities arose for female children as a result of the World Declaration on the Survival, Protection and Development of Children and Plan of Action adopted by the World Summit for Children on September 29-30, 1990. Special mention is made of female children.

The 1991 UNICEF Report (E/ICEF/1991/L5) presents principal means to sensitize the international community to the problems facing women and girls [16]. It notes the importance of interdependent relations and structural factors regarding their situation. Female children are now declared a priority group for the implementation of human rights.

DISCRIMINATION AGAINST GIRLS: SOME EXAMPLES

While the burden of poverty is heavy for women and men, girls and boys alike, it is far heavier in developing countries. There, conditions for women and girls are even worse than for their male counterparts with regard to:

• food and health care;
• enrollment in and number of years spent in school; parity in literacy;
• unpaid domestic and other work and, where remunerated, lower salaries;
• professional training and a say in decision making;
• equal, if any, leisure time.

In addition, maternal mortality is unnecessarily high among both adults and teenagers. According to the World Bank [17], for instance, 99 percent of the half million women who die each year in childbirth occur in the developing countries. Of these, 25 percent are teenage girls.

As *The Girl Child: An Investment in the Future* (UNICEF, 1991) [18] stresses, food, household labor, health care and access to schooling, benefit boys more than girls. This is a family decision depending on the customs and social practices. The same publication notes that 60 million girls have no access to primary schools, as compared to 40 million boys. Primary school enrollment for girls is about 80 percent that of boys; secondary school enrollment is 70 percent.

In the absence of national statistics, surveys indicate that in many developing countries, especially in the poorest families, the child mortality rate for girls is higher than for boys [19]. For instance, according to surveys, one in six deaths of girls in India, Pakistan and Bangladesh may be the result of neglect or discrimination [20]. Household chores are heavier for girls. Furthermore, girls marry earlier than boys in spite of the maternal risk during the teenage years. Early maternity has adverse effects on health, nutrition, education and employment for the young mothers. According to a report cited in UNICEF's *The Girl Child* [18], 20 percent of Bombay's 100,000 prostitutes are minors, while a situation analysis quoted in the same publication indicates that there are 800,000 girl prostitutes under 16 years of age in Thailand.

Gender status has an impact on nutrition: women have a self-abnegating attitude and, according to customs, they pass it on to their daughters and granddaughters [21].

Inferior gender status is also reflected in the distribution of household tasks and in the underrating of the value of girls' labor (a form of discrimination, it should be noted, that has not yet disappeared in industrialized countries). Boys are valued more than girls by both parents, who give more opportunities to their sons to learn economically valuable skills [22].

Parents invest less in education for girls than for boys. This derives from the fact that women's skills earn lower pay and girls are "born to marry." These assumptions held true for certain social groups in the industrialized countries as recently as twenty years ago. Compounding the problem in developing countries, school dropout rates for female pupils are very high. In Benin, Guinea, Pakistan and Yemen, the gap between girls and boys has been widening since 1970. However, most countries in the Caribbean, Latin America, East and South East Asia are achieving parity between girls and boys in primary schools [23].

All the problems currently affecting female children arise from a complex combination of factors. Fundamental structural changes are necessary before they can be eliminated. Even if poverty and underdevelopment are important contributing factors to these problems, we must also note that traditional values and attitudes contribute substantially to this under-valuation of women and female children. This under-valuation is aggravated by extreme economic and social difficulties common to men and women, boys and girls. It is perhaps most clearly manifested by the widespread preference for sons which is seen as both consequence and cause of the second-class status accorded women and girls. The roles they play are considered unimportant and, accordingly, are valued less. They are the lesser human beings. As a result, investment in females is lower—causing a further lowering of their status.

This sexism implies lower allocation of prestige, power and resources, which often results in the neglect of essential needs, a situation worsened by the lack of awareness of the discrimination which affects women and female children.

Daughter neglect is lower where there is respect for a woman's freedom of movement and/or her right to retain property, or where the value

Table 1. Preference for the sex of children

Country	Index of son preference*	Country	Index of son preference*
STRONG SON PREFERENCE		**EQUAL PREFERENCE**	
Pakistan	4.9	Guyana	1.1
Nepal	4.0	Indonesia	1.1
Bangladesh	3.3	Kenya	1.1
Korea	3.3	Peru	1.1
Syria	2.3	Trinidad & Tobago	1.1
Jordan	1.9	Colombia	1.0
		Costa Rica	1.0
MODERATE SON PREFERENCE		Ghana	1.0
Egypt	1.5	Panama	1.0
Lesotho	1.5	Paraguay	1.0
Senegal	1.5	Portugal	1.0
Sri Lanka	1.5	Haiti	0.9
Sudan	1.5	Philippines	0.9
Thailand	1.4		
Turkey	1.4	**DAUGHTER PREFERENCE**	
Fiji	1.3	Venezuela	0.8
Nigeria	1.3	Jamaica	0.7
Tunisia	1.3		
Yemen A.R.	1.3		
Cameroon	1.2		
Dominican Republic	1.2		
Ivory Coast	1.2		
Malaysia	1.2		
Mexico	1.2		
Morocco	1.2		

*Index of son preference = Ratio of the number of mothers who prefer the next child to be male to the number of mothers who prefer the next child to be female.

SOURCES: *World Fertility Survey, Cross National Summaries*, Number 27, October 1983; and *First Country Reports*.

placed upon her work in the labor market is higher. These factors also hold true for the industrialized countries.

In addition to economic factors, strong son preferences are often attributed to religion and culture [24]. In many societies, sons are needed to carry on the lineage and to perform religious rituals, especially in memory of their parents. The main economic onus of caring for aging parents also falls on the son, further diminishing the perceived importance of a daughter's family role and consequently affecting her self-esteem.

This strong son preference will diminish or disappear in developing countries with the acceleration of social-human and economic development if accompanied by political will and specific plans of action. Efforts to enhance the female child's sense of self-esteem also demand support.

The World Fertility Survey, Cross National Summaries [25] presents a table of preference for the sex of children (see Table 1).

UNDER-FIVE MORTALITY RATES AND EDUCATION

Disaggregated data on life expectancy could suggest that females have better living conditions than males. Women live longer and they are more resistant to disease, especially during the months after birth. In populations where girls are treated much the same as boys, there are about 106 females for every 100 males. However, according to UNDP's *Human Development Report 1991* [15], "in most of Asia and North Africa far fewer female children and women survive because they suffer active discrimination." In South and West Asia and in China, according to the same report, "there are only 94 females for every 100 males."

Genuine social-human development progress is correlated with a decreasing child mortality rate, which fell by half between 1960 and 1989. For this reason, in the next two tables, we used groupings of countries according to their child morality rates.

Let us now examine some figures about girls and education. In 1986-88, Table 2, the enrollment ratio for females as a percentage of males enrolled in primary and secondary schools was correlated with under-five mortality rates. The medians are shown in the table.

Let us note the significant inverse correlation between those countries with a decreasing under-five mortality rate and the enrollment ratios for girls as a percentage of boys in primary and secondary schools. The same correlation is found for literacy. Both sets of indicators point to the need and the evident benefits of investing resources in girls' and women's education. The acquisition of knowledge and a deeper understanding of problems are important factors in social-human development and have an impact on under-five mortality rates.

Table 2. Correlation between female education, literacy and child mortality

Countries grouped according to under-five mortality rate	Enrollment Ratio: Females as % of Males, Primary School, 1986-1988	Enrollment Ratio: Females as % of Males, Secondary School, 1986-1988	Adult Literacy Rate: Females as % of Males, 1985
Very high (over 170)	65	48	50
High (95-170)	83	67	50
Middle (31-94)	98	99	93
Low (30 and under)	100	103	93

SOURCES: Derived from *The Girl Child: An Investment in the Future* [18]; figures based on UNICEF, *State of the World's Children 1990* [26].

Table 3 points to the importance of care given during delivery by trained health personnel and the links between under-five mortality, maternal mortality, the percentage of pregnant women immunized against tetanus (1987-1988) and contraceptive prevalence. Table 3 highlights further the importance of girls' education in terms of its positive effects on attitude and behavior.

Table 3. Correlation between female education and health

Countries grouped according to under-five mortality rate	Enrollment Ratio: Females as % of Males, Primary School, 1986-1988	Enrollment Ratio: Females as % of Males, Secondary School, 1986-1988	% of Births Attended by Trained Health Personnel, 1983-1988	Maternal Mortality Rate, 1980-1987	Contraceptive Prevalence (%), 1980-1987	% of Pregnant Women Immunized Against Tetanus, 1987-1988
Very high (over 170)	65	48	25	600	5	20
High (95-170)	83	67	41	300	12	26
Middle (31-94)	98	99	78	78	49	40
Low (30 and under)	100	103	99	10	71	--

SOURCES: Derived from *The Girl Child: An Investment in the Future* [18]; figures based on UNICEF, *State of the World's Children 1990* [26].

Contraceptive prevalence linked to equal educational opportunities for girls seems to indicate that fertility rates decrease with female educational advancement. The lowest under-five morality rates are linked to falling maternal mortality rates and deliveries assisted by qualified health personnel, conditions associated with increased access to education for female children and women.

In countries with the highest under-five child mortality rates, 20 percent of pregnant women are immunized against tetanus, according to 1987-88 figures. The percentage immunized increases to 26 percent in countries with a high under-five morality rate and to 40 percent in countries where the under-five mortality rate is in the middle range. (Percentages immunized against tetanus are generally not available as a median for countries with low under-five mortality rates—where available, the percentage is high). Tetanus is, of course, a cause of mortality.

It is important to stress that fertility rates seem to decrease when more children survive. Furthermore, contraceptive prevalence has an influence on the reduction of maternal mortality in reducing the number of abortions. Better health care for women and girls could halve maternal deaths. This has special significance for the female child since the risk of maternal mortality for teenage mothers is twice that for mothers aged 20 to 24 [17,27].

While many of these observations are encouraging, the situation of boys and girls in the developing countries nonetheless remains precarious. Development policies should focus not only on the disparities between girls and boys, but also on disparities between rich and poor, cities and rural areas, between the employed and the under-employed. Poverty means reduced access to services. In this context, a necessary prerequisite for social-human development continues to be the reduction of the debt burden whose adverse effects on the children of the developing world have been well documented.

Perhaps the historic breakthrough in terms of acknowledging the situation of children in general and female children in particular came with the landmark decisions of the Heads of State and Government attending The World Summit for Children described earlier.

SUGGESTIONS AND CONCLUSIONS

The improvement in the situation of women and girls must be carried out through education, health services and income-generating activities.

Education provides the necessary tools to enable girls and women to take more control of their lives, develop more confidence, and in turn improve the situation and prospects of their children. This is as valid for girls as it is for women since, especially in developing countries, girls are expected to take care of children from an early age.

Education facilitates not only the acquisition of knowledge but also new roles and status. Attitudes toward both roles and status as well as new perceptions of the rights and obligations inherent to them are changed through education. Adolescence is the time of changing relationships between the sexes, a time when adolescent girls and boys alike should be encouraged to analyze the constraints and opportunities of their potential within both family and community.

This could be the basis for a policy objective to improve the quality of life based on a more democratic relationship between the sexes.

Health education is also necessary if essential needs are to be met. Health policies take this into account when they provide health care but also when they raise parental awareness of the adverse effects of gender discrimination against female children. Health is a right and this entitlement plus the attendant knowledge about service access and self-help should be widely disseminated by health and social workers and concerned members of the community.

Practical training, a theoretical approach and awareness-raising are three dimensions of education. Education will help to assess the opportunities and limits of knowledge of young people and adults with an aim of increasing the development potential of individuals and communities.

Elimination of discriminatory processes is a key principle in education as is the evaluation of their successful elimination. With this in mind, it is necessary to identify the problems and to combat the practices perpetuating a lower status for women and girls as well as the lesser roles, activities and unequal salaries that go with this status.

New categories of perception have to be thought up—i.e., new ways of perceiving the world we live in and its disparities are necessary so that the classification of things, activities, human beings and groups can be expressed through new words which shed new light on things previously taken for granted. The disparities resulting from the "totalization" and "exclusion" processes described earlier in this paper can no longer be taken as "immutable givens" or part of the natural order of things. Discriminatory marginalization has already been described as an obstacle to the fulfillment of human rights and a barrier to social-human development progress.

Development policies, therefore, must address and eliminate underlying causes of discrimination. This requires first of all that the factors be identified. It is vital to collect data and to elaborate statistical systems which will take disparities into account. This process would clearly reveal the preferential treatment given to boys and the concomitant deprivation of girls, and identify all the areas where a non-discriminatory approach should be substituted as a matter of immediate priority.

Gender-disaggregated data should not be confined to the realms of research or to elaborate statistical systems to produce indicators. It is necessary also to make them widely known through the media; to share them with non-governmental organizations; and to present them, accompanied by short- and medium-term plans for their implementation, to relevant authorities. In other words, it is necessary to mobilize all existing services to produce valid data and programs which include girls and women in the main orientation of development policies.

Even in countries—developing as well as industrialized—where rights are equal by law, inequality of rights continues to exist in fact.

We must put an end to such devaluation and undervaluation of women's work which many governments and employers still continue to consider as non-productive. "Women's work"—so called because it is left to "second class citizens"—is ignored by statistics. This amounts to a bias in the research possibilities of the social sciences and perpetuates the process of prejudice and discriminatory marginalization.

Access to credit by women is nearly non-existent. It is therefore difficult for them to invest in the more productive sectors. In addition, they are pushed into lower-paid occupations, and often they have no other choice except to work in activities in the informal sector of the economy—a typical situation for women of the fourth world. If these are the conditions of existence of women, then this is the future of girls who will have no other choice than to reproduce these conditions.

It is only by obtaining a higher social status, a greater freedom of action, more economic and cultural resources that women will escape the vicious circle of disease, illness and poverty and numerous childbirths which closes to them those roles in society which are necessary to improve their conditions.

When one examines women's conditions, the words "quality of life" become ludicrous when speaking of the future of girls. What is involved is rather quality of survival. And yet, when we look back on progress achieved in development programs during the past thirty years, one remains confident that real possibilities and opportunities exist to reduce the underdevelopment of women and girls in an environment of poverty. Everywhere, sexual discrimination is apparent in the workplace, both in industrialized and developing countries. Women are barely present at higher decision-making levels in development policies, whether in national or international organizations. And when they are consigned to the world of the poor, impoverishment remains their lot; reproduction gives them their only status, their only possibility is enslavement to work which goes unrecognized. Such will be the future of their daughters if nothing is done.

Significant changes will have to be brought about for all these levels.

The monetary costs of such changes are often less than one would think. Equality of opportunity in the legal system, in work, in health and in education is not more expensive than is inequality.

And let us not forget this poor relation, always left behind by poverty and inequality. We are speaking of free time. Leisure time is necessary to increase girls' opportunities. It will benefit all, regardless of gender—men and women, boys and girls, families and communities.

References

1. *World Declaration on the Survival, Protection and Development of Children*. World Summit for Children, United Nations, New York, Sept. 29-30, 1990. New York: UNICEF, p. 2.

2. *Plan of Action for Implementing the World Declaration on the Survival, Protection and Development of Children in the 1990s*. World Summit for Children, United Nations, New York, Sept. 29-30, 1990. UNICEF, p. 11.

3. *Country Report on the Situation of the Female Child in Sri Lanka*. SAARC Meeting on the Female Child, Sept. 19-23, 1988. New Delhi: Women's Bureau, Ministry of Women's Affairs, Teaching Hospitals.

4. *The Girl Child in India—A Data Sheet* (SAARC Year of The Girl Child—1990). New Delhi: Government of India, Department of Women and Child Development, Ministry of Welfare.

5. *The Girl Child in Maldives*. SAARC Workshop on the Girl Child, Sept. 19-23, 1988. By Naseema Mohamed, Director MCH, Department of Public Health, Republic of Maldives. New Delhi: 1988.

6. *The Girl Child in Pakistan: Priority Concerns*. By Sabeeha Haffeez. Paper prepared and presented in the Strategy Meeting, SAARC Year of the Girl Child, Islamabad, Jan. 28-30, 1990. Sponsored by UNICEF.

7. *The Girl Child in Uttar Pradesh*. Symposium on Girl Child, Lucknow, April 29-30, 1988. Major Recommendations. Lucknow: Forum for Development of Women and Children in collaboration with the Department of Rural Development and UNICEF.

8. *The Lesser Child, the Girl Child in India*. Department of Women and Child Development, Ministry of Human Resource Development, Government of India, 1984.

9. *National Health—1990 The Year of the Girl Child*. Special Supplement, January 1990.

10. *Report of the National Seminar on the Girl Child*. Kathmandu, Nepal, Sept. 25-27, 1989.

11. *Report of the National Workshop on the Girl Child*, Dec. 27-29, 1987, India International Center. New Delhi: Women's Development Division, National Institute of Public Cooperation and Child Development.

12. *Report of the SAARC Workshop on the Girl Child*. New Delhi, Sept. 19-23, 1988.

13. Shanti Ghosh. 1990. "Girl Child in the SAARC Countries." *The*

Indian Journal of Pediatrics 57(1) (Department of Pediatrics, India Institute of Medical Sciences, New Delhi):15-20.

14. *West Bengal–State Level Workshop on the Girl Child,* June 20-22, 1988. Sponsored by CINI-Child in Need Institute and supported by UNICEF.

15. UNDP. 1991. *The Human Development Report 1991.* New York: Oxford University Press for the United Nations Development Programme, Ch. 2 and p. 27.

16. UNICEF. 1991. *Progress Report on Achievement Made in the Implementation of UNICEF Policy on Women in Development.* E/ICEF/1991/ L/5. Feb. 4, 1991.

17. Work Bank. 1990. *Poverty: World Development Report 1990 and Development Indicators.* Washington, D.C.: Oxford University Press for the World Bank, p. 83.

18. UNICEF. Program Division. 1991. *The Girl Child: an Investment in the Future,* rev. ed. New York: UNICEF, p. 4.

19. United Nations Development Programme (UNDP). 1990. *Human Development Report 1990.* New York: Oxford Univ. Press for UNDP, p. 31.

20. Sundari Ravindran. 1986. *Health Implications of Sex Discrimination in Childhood.* Review paper and annotated bibliography prepared for WHO and UNICEF. Geneva: WHO/UNICEF/FHE 86.2.

21. Salwa Marsi. 1985. "Sex Discrimination against Girls in Nutrition and Health Care." In UNICEF, *Girls Adolescence: the Best Opportunity, the Vital Need for Equality, Development and Peace.* Mena, Amman, UNICEF, pp. 26-27.

22. Oyetunji Orubuloye. 1987. "Values and Costs of Daughters and Sons to Yoruba Mothers and Fathers." In *Sex Roles, Population and Development in West Africa,* edited by Christine Oppong. Portsmouth, N.H.: Heineman Educational Books, Inc.

23. Elizabeth King. 1990. *Educating Girls and Women: Investing in Development.* Summary Report. Washington, D.C.: World Bank.

24. M. A. Mannan. 1988. "Preference for Son, Desire for Additional Children and Contraceptive Use in Bangladesh." *The Bangladesh Development Studies* 16(3).

25. *The World Fertility Survey, Cross National Summaries.* No. 27, October 1983, and *First Country Reports.* In WHO/UNICEF/FHE 86.2

26. UNICEF. 1990. *The State of World's Children 1990.* New York: Oxford University Press for UNICEF.

27. United Nations. 1991. *The World's Women, 1970-1990, Trends and Statistics.* Series K, No. 8, *Social Statistics and Indicators.* New York: United Nations.

Chapter 10

HIGH TECHNOLOGY: INDUSTRIALIZATION AND PROBLEMS OF DEVELOPMENT

G. Széll

Osnabrück University

INTRODUCTION

Under the title *The Informational City*, the Spanish urbanist Manuel Castells has already published, in 1986, his visions of the reality and the future of the world. In this book he foresees that due to the possibilities and the use of high technology, the process of centralization will increase on the global level. In the year 2000 we will have—if today's tendencies will go on without a break—only seven metropolitan centers worldwide: New York, Los Angeles, Tokyo, London, Paris, Frankfurt or Berlin and Toronto or Milano. It is evident that only centers in private-capitalist countries are enumerated. The rest of the world will be graded down to be periphery. Beijing and Kobe, Lyon and Moscow will have in this context the same irrelevance for the future global decision-making structures. The decisions of the future of the world economy will be taken in these centers by a few worldwide acting trusts and banks. Participation and democracy, trade unions and political parties, parliaments and governments will become decoration. Is this another "Brave New World"? Have the Marxian and Rosa Luxemburgian prophecies of the increasing centralization of capital and the globalization of the economy not finally become true? Is this tendency unavoidable or are there alternatives?

SMALL IS BEAUTIFUL

At the same time we notice the revival of the region and the local in the past couple of years. Nearly everybody speaks of them. Also the sciences have rediscovered them: from the early citizens' movements to projects as "Small is beautiful."[1] But is this a reintegration, backward struggle, nostalgic fashion or a fundamental development which in the next years will lead to substantial transformations in the political, economic, social and cultural landscape? Is this a practicable counter-model to the demonstrated centralization and globalization tendencies? The rediscovery of the local and regional level has various reasons:

- the conservative rollback on the national level in a number of Western states;
- the failure of neo-Keynesian economic policies on the national level;
- the crisis of the welfare state;
- the identity crisis of the workers' movements and their trade unions;
- the increase of regional disparities in and through the economic crises of the last twenty years;
- the discovery of environmental issues.

THE DEBATE AROUND "THE LOCAL STATE"

In the Anglo-Saxon countries especially critical social scientists have started a debate around "The Local State." The commune in these countries had always had a greater autonomy than on the European continent, where the local autonomy not only in Prussia but also in Jacobin France and Tsarist Russia was massively restricted—not to speak of other continents. Perhaps on this background the renewal in Great Britain is understandable as it culminated in the Metropolitan Areas with the Greater London Council at the top in the 1980s. "The Red Republic of Sheffield" as well as other areas confronted the conservative Thatcher government with their own model of economic policy which, instead of the orientation towards the world market and international competitiveness—the credo of conservative politicians—was oriented towards social needs and socially useful products (Cooley 1980). This alternative economic and social policy was the reason for the, from a constitutional point of view, most doubtful dissolution of all Metropolitan Areas in Great Britain in 1986. But the ideas and approaches have not been destroyed with the dissolution of these institutions.

The starting point of the Local-State debate is the question about the reasons for local inequality between regions and social groups (Duncan, Goodwin & Halford 1987, p. 8). The explanation goes like this: social and economic differences between groups, as gender and class differences, have been transformed in legal relations between supposedly free and equal citizens (Duncan, Goodwin & Halford 1987, p. 17). This leads instead of more equality to the cementation of inequality. Local groups can now use the local state to push through their own interests. Conflicts with the central state become inevitable, but are not necessarily an expression of different political opinions. Institutions of the local state are in a situation of mediators between the sphere of work and the sphere of the organizations of the civil society. Both are constituted in a specific way in space and interrelated themselves specifically at specific places. This heterogeneity and the multitude of social conflicts and links which derive from it are the reason for the uniqueness of the local state.

We can derive from this argument that the local state is located in an interest contradiction to a centralization tendency but is necessary in an economy which is oriented towards the world market for the realization of profits and dominance.

Guy Kirsch (1988) has argued accordingly in an article "When Change Becomes Crisis" with the subtitle "Welfare and Growth Ask for the Courage to Change the Accustomed Living Conditions/The Costs of Stagnation/The Exhausted State." There it reads:

> It is therefore not so that we can control in a fast changing world societal and economic instabilities. It is even not to be wished to prevent them, because individual, sectoral and regional, i.e. micro-instabilities are the means, the only means to guarantee that flexibility for a society without which the society will break apart. The prevention of micro-instabilities leads not to stability, but to the rigidity of a society. Without micro-stabilities there is no macro-stability. The small instabilities limited to regions or sectors allow us to accommodate the change and to work it out almost in small portions. They allow us to soften the shocks of the whole society induced by the change so that the whole context is not destroyed.[2] (p. 13)

If this thesis by Kirsch is valid, it would give an explanation for the economic and social problems of the states of the real-existing socialism because those had destroyed the autonomy of the micro and meso levels through overcentralization. Adaptation and transformation were therefore only from above—if at all and then only in a very clumsy way—possible. The fate of *perestroika* and *glasnost* are striking examples.

Guy Kirsch sees the problem of the market economies that the efforts of adaptation are mostly performed by the economically and socially weak: "The distribution of the efforts of adaptation is following the rules of the strong, and that is when the law of the strong is realized through the strength of the law." A further tendency is that those companies, sectors, professional groups which are not capable or ready to adapt and transform apply to the state to regulate their problems.

> The result is that in the state almost as in a concave mirror the instabilities of the society and the economy are focused. Those small instabilities which one could have absorbed and worked out decentrally are now to be confronted centrally. Those instabilities which on an individual company, sectoral, regional level could and should have been regulated through transformations and adaptations are endangering the state in his functioning, and even in his very existence. (p. 13)

This over-demand of the state in binding a large part of its budget (especially in the social affairs) leads to the restriction of the scope of action in the form of lacking investments and initiatives for the future. And with this the state is also not present as a factor of order and regulation. The socially weak will in the long run not accept this situation. A state of lawlessness and anarchy is to be feared. Guy Kirsch therefore pleads against the dominating conservative redistribution policy in favor of the rich, the companies, the well off—though he sees the limits of the welfare state:

> The liberal politicians point to the fact that macro-stabilities are only to be preserved . . . through micro-instabilities. With good reason those opposed to this opinion argue that the adaptations in detail asked for are often overwhelming the capacities of the individual and that from this side the stability of the whole may be endangered. (p. 13)

Other authors recognize with the recent developments also an increased importance of the local level (Krätke & Schmoll 1987). They ask if the local state is a "counter-power" or only an "executive organ" of or the "incorporation" into the central state. Definitely through modern traffic systems and mass media, an enormous "socialization of space" is happening in all countries since the Second World War (Ipsen 1987). This socialization not only includes the economization and monetarization of social relations but also the political and cultural integration with the help of institutions, parties and the mass media. A *social* theory of space, which includes the economic, cultural and social dimension and which is a prerequisite for a regional strategy, remains to be developed. Already the determination of the relationship between communities within a county or between townships and their neighborhood is still largely undefined.[3] With the technological and economic transformations of the last decades the relevance of space as such has been changed. We could speak formerly of a dichotomy between city and countryside, of qualitatively different working and living conditions; they have now to be placed on a continuum. In this context, what does local and regional identity mean (Brüggemann & Riehle 1992)? A change of the use and meaning of space and their relations is to be found. Their inner organization and stratification is at disposition. The future conflicts of the coming years and decades will not be at first hand those of the military control of space and regions, but of their political and social control. (Though the Gulf War and the conflicts in Yugoslavia seem to teach us the contrary.)

Henri Lefebvre, who passed away in 1991, has delivered very important contributions to this theory. So it is not surprising that the problem of the urban in global dimensions is one of his central topics. Lefebvre, Marxian and one of the "fathers" of the 1968 rebellion in France, has analyzed, with the help of a number of empirical studies, the crisis of the cities. For him the city is the great social laboratory of the 19th and 20th centuries in which the industrialization has been realized and the proletariat has been born. Space is an historical product, the meeting point of material, financial and space-temporal planning of society. We are right now at the historical moment of "post technology": the metropoles absorb all forces of society and subdue the rest of the nation under their needs. This leads also to the destruction of the working class in space. Is the company still the point of reference? Is it not space? Each society produces its own space. But with the creation of a global space the independence and autonomy of most cities and local communities are destroyed. Against this tendency Lefebvre postulates—as Marx already did—the "right to the city" as a social space. The strategy of the reappropriation of one's own space against capitalist economization and subordination is based on the following three principles:

1. the question of the design of humans living together in space has to receive the highest priority in politics;

2. a program of generalized self-management has to be developed in which regional and industrial self-management will be combined;

3. the right to the city, i.e., the participation at the centrality and the movement linked to it.

The dialectics of general and specific are also valid in space in the relationship between local and global.

Until recently the local state and the counties were in first line dominated by local economic interests and the local bourgeoisie. Corruption and speculation in the context of ground and construction were important elements. Nowadays the world market influences the local specificities. But this influence is not at all a direct one as dogmatic Marx-scholars think. Because the contradictions of the logic of capital are even to be found within a company where the logic of capital is much more evident and clear-cut. But here—as in space—local and historical specificities are working which do not allow "one best way," but, e.g., with the same technology different models of work organization are possible: *rationalization in contradiction* as we phrased one of our publications. These contradictions allow for trade unions and workers' representatives a great scope of action (Hartmann 1984).

But how great is the scope of action on the local and regional levels finally? Krätke and Schmoll (1987) point out that the new (and old) tendencies of self-help and local participation only transmit the solution of social problems to the concerned instead of a societal solidarity as in the welfare state. The demand to solve the problems of the quarter within the quarter is okay for the powerful. Even if a local counter-power establishes itself, it is an "accident" or a "class compromise." Local actions would only overlay class conflicts. And consequently they question all approaches of a strategy oriented towards an endogenous development.

> As reasonable as it may be in the concrete case in the lack of global and national development impulses to concentrate the attention more to the locally present potential, as contradictory remains the effect of such approaches: they always present a contribution to the integration of oppositional forces, integrate them into processes of geographical and social transformation, are an important domain in which—with transformations and restructurings at the societal centre at the same time—the stabilisation of the new periphery is organized. (Krätke

& Schmoll 1987, p. 68)

Also, Bullmann and Gitschmann (1987) see the endangerment of local politics in the shadow of neo-conservative modernization strategies in the form of new subsidiary and privatization strategies. These are accompanied on the societal level with through-capitalization and through-étatization of large not yet explored domains, of the deregulation of working and social conditions, of the flexibilization and fragmentation of the work force.

To prevent this kind of socialization Krätke and Schmoll (1987) plead against an empty concept of decentralization, and instead for the democratization of the commune through the participation by the concerned. Very often the local level is under pressure of so-called *Sachzwang* (force of things) and this leads easily to a depolitization—to be recognized by the unanimous decisions in the councils. Against this trend a "repolitization," a concentration of different projects and approaches as well as an interregional network should be opposed.

THE SHORT DREAM OF EVER-LASTING PROSPERITY

Many authors who speak of the "post-modern," "post-industrial" age argue that we live in the "information society." And in this new age class conflicts and debates linked to them have become obsolete. This is in my eyes pure propaganda or an illusion, because productive work was, is and will always remain the only base of the reproduction of society. You cannot eat information, or house or clothe yourself with it. The power question will always remain who decides on what is, where, how and for whom produced as goods or services.

Burkart Lutz (1984) refers in his excellent contribution to the post-war history of Germany, that the naive modernization model of the labor movement, represented by the SPD and the trade unions, has failed with the global crises of the 1970s. He demonstrates convincingly that the development after the Second World War until the mid-1970s has not been the morality of capitalist development but the exception. In a unique way successful welfare politics have opened a large sector of traditional economic, production and living modes to the conquest through industrial technology, big enterprise organization and market economy profitability calculations.

But this development pattern is not repeatable nor reproducible. In the comparison of the 1920s and the 1980s the different character of *systemic instability* becomes apparent. The common denominator is that the economic basic constellation is apparently not any more capable to use the productive resources of an economy in the long run in a partly satisfactory way. This holds especially true in regard to employment and the work force. The historical uniqueness of the given situation may be resumed in the following way:

1. A long period of economic stagnation with considerable non-use of economic production capacities, but altogether with a relatively high level of welfare, is imaginable.

2. A homogenization of interests and living conditions historically without comparison allows tiny signs of a rational-experimental electoral behavior.

3. The internationalization of flows of resources and decision-making processes.

4. The risk of systemic disturbances of the overall balance.

The systemic instability is, according to Lutz, based on the fact that

- the traditional sector has been absorbed or has been destroyed;
- follow problems and costs of the post-war prosperity appear now more and more;
- the political administrative system of the European industrial nations is so cemented that it is not capable to give enough guidance nowadays.

In this analysis we recognize the parallels of so different positions as those of Kirsch and Lutz. Also, the solutions which are shown are not too different. A new prosperity constellation is only thinkable for Lutz if it is possible to find:

— a target system which *ex ante* has a very high power of mobilization;

— to realize *explicitly* the pattern of order which guarantees the orientation of particular interests and the forms of their realization towards this target system.

As just the ecological problems and the finity of resources lead to further destabilization, Lutz pleads for a political process at which all groups of the population and particular interests participate. At the end of this process a new explicit "social contract" has to come out, which determines the basic structures of a new political-institutional arrangement.

ENVIRONMENT AND NO END?

The environmental problems have entered public debate through the reports of the *Club of Rome* and the *Global 2000* Report to the President of the United States. The topic of the environment has in general not been raised by the dominant forces in society, and still it is subsumed under the economic interests expressed through economic growth rates. Trade unions and trade unionists—although we can state enormous learning processes—regarded and regard still economy and ecology as contradictory.

A reason for this may be that many fundamentalist ecologists interpret the current ecological problems as a crisis and the end of the industrial society and of industrialism. In this context trade unions as well as entrepreneurs and politicians are made responsible for the state of the world. This is certainly partially correct, but leaves aside cause and effect and is an expression of lacking historical and theoretical reflection.

A radical theoretical position is taken by the German sociologist Ulrich Beck in his two much discussed publications: *Risikogesellschaft. Auf dem Weg in eine andere Moderne* [*Risk-society. On the Way to Another Modernity*] (1986) and *Gegengifte. Die organisierte Unverantwortlichkeit* [*Counter-Poison. The Organized Irresponsibility*] (1988). According to Beck humanity has always faced risks, especially in the early industrialization process. The risks with which we are faced in the technological high civilization have a qualitatively completely different character:

— they are not limitable—not in space nor in time or socially;
— the established rules of accountability and responsibility fail;
— the dangers can only be minimized but never be excluded;
— we are, as we are mixing up the centuries, without the necessary preventive cure, as we think that we are able to solve all problems through economic compensation.

Without any doubt ecological problems are not technical, but social and political ones. And they can only be solved in this way.

TRADE UNIONS HELPLESS?

I am discussing now the role of trade unions as they are in my view the most important democratic mass organizations in industrial societies. They have developed with these societies and have become one of their main pillars.[4]

Neo-Keynesian politics seemed in the 1960s and 1970s to be the egg of Columbus. So the worldwide economic crisis of 1973/74, which became known as the first "oil crisis," was relatively well managed and controlled. A radical rethinking did not seem to be necessary. Reduction of working time nor regional inequalities or ecological problems were discussed.

The belief that with steady economic growth all social problems may be solved and that the role of trade unions is to arrange through collective bargaining—nearly without strikes or just symbolic strikes—a wage increase which corresponds to the productivity increase plus inflation, diminished in the 1980s. This *iron wage contract* was questioned by entrepreneurs and management in the wake of increasing international competition, mainly pushed through Japanese companies and the "four tigers" of Southeast Asia. In the last years we face a relative decrease of income for wage earners, the marginalization of whole wage groups, the increase of precarious jobs.

So, trade union policy of the last decades has reduced the income disparities only a little bit, not to speak of the distance between salaried and independent workers. But especially the regional disparities have increased worldwide.

The Federal Republic of Germany and Japan have managed best within the international competition so far. This depends in my opinion on the following three factors:

- the relatively high level of qualifications of the work force;
- participation of the employees at decision making;
- the relatively low part of military expenses of the GNP.

These factors are also preconditions for sustainable development. But the relative success of trade unions in the industrial societies may also be an explanation for their stagnation or even decline today. That means that some bureaucratic and/or centralized structures which developed over the last decades become now an impediment to further development. Those people who had led the unions relatively successfully are not able to change strategies radically and to face new challenges as the ecology.

SOCIALLY USEFUL PRODUCTS AND SERVICES

According to Beck (1988, pp. 239 ff.) it is not any more the ownership of the means of production which is the decisive social criterion of differentiation but the differentiation across capital and capital, labor and labor: capital *and* jobs in "risk-winning" and "risk-losing" sectors become decisive. This also leads to a new kind of conflicts between sectors, industries and enterprises as well as their trade unions, but also to new coalitions. New research findings have taught us that workers may be mobilized for ecological questions also through their work and within the enterprise, so that corporate identity and clan-thinking is not the only variable for political action. The reception and acceptance of ecological debates is rather independent of or in contradiction to social class interests (Heine & Mautz 1988).

But we have to keep in mind that risk-production and risk-definition are mostly connected with the production line which is normally not controlled by trade unions or work councils, and is generally only controlled by management. We have now to pay the price for the decoupling from the product, the legendary "indifference" from the product, forced through the system of wage labor and historically trained. In the wage contract the question of the use and reason of the work result and of the own work force is delegated from the worker to the management. Beck defines this as the main reason for the crisis of the trade unions. A practical-political outlook for him could be:

> If the labour movement will not be pushed on the historical siding—and from this the democratic future will largely depend—then on the background of the above reflections they must start at once, to design and to practice an offensive, politically oriented "production policy," and to demand and to fight for

a "production codetermination" somehow, within the company and the society. The trade unions must denounce and reduce the centre of the "ecological question," the extreme inequality of the "definition relationships"; to create values for the ecological critique of their basis inner-company; to fight for a right for inner-company technique critique out of the real experience and the responsibility of the "executive actor." To say it the other way round, they should not react on ecological et al. critique "harshly," but to pick it up active-ly, preventively, to put oneself even in unconventional coalitions at the top of the critique, and especially to develop within an *ecological learning capability* and to push it socially forward and realize it with proved means. Such a "greened" trade union movement could very well have its political spring. (Beck 1988, pp. 246 ff.)

The new orientation started more than a decade ago with the debate on *socially useful goods and services*. The debate centered mainly around the question of arms conversion (Cooley 1980; Paukert & Richards 1991; Széll 1987; Dünnwald & Thomsen 1987; TGWU 1988). As we see right now with the restructuring of the former socialist countries this is a core problem of the future of industry, ecology, world resources and the quality of social life. Eighty percent of the Soviet arms industry should be converted, as Michail Gorbachev explained at the world economic summit in July 1991 in London. China already started a similar program a couple of years ago. It is evident, if mankind continues to waste its main resources for armament, we will not be able to cope with the ecological crisis. About one trillion U.S. dollars are spent annually for military purposes. Some of the Third World countries dedicate the major part of their state budget for military expenditure. Nearly half of all scientists and technicians are employed worldwide for military activities. And the waste of resources is accordingly. So, disarmament and conversion are the main demands for a survival of humankind.

But armament and military are just the tip of the iceberg of wasted resources and wasted wo/manpower. Arms conversion is a specific and the most critical case of restructuring of production and services. Some argue that within a market economy this restructuring is realized through the market forces themselves. But in the case of arms conversion we find specific conditions. As the state in general is the only demander and user it has a special responsibility in regard to the conversion process. The conver-sion has to be realized in a socially oriented way. Military and arms produc-tion are mostly unequally distributed in space. Regions are touched differ-ently. The decision to buy arms is not an economic but a political decision. Disarmament has therefore to follow also political and social criteria. It is hence not an economic optimization problem but one of global social optimi-zation.

The last centuries have brought not only the industrial revolution and the globalization of market economy but also a worldwide process of democratization. (How these are linked together is another topic.) This means that we have to decide in the knowledge of issues ("en connaissance de cause," as the French say), to decide consciously of the priorities in our life and for our future instead of leaving it to market forces in the dark or through mafia-like gangs of speculators, bankers, drug dealers, etc.[5] Politics is the decision-making process of setting priorities. Eastern Europe just demonstrates to us this principle anew. And we have to add that the economy has no reason for itself, but its reason is to fulfill needs and wishes. In this light the primacy of politics becomes even clearer. What is the reason of the quality of social life? A higher productivity, more profits? Or is it not at the end more freedom, liberty, autonomy, democracy for the individual and the society at large? Or, if we have already reached the end of the history of human society, as some propagate, does this mean we already live in the best of all possible worlds (cf. Voltaire's *Candide*)? Do we not continue to create a large mess around us? If this is so, a further democratic development is possible and necessary (Széll 1988).

So, the struggle for the future is fully developed. Though fundamentalism and national-chauvinism seem to spread all over the world, on the other hand democratic alternatives develop as well. There are social, political, economic and cultural alternatives. A democratic and ecological future will not come by itself, but we have to fight for it against many vested interests and narrow-minded citizens. It is not possible and reasonable to present an elaborated utopia of this better future. This has to be realized at each place, in each region according to its needs and historical as well as cultural specificities. This future should be as diversified as the regions are themselves. There are two main alternatives according to Beck: *the authoritarian technocracy* or *the ecological democracy.*

> If the definition relationships remain constant then
> — catastrophes will result in power enlargement of technocratic elites;
> — it will be demonstrated with 'unprovable proves' that the protest is absurd;
> — small groups of experts and expert institutes will decide for all how safe *safe* is;
> — the talk of democracy in decision making, which determines the life of generations, becomes more and more thin, unreal, sarcastic;
> — the shunts are directed towards authoritarian technocracy. (Beck 1988, p. 272)

Though the signs are all put into the direction of an authoritarian technocracy the counter-strategy in the form of *counter-poison* is ready: within citizens' movements, at the work place, in the mass media, the legal institutions, in the parliament, the government. Three types of counter-strategies may be discerned:

> • cancellation of the tolerance vis-à-vis and non-acceptance of technocrats;

• de-monopolization and enlarged security definitions;
• redistribution of the prove obligations and creation of accountability.
(Beck 1988, pp. 277-79)

The possibility of an ecological democracy will be decided through the answer to the following question:

> Are we dependent in all details of survival from experts or counter-experts, or are we winning back the competence of our own judgement with the culturally re-established sensitivity for dangers? Is the alternative only: authoritarian or critical technocracy? Or is there a possibility to overcome the interdiction and expropriation of everyday life in the civilisation of danger? (Beck 1988, p. 293)

THINK GLOBALLY, ACT LOCALLY

A number of authors—namely from the U.S.A.—are convinced that the future center of global development will not anymore be the Atlantic but the Pacific region. This statement is in my eyes premature, because it is mainly based on the over-average economic increase of the newly industrialized countries which is by nature higher than in more developed countries. But that these countries are an economic challenge, the United States have felt it strongly.

The answer of Europe is the decision to integrate Europe after 1992 in the fields of the economy, social affairs, politics, culture and the military. But is the international competitiveness the only criterion? Or is it not more quality of life?

K. Weiermaier (1986) is convinced that the result of the democratization of the enterprises will be a convergence, a symbiosis of the German, U.S.-American and Japanese systems.

Regionalization of politics and economic policy is in the first place a reappropriation of one's own history, a re-sensibilization for social needs, a rediscovery of local and regional potentials for action. It is a collective learning process. *Gräv där du står!* (Dig where you stand) is the slogan phrased by the Swedish labor movement to express that we have to reflect our own traditions and roots, and based on them to design our future. The counter slogan, "me, myself and my family," expresses individual, egotistic strategies instead of collective solidary action.

Dimitrios Roussopoulos, Murray Bookchin and R. Buckminster Fuller—like Henri Lefebvre—have propagated in North America the revival of the cities as a social space worthwhile living. This demand is important but not enough. The city is not autonomous anymore, and even in the case of million-cities they comprise a very limited area. The local community today has flowing borders to the neighboring areas. Regional development limited to a city is as senseless as to consider only the neighboring areas.

The point of reference of the region to unite ecology, resources and the quality of social life is proposed here because it expresses an orientation towards endogenous, sustainable development, as it is named by the United Nations World Commission. A local community is certainly not large enough for such a strategy. How big a region has to be defined depends on a number of factors which to enumerate and to explain here is not possible (Széll 1989). The danger of local and regional egotism (like enterprise egotism) is not to be underestimated. Many communities, regions, states and nations compete, e.g., for investments in their area. Globally speaking, this is a zero-sum game where not a single supplementary job is created.

More reasonable seems to be the concept of the *autonomous workbenches* developed by the Swiss Willy Bierter (1986). In his book subtitled "Report from an alternative economic conference in the year 2003," he describes the demands and criteria for a democratic and ecological future. Table 1 contains the main elements for such a strategy. Bierter designates six criteria for the choice of technologies: (a) fulfillment of basic needs; (b) development of local conditions; (c) social development; (d) cultural development; (e) human development; (f) ecological development.

The aim is the development of autonomous production tools which are largely decoupled from the world market, which use the world market only in a subsidiary way. In front stands the fulfillment of regional needs. Precondition for such a concept is, according to Bierter, a network of human relations, the assertion of social life and a social identity as well as recognizable efforts by the concerned. Helpful for this is an explicit professional ethic, the existence of a number of small- and medium-sized enterprises, social forms of direct solidarity and social integration.

SUSTAINABLE DEVELOPMENT

The United Nations have founded under the chair of the Norwegian Prime Minister, Gro Harlem Brundtland, a world commission, "Environment and Development," which published its report, "Our Common Future." In this report the concept of *sustainable development*, i.e., a global development which equilibrates ecology and human needs, is elaborated.[6] In this Commission, all parts of the world and different political affiliations were represented. The final Tokyo declaration had not the assumption to solve all problems but to establish eight principles for sustainable development:

1. revive growth;
2. change the quality of growth;
3. conserve and enhance the resource base;
4. ensure a sustainable level of population;
5. reorient technology and the management of risks;
6. integrate environment and economics in decision making;

7. reform international economic relations;

8. strengthen international cooperation.

Of special interest in this context is the chapter on industry, and there the part on new technologies which is headed by the terms of promises and

Table 1. Demands for an adapted technology

The reason of technology is to fulfill basic needs of humankind.	
Material needs: Food, clothing, housing, health, education, transport, communication	Economic demands
Immaterial needs: Creativity, identity, autonomy, sociability, participation, self-expansion, philosophy	Social demands
Necessary conditions	
Structural conditions: Justice, autonomy, solidarity, participation, integration	Ecological demands
Ecological conditions: ecological balance	

Source: Bierter 1986, p. 108.

risks. Point 5 of the recommendations of the Brundtland Commission reads like this:

> Technology creates risks, but it offers the means to manage them. The capacity for technological innovation needs to be greatly enhanced in developing countries. The orientation of technology development in all countries must also be changed to pay greater regard to environmental factors. National and international institutional mechanisms are needed to assess potential impacts of new technologies before they are widely used. Similar arrangements are required for major interventions in natural systems, such as river diversion or forest clearance. Liability for damages from unintended consequences must be strengthened and enforced. Greater public participation and free access to relevant information should be promoted in decision-making processes touching on environment and development issues. (p. 365)

Before continuing further, we need some clarification in regard to what we understand under the term of "high" or "new technologies." They are generally associated with micro-electronics, but we should include as well biotechnology and new materials.

High technology, by its very principle, can save energy and resources, because we are able to plan and control much better, and to increase productivity by them. And it is said that the information society wastes much less resources than the industrial societies. This assumption is certainly only partially true—if we look into the enormous waste of energy and space for distraction parks like Disney World, the transport you need to get there, the destruction of nature through tourism and other leisure-time activities which become more and more commercialized. The package for consumer goods is sometimes more expensive than the product itself. And what is the difference between industry and service jobs? If we look closer at the work place level, we often cannot distinguish, in regard to quality, between an industrial and a service job, e.g., if we look to McDonald's hamburger preparation.

High technology definitely has the potential of increasing the quality of social life, preserving world resources and the ecology, but it depends very much on the concrete conditions of their application and even of their logic. For example, computer software is mostly designed to preserve hierarchical structures and expertise with the experts, strengthening the authoritarian technocracy as Beck named it. So, it is necessary, if we want to democratize society, to democratize also the technology. Figure 1 may demonstrate the complex interrelationships of our topic.

What has been realized of the Brundtland Commission program during the last four years? We had a number of international conferences where the outcome may be resumed in some simple words: the rich are not ready to reduce substantially their pollution, waste, etc. Economic growth remains still the dominant factor for action and production. And the Third World countries rightly insist that the biggest polluters start first and give them appropriate financial help instead of continuing to export hazardous waste and industries to them.

What is even more frightening is that the largest part of economic growth has become negative goods. The German economist Christian Leipert has calculated for the old Federal Republic of Germany in 1989 that the economic growth between 1983 and 1988 was three-quarters due to repair and compensation of environmental, social and health damages. And this negative tendency goes increasingly on. So what Marx already foresaw more than one hundred years ago might become true: the productive forces of the industrial, capitalist society increasingly become destructive forces.

The only alternative is, in my opinion, what I named in 1987 a *socially oriented technology*. This means that it is not enough to make new and high technologies socially acceptable and adapted, but instead we have to *think* and assess first our needs and *all* long-term costs before we produce. Technology assessment is the term used for this process for nearly 25 years. But once again the effects of technology assessment are not nearly visible. Is technology assessment just an alibi? So we have to go even one step further: there will be no democracy without democracy at the work place, a strategy which has to be supported by democratic scientists.[7]

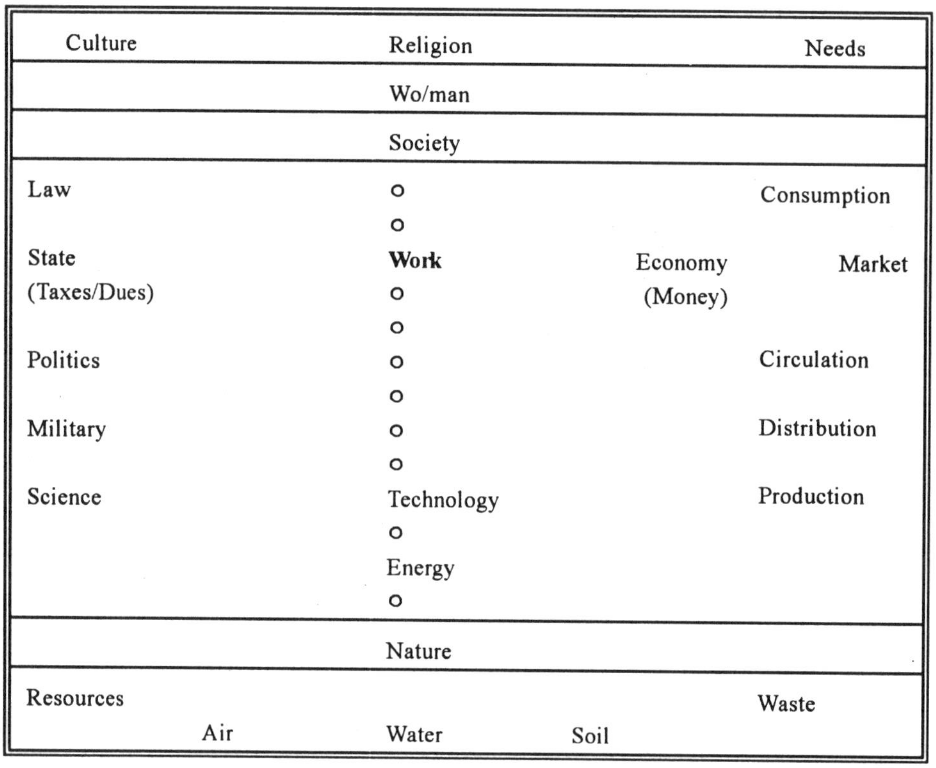

Culture	Religion		Needs
	Wo/man		
	Society		
Law	o		Consumption
	o		
State (Taxes/Dues)	**Work**	Economy (Money)	Market
	o		
	o		
Politics	o		Circulation
	o		
Military	o		Distribution
	o		
Science	Technology		Production
	o		
	Energy		
	o		
	Nature		
Resources			Waste
	Air	Water	Soil

Figure 1. Wo/man and nature: some interrelationships

CONCLUSIONS

The ecological crisis which we live in today—and the burning of Kuwait is just another striking example—is the greatest challenge of human history. We have to rediscover the political dialogue, to understand that blind market forces will not solve our problems which they have created. Humankind seems to be in the situation as the German poet Johann Wolfgang von Goethe described nearly two hundred years ago with his poem on the witch apprentice: we may not be able to control those forces which we have awakened. Policy in its very sense has to be rehabilitated as a discourse on the reason of life and the priorities in it. Looking simply back and asking for fundamental solutions of the "good old times" with the help of religion or other ideologies, with strong authoritarian leaders, will create more social conflicts and wars. But this danger is apparently a real one.

Today's historically unique situation represents a challenge for all scientists as well. Once again it is not enough to interpret the world differently, but we have to change it, to save it. Disciplinary approaches are not sufficient—the world, the environment, the region, the enterprise is not divided into disciplines. We should concentrate our efforts on issues of democratic planning and the further democratization process in all realms of life to mobilize everybody in this great moment. We need all and everybody, and a broadening of consciousness, so that democracy becomes real and we all decide in elections or plebiscites "en connaissance de cause." A second age of *Enlightenment* is necessary, to prevent our leaving the definition of the problems and with it the solutions to the so-called and self-named experts. But this broad public sphere and debate has still to be created against all those who think they are losing something in a more democratic world.

"More democracy or more destruction" are the alternatives we are confronted with. We have to take sides.

Notes

[1]This term, phrased by E. F. Schumacher (1974), is not as idyllic as supposed: the size of enterprises envisaged is about 1,500 employees.

The exceptions in regard to this general tendency to more regional and local orientation are the dominant economic schools.

[2]All translations are by the author.

[3]The hierarchical space theory which supposes space centers on the different levels does not contribute substantially to this kind of relation.

[4]See for that the debate about corporatism and neo-corporatism (Van Waarden 1992).

[5]The three drug mafias control an estimated $1 trillion (U.S.) investment, a large and increasing part of our economies (Ziegler 1990).

[6]In 1990, the *International Social Science Council* decided, in the follow-up of this debate, on the program "Human Dimensions of Global Environmental Change," where the social sciences were asked to contribute as effectively as the natural sciences to preserve and save our planet.

[7]See, for the debate around democratic and authoritarian democracy, the writings of Lewis Mumford.

References

Beck, Ulrich. 1986. *Risikogesellschaft. Auf dem Weg in eine andere Moderne*. Frankfurt: Suhrkamp.

Beck, Ulrich. 1988. *Gegengifte. Die organisierte Unverantwortlichkeit*. Frankfurt: Suhrkamp.

Bierter, Willy. 1986. *Mehr autonome Produktion—weniger globale Werkbänke*. Karlsruhe: Verl. C. F. Müller. (Alternative Konzepte 55)

Bookchin, Murray. 1983. *The Limits of the City*. Montreal: Black Rose Books.

Bookchin, Murray. (1980) 1986. *Toward an Ecological Society*. Montreal: Black Rose Books.

Brüggemann, Beate and Rainer Riehle. 1992. "Countryside." Pp. 206-11 in *Concise Encyclopedia of Participation and Co-Management*, edited by G. Széll. Berlin/New York: de Gruyter.

Brundtland, Gro Harlem, et al. 1987. *Our Common Future*. Oxford: Oxford University Press.

Bullmann, Udo and Peter Gitschmann. 1987. "Renaissance des Kommunalen? Zum Stand alternativer Kommunalpolitik und -wissenschaft." *Das Argument* 163(29/3):401-13.

Castells, Manuel. 1986. *The Informational City*. Oxford/Cambridge, Mass.: B. Blackwell.

Cooley, Mike. 1980. *Architect or Bee?* Slough: Langley Technical Services.

Duncan, S., M. Goodwin and S. Halford. 1987. "Politikmuster im lokalen Staat: Ungleiche Entwicklung und lokale soziale Verhältnisse." *Prokla* 68(17/3):8-29.

Dünnwald, Johannes and Peter Thomsen. 1987. *Sinnvoll arbeiten—Nützliches produzieren*. Frankfurt: Fischer Taschenbuch Verlag.

Greater London Council. 1985. *The London Industrial Strategy*. London: Greater London Council.

Hartmann, Michael. 1984. *Rationalisierung im Widerspruch*. Frankfurt/New York: Campus.

Heine, H. and R. Mautz. 1988. "Haben Industriefacharbeiter besondere Probleme mit dem Umweltthema?" *Soziale Welt* 2:123-43.

International Social Science Council. 1990. *Human Dimensions of Global Environmental Change*. Paris.

Ipsen, Detlev. 1987. "Räumliche Vergesellschaftung." *Prokla* 68(17):113-30.

Kirsch, Guy. 1988. "Wenn Wandel zur Krise wird." *Frankfurter Allgemeine Zeitung.* 17 December, p.13.

Krätke, Stefan and Fritz Schmoll. 1987. "Der lokale Staat—'Ausführungsorgan' oder 'Gegenmacht.'" *Prokla* 68(17):30-72.

Lefebvre, Henri. 1968. *Le Droit à la Ville*. Paris: Anthropos.

Lefebvre, Henri. 1973. *Espace et Politique*. Paris: Anthropos.

Leipert, Christian. 1989. *Die heimlichen Kosten des Fortschritts. Wie Umweltzerstörung des Wirtschaftswachstum fördert.* Frankfurt: S. Fischer.

Lindqvist, S. 1978. *Gräv där du stär*. Stockholm: Bonniers.

Lutz, Burkart. 1984. *Der kurze Traum immerwährender Prosperität.* Frankfurt/New York: Campus.

Marx, Karl. (1857/58) 1968. *Grundrisse der Politischen Ökonomie.* Wien/Frankfurt: Europa Verlag.

Paukert, Liba and Peter Richards, eds. 1991. *Defence Expenditure, Industrial Conversion and Local Employment.* Geneva: ILO.

Roussopoulos, Dimitrios, ed. 1979. *The City and Radical Social Change.* Montreal: Black Rose Books.

Schumacher, E. F. 1974. *Small is Beautiful.* New York: Harper & Row.

Széll, György. 1987. "Sozialorientierte Technikgestaltung im Jahr 2000." *WSI-Mitteilungen* 8:464-71. (English translation available)

Széll, György. 1988. *Participation, Worker's Control and Self-Management.* London/Beverly Hills/New Delhi: Sage.

Széll, György, ed. 1989. *Konzepte alternativer Regionalentwicklung und gewerkschaftliche Handlungskompetenz.* Osnabrück/Münster: WURF.

Transport and General Workers Union (TGWU), ed. 1988. *Arms Jobs Conversion—A TGWU Report. The Proceedings of a TGWU European Trade Union Conference on Arms Jobs Conversion. Eastbourne 1987.* London: TGWU.

Waarden, Frans van. 1992. "Corporatism and Neo-Corporatism." Pp. 193-205 in *Concise Encyclopedia of Participation and Co-Management,* edited by G. Széll. Berlin/New York: de Gruyter.

Weiermaier, Klaus. 1986. "Industrial Democracy and Labour Market Behaviour." Pp. 135-52 in *Die Unternehmung in der demokratischen Gesellschaft,* edited by Wolfgang Dorow. Berlin/New York: de Gruyter.

Ziegler, Jean. 1990. *La Suisse lave plus blanc.* Paris: Seuil.

Chapter 11

THE GRANDEUR AND DECADENCE OF THE DEVELOPMENT SCIENCES: A STUDY OF THE SOCIOLOGY OF KNOWLEDGE

Raymond Boudon

University of Paris–Sorbonne

Development, of course, remains essentially a political problem. The numerous migratory movements from the south to the north are there to remind us that paradoxically one has the impression that the developmental sciences have exhausted themselves. More precisely, when one lists the works in sociology, political science or economics, which got attention, the works of the great names associated with the idea of development, it becomes clear that these works date mostly from 1950s and 1960s, the decline beginning in the 1970s. It is enough just to mention the names of Hoselitz, Gerschenkron, Rostow, Hirschman, etc., to be aware of this. In 1970, the Israeli sociologist, Eisenstadt (1970), published an important work which selected classical texts from the 1960s. It is unlikely that twenty years later we would be able to find a sociologist tempted by an undertaking of the same sort. It would be difficult to find recent texts which could be presented as an essential contribution to developmental theory. The fiasco of developmental sciences was dutifully diagnosed in a special edition of *L'Année Sociologique* (1991).

One may wonder what the origin of this exhaustion may be. It does not result from the developmental sciences being a failure in the sense that they have taught us nothing. From this point of view we can contrast them with that which we can conveniently call post-modernism. This "theory" is purely interpretive. Most often it is the work of essayists attempting to present objectively their subjective impressions of contemporary societies. That is why this "theory" is more important from a doxographic perspective, from the point of view of the history of ideas, than from the point of view of knowledge of societies. The case of developmental sciences is completely different. Here, authors rely on controlled observations. They implement the principles of the scientific method. Undeniably, they have instructed us in developmental processes and more generally in social change. So, why this abrupt stop?

One cannot ignore the fact that part of the answer to this question lies in the skepticism which is developing today in regard to all forms of knowledge and which is a response to the somewhat overindulgent "positivism" of the 1950s and 1960s. But this general answer is not enough. The main reason for the discrediting of studies on the subject of development is that although undeniably they have taught us about the world in other respects, and rightly so, they give us the feeling that they have helped to lead political action astray. They have taught us, but they have also filled us with illusions.

How could this paradox have been possible?

The heart of the answer likely lies in two main ideas of the sociology of knowledge. The *first* is expressed by the American sociologist, De Gré (1979, pp. 35-112; see also Chazel 1987). When the social subject does not know the answer to a question, he/she has a tendency to resort to the strategy of extrapolation, a perfectly legitimate method which occupies a central position in the scientific process. But by doing this, he/she runs the risk of believing to know more than he/she does. De Gré illustrates this by using a didactic example. He asks us to imagine four people, each one of them seated on a different side of a pyramid in such a way that they are not able to see the other sides. Each side is a different color. If the subject is asked what color the pyramid is, according to De Gré, he/she will normally answer that the whole pyramid is that color which he/she sees before his or her eyes. This procedure of extrapolation is at the same time a fundamental source of knowledge but also of illusion.

The *second* idea which completes the first is that knowledge does not reflect what is real but rather is composed of the answers the social subject gives to his or her own *questions*, or to those *one* asks him or her in his or her environment. But the *form* that the questions take *can* contribute to determining their answers. In this case, even if one adopts a rigorous approach to answering, the answer depends on the question and one can end up with a false belief. This example represents another fundamental source of illusion (Boudon 1986a, 1986b).

To illustrate, let us imagine a simple example. Let us suppose that a subject asks him or herself a question in the form of X or Y; for example, is it X or is it Y who is the cause of such and such an event? And let us suppose that he or she has convinced him or herself, through entirely objective reasoning, that Hypothesis Y must be dismissed. In this situation, the belief that X is the cause of the event in question will become implanted in his or her mind, but this belief will be due to the form itself of the question.

In its simplicity, this example involves important consequences. It indicates how sociology and epistemology structure themselves on a well-established point. In fact, often the way of asking questions, the *form* of questions, has a social origin. Explaining this is a matter for *sociology*, but the procedures of the production of answers are a matter for *epistemology*.

The viewpoint that I would like to defend is that the disillusions of developmental sciences above all are due to the fact that theoreticians and practitioners of development have behaved much like the subject of De Gré, or like the questioner that I have called to mind. They did not see that the questions they asked strongly contributed, in many cases, to determining their answers. Thus, with complete confidence they propounded ideas that reality ended up contradicting and thus they themselves provoked this movement towards disillusion which we witness today.

It is important to reflect on this period in the social sciences which is represented by the grandeur and decadence of studies on the subject of development. In fact, it is of interest not just from the point of view of the sociology of knowledge; it also allows one to determine to what degree and in what manner scientific research can guide political action.

In Search of the Factor

It is easy to find a first illustration of these two cases which I have just brought up. When one examines developmental literature, one recognizes that in large part the discussions of developmental sociologists and economists consist of determining *the principal factor* responsible for development. In his noted book, Hagen (1970) described the situation well. Some claimed that a leading or dominant industry is a prerequisite for development; that is, sometimes the case is clear. It was in this way that English development in the 18th century sprang from the textile industry and Danish development in the 19th and 20th centuries sprang from the dairy industry. But it is easy to find instances where a dominant activity has been the source of problems, as is the case with Chile and its copper industry. Furthermore, modern Italy is not centered on the dominant industry.

A whole series of other factors has in turn been suggested as the source of development. Economists, for example, have suggested that the development of means of transportation is a necessary and sufficient condition for development. Others have pointed to stagnation and the persistence of an underdeveloped state caused by insufficient available capital. Still others have supported the idea that persistent underdevelopment is due less to the lack of financial resources than to very strong social inequalities and the two-tiered social structure which often characterizes underdeveloped societies.

According to some, this dualism could imply an insufficient domestic market which blocks development. According to others, the result could be that the elite identify themselves with their own society rather than with advanced Western societies.   This causes in the elite a phenomenon of conspicuous consumption which shifts their available financial resources from savings and investments towards consumption.   From this lack of domestic resources, many have found the notion of injection of foreign capital is the necessary and sufficient condition to set in motion as a mechanism for development (on "foreign aid," see Bauer 1971).

The list could thus continue (Boudon 1991). As for the sociologists, some have tried to show that education, while others the form of the means of mass communication, are the necessary and sufficient conditions for development. As well, others have stressed questions of *ethos*. The most remarkable research in this regard is perhaps that of McClelland (1961). Incredible in its breadth because it touches on almost all historical societies, it posits the notion that above all it is the collective psychological disposition that determines whether a society appears dynamic or not. To confirm this, McClelland has studied notably the literary production of said societies and has attempted to illustrate that dynamic societies are those in which the need for success and the need for achievement appear to be well developed, where the values of personal success and achievement are considered to be of utmost importance.

Other authors believe very strongly that centralized economic planning is the only way to achieve harmonious development.   Still others believed that a market economy free of all central control was the only harmonious way to achieve growth.

This list is sufficiently long to bring to light the point I wish to make: that a large portion of research for development tries to explain how development appeared at such and such a moment in such and such a country, not by using examples but rather by answering a question which is much more "closed" in its form: what is the determining factor of development? Alternatively, of underdevelopment? If one does not see that a question of this type underlies this research, one does not understand the nature of the research undertaken by the different authors that I have mentioned or by those it would be possible to mention. Yet, on the other hand, when one lays the cards on the table, as I have done, one immediately notices that the question is not an innocent one, but in fact carries a lot of baggage. This question presupposes that *a dominant factor of development does exist and that the research mainly consists of determining the nature of it.*

Of course, the questions that dominate all of this research remain implicit. It is for this reason that I talk about "laying the cards on the table." These questions remain implicit because they are considered by their authors to be self-evident. They are not elucidated and consequently they are not criticized. Why does this continue?

THAT THE NOTION OF A SINGLE CAUSE HAS A STRONG APPEAL

Why is the idea of determining *the* factor of development or of under-development so easily considered to be perfectly natural? The answer to this question is that it is completely natural and normal, when seeking to explain a phenomenon, to research *the* cause. This is true in everyday life. Thus, John Stuart Mill (1974) points out that someone who has just caught a cold will likely contribute this change to *one* unique cause. "I caught a cold because I got a chill." Of course, a cold is a complicated physiological process which is poorly understood, but the proposition which I have just quoted would shock no one. In other words, often one can legitimately introduce the supposition that it is legitimate to research the *cause* of a process even when the said process is complex. Most often one will do this implicitly.

One reason, therefore, why the theory of the single or dominant factor is so common is due to the fact that it is often legitimate and productive in everyday life, as in the practice of science. The intrinsic complexity of a phenomenon does not mean that this theory must be rejected. Moreover, it appears, when one is in doubt, to be the most natural in the sense that it is "natural" for De Gré's subject to reply that the pyramid is all of the same color as the side that is before his or her eyes.

Similarly, in *La Démocratie en Amérique* [*Democracy in America*], Tocqueville explains an enormous number of differences between England and the United States by a single factor, which he describes by the famous opposition between "democratic" and "aristocratic" society.

Of course, it also sometimes happens that the factor is put forward as a candidate for being the cause of a given phenomenon. This furnishes an incomplete explanation, but the discussion which will accompany such a diagnosis will consist most often of proposing to replace that factor with another candidate, rather than putting in question the theory which suggests the existence of a dominant factor: the form of the assumption will usually be conserved; only its content will change. There is more. In fact, when a factor appears to be insufficient, not only do we try to replace it with another, but we prefer to turn to types of factors as far removed as possible from the rejected factor.

One may cite many classical examples showing that scientific dialogue often takes such a twist, so, when Weber considers the reasons why there developed in Europe a novel form of economic organization to which, following Marx, he affixes the label "capitalism," he finds before him an established idea; namely, that this transformation was the result of what Marx called the *forces of production*. In contrast with his standard interpretation, Weber suggests *religious and moral* factors as the principal cause of the change in question.

THE STRUCTURING OF DIALOGUE IN THE SCIENTIFIC COMMUNITY

Weber's *The Protestant Ethic* illustrates a typical structuring of scientific discussion. If his book had such a great success, to the point where it is one of the most cited and discussed books in the whole history of the social sciences, this is of course attributable to its intrinsic qualities, to the audacity of the theory which it defends, but most of all to the fact that it proposes a framework for understanding which is different from the Marxist framework. The attention which focused on McClelland or Hagen is without a doubt partly attributable to the quality of their work, but first and foremost to the fact that they have contrasted with the *economic* viewpoint predominant in the theory of development a *psychological* viewpoint which could easily be seen as very remote from the current economic theories. Similarly, P. Berger (1978) has well demonstrated the neo-Marxist claim that the interaction between the West and underdeveloped countries is the principal cause of their lack of development, while the developmentalists see in the same interaction the possibility for general development.

Generally speaking, discussions relative to social change are often structured around a series of binary questions; personality factors versus anonymous factors, materialism versus idealism, positive versus negative effects of international trade, etc. The same oppositions are found in history. Carlyle claimed that great men make history, whereas Le Bon claimed it was the commoner (Stoetzel 1978). This tendency toward binarization of discussion appears elsewhere in the field of natural sciences (cf. the examples in Boudon 1986b).

This phenomenon suggests there is good cause to be aware of the limits of this "communication," which some thinkers today want to view as a panacea for the perspective of both the progress of knowledge and of knowledge of the democratic functioning of societies (Habermas 1986). The tendency toward binarization, to which many discussions refer, reminds us that all discussion normally is situated inside a framework which, without a doubt, makes the discussion possible, but at the same time limits the truths. Discussion itself can reinforce the undesirable assumptions instead of placing them in a central light.

The structuring force of the *framework* of discussion is so powerful that some authors are not able to see what they have actually found. They are so preoccupied with the goal of demonstrating that it is not such and such a factor, but rather another, which is at the origin of change or of development, that they do not in fact see that their analyses have gone beyond this framework.

From this perspective, the case of Hagen is very instructive. Unsatisfied by the theories that see in economic factors the principal cause of development and underdevelopment, Hagen begins by reviewing all the objections one might have to all these economic theories. Having made this criticism, he examines some case studies with the intention of showing that economic theories cannot explain them. Without a doubt the most interesting case is from Colombia. Hagen wonders how the spectacular development of this country at the beginning of the century might be explained, an episode which has intrigued economic historians and economists. This case holds Hagen's attention because it contradicts almost all economic theories. Colombia's infrastructures, in terms of transportation, were at this time rudimentary. The country was internationally isolated. Foreign investment was non-existent. One sees no trace of development of pilot industries. In short, none of the economists' favorite factors explains the remarkable burst of development that economic history reminds us of.

Hagen's explanation is the following. When analyzing the identity of economic actors responsible for this period of development, one notices that it mainly involves people originating from Medellín, an area which exhibits, as we know too well, its spirit of enterprise and innovation. Why? As Hagen explains, it is because historically the province has always been marginal. In the wars which Colombia led against its neighbors in ancient times, the soldiers originating from Medellín always appeared to be bad fighters, ready to flee at the first opportunity. Generally, the Medellínos had a negative image compared to their fellow citizens, especially those from Bogotá. They themselves appeared to identify but little with Colombia. In summary, Hagen develops the idea that the Medellínos had a collective feeling of rejection, their personality having been structured around the unconscious motivation transmitted from generation to generation by the socialization process to regain lost status. In other words, the Medellínos would suffer from the chronic need for recognition. It is this need that would lead them to engage in superior activities to those of the Bogotáns, for example. Through their desire to assert themselves and succeed, they showed their desire to escape their position as second-class citizens. These complex mechanisms, which introduce hypotheses arising from the collective unconscious, would explain the successes of the Medellínos and allow us to understand why these enterprises were founded more than proportionately by Medellínos.

ONE MUST LET THE SUGAR MELT

The prolonged discussion which followed *The Protestant Ethic* allows another essential point to be brought to light; namely, that it is often a discussion which brings with it an effort to determine *the* factor responsible for such and such a phenomenon that finishes with the report that absolutely no explanation of the said phenomenon can be found in the language of factors. Weber situates himself firmly in the framework of the factor: such and such a factor, and not another one, is responsible for the exceptional progress of the West. In fact, the solution to the problem can only be obtained by renouncing the language of factors.

The correlations between Protestantism and capitalism, which were Weber's point of departure, demonstrate neither a causal influence of the Protestant ethic on the genesis of capitalism nor that the Protestant *ethos* is the original cause of the acquisitive behavior which characterizes capitalism nor even that it is one of its important causes. In fact, the over-representation of the elite Protestants in the economic elite (for example in France), the warm way in which "capitalism" was welcomed to Protestant countries and the other "correlations" that inspired Weber's theory can be explained in a way that is at the same time simpler and more complicated than this theory, in a way which is simpler *psychologically* and more complicated *sociologically*.

Weber's own psychological hypotheses are in fact difficult and arbitrary. This has been noted many times (Schneider 1970; Eisenstadt 1967). They assumed that the belief in predestination creates for the believer a state of anxiety that he tries to dispel by reassuring himself through his success in this world. According to Weber, this would have prompted a valuing of methodical behavior, a tendency to prefer investment to consumption, and, in general terms, a valuing of effort of success and of "achievement." These brilliant hypotheses have three drawbacks in that they are complex, ad hoc, and, to the extent that they can be empirically tested, not very compatible with such testing.

The polycephalic theory which emerged from the works of various authors emphasizes on the one hand that Protestantism tended to establish itself in weak and relatively uncentralized states, such as Holland and a number of small German states. As a result, there is a correlation: the autonomy given to institutions of the civil society, such as banks, was in general greater in the countries that had turned to Protestantism.

This "new theory" leads ultimately to reversal in the causality postulated by Weber. It is because one belongs to the business class that one feels attracted to Protestantism.[1] The causality goes from the social to the mental rather than from the mental to the social.

Then came the Counter Reformation. Protestant businessmen were neither persecuted nor harassed, so they emigrated en masse to Protestant countries, helping, for example, to energize Amsterdam at the expense of

---

[1] Protestantism, as any rebellious movement, also attracted people who felt excluded and exploited. Its success among lower class people in Paris in the 16th century has been accurately described by Balzac in his novel *Catherine de Médicis*.

d'Anvers, or assuring the development of Geneva or the Palatinat and, of course, Holland.

One sees that the diverse correlations from which Weber began are no longer explained by identifying *the factor or factors* that would be responsible. The "polycephalic" theory that I have just summarized abandons the language of factors and suggests that an explanation which presents itself is a tangled network of causes and effects.

THE TENDENCY TO SIMPLIFY: THE EFFECTS OF *GESTALT*

In general, and although this may appear a little paradoxical, a good number of illusions that we have about society are derived not from "ideological thought"[2] but through *scientific* thought for the reasons that I gave at the beginning. In fact, all new theories, including the most scientific, are based on assumptions which can result in giving a scientific "basis" to false beliefs, or at least in giving the "understandable" illusion that they are scientifically based. This is true in particular for works on development. I will illustrate this by using two examples.

The first is the theory of Nurkse (1953). This theory, along with other theories of the same type, had a lot of influence and contributed in establishing as a scientific truth the idea that foreign aid is essential to rescue a country from underdevelopment. Reduced to its logical skeleton, the theory can be summarized in the following way:

(1) A poor country is by definition a country where there is little opportunity to save; (2) Consequently, the opportunity for investment is poor; (3) As the possibility for investment is poor, the possibility of developing productivity is poor; (4) Increasing productivity is the way to reduce production costs and consequently to increase buying power and the standard of living; (5) When productivity stagnates, the standard of living stagnates; (6) *Ergo*, a poor country will remain so; (7) Unless it benefits from foreign aid, which is therefore the necessary condition for development.

The first thing that must be noted is that this theory is as scientific as a theory can be. The propositions from which it is derived are all acceptable. Yet, we know that its conclusion is wrong, simply because one can cite the examples of numerous countries which developed without foreign aid, starting with Japan or England.

As the argumentation is valid and the conclusions are wrong, the failure can only be attributed to the fact that the conclusion is not drawn only from the explicit arguments of the theory but also from the implicit proposi-

---

[2]I take this expression in its common—some would say "ideological"—meaning: ideas as they are influenced by irrational affective factors.

tions which must be viewed as being of doubtful validity as they lead to unacceptable conclusions.

It is not difficult to detect these implicit propositions. Thus, the first proposition, explicit, assumes implicitly that in the typical, ideal society considered, *everyone* is poor. But in most underdeveloped countries there is not a great deal of wealth, but a minority holds a large part of it. In fact, the observation shows that often the poorer the country, the greater the inequalities. The third proposition is equally full of assumptions: in fact, one can notably increase productivity through uncostly means of modifying, for example, the organization of work. But this third proposition assumes implicitly that the productivity gains are *always costly*. Other implicit propositions include the fact that the theory presupposes that the typical, ideal society that it describes does not trade with other nations. Otherwise, in fact, there could be a rise in the standard of living through the importation of enhanced productivity. Of course, the standard of living depends not just on productivity, as the theory implicitly assumes, but on many other factors, such as the reduction of the tax burden.

It is clear the conclusion with regard to the need for foreign aid only follows if one makes all these implicit assumptions. But, as soon as one accepts them, one sees that they are far from indispensable. Furthermore, the premises do not themselves demand the conclusions which Nurkse draws from them: foreign aid is not the necessary precondition for development. But, since the implicit is not made explicit, one might easily believe that the theory scientifically demonstrates the proposition that development is impossible without foreign aid. The genuinely scientific appearance of this theory explains why it has considerable influence.

Let us take a second example in the same vein; that of the neo-Marxist theory which holds that sometimes labor relations alone are enough to determine the nature of the economic system and to cause development or economic stagnation. I refer here to a theory proposed by an Indian economist which represents, if you will, a modern mathematical version of the Marxist theory of Asian means of production (Bhaduri 1976). The study deals with West Bengal. Labor relations there are described as "semi-feudal": they are not feudal because there is a labor market. Nonetheless, they recall the feudal system to the extent that the tenant farmer cannot survive on his own income but must borrow from his landlord, who is the only person likely to give him credit considering the fact that there is little to guarantee a loan. As he is chronically indebted, this creates a dependence from which he cannot free himself.

The theory in question shows that in such a system progress is not possible: the system perpetuates itself forever. Why? Because the landowners garner their income, not just from the sale of that part of the harvest which they receive, but from the financial exploitation of the tenants they employ. Suppose they adopt an innovation hoping to improve the productivity of their land. They may, perhaps, increase their commercial income, but will run the risk of seeing their interests reduced with no guarantee that the loans will be compensated for by increased commercial revenue. Due to this uncertainty, they will forego the opportunity. Unable to reform from the inside, such a system must be reformed from without, and as labor relations are *the cause* of stagnation, the intervention must consist of a transformation of labor relations.

Once again, we see a theory as scientific as any theory can be. Note that the radical conclusion which emerges does so only if one introduces the implicit reasoning as well as the explicit. In fact, the theory assumes (implicitly) that the landowners have a terrible aversion to risk. Indeed, nothing suggests that the commercial benefits might not more than cover the loss of interest that the landowners could suffer from, by the fact that the tenant farmers could take advantage of their own increased income to reduce their indebtedness. But there is more. One must assume that the aversion to risk is common to *all* landowners. Otherwise, if some landowners attempt to innovate, they could produce their rice at less cost, sell it at a lower price on the market and would thus indirectly force the others in turn to adopt their innovation.

For the conclusion to follow from the premises, one must also assume that the power to make innovations is exclusively in the hands of the landowners. If the innovation is costly or not subsidized, the hypothesis appears plausible; otherwise in principle nothing precludes more or less direct pressure, either from political authorities or from the tenant class, from making the rejection of innovation difficult.

Briefly, as in the preceding case, the radical conclusion does not flow from the premises, but it does *appear* to flow from them, and it is by that fact alone made very convincing. In fact, it seems to flow from a theory which not only appears scientific but is as scientific as possible.

At the same time, these examples show that the normal functioning of scientific thought may have the effect of suggesting the existence of inflexible social laws of the form "if A, then B," calling to mind those that one may establish in the domain of the natural sciences. Nurkse's theory scientifically demonstrates "without foreign aid, no development." Bhaduri's theory shows in a similar fashion that "a semi-feudal system is bound to perpetuate itself."

In reality, this inelucidable character disappears as soon as one takes note of the implicit propositions which allow such conclusions and are at the same base of their rigidity. Thus the idea itself of a *law* disappears, giving way to the notion of a *model*, and any conclusion from this point on is framed in a cautious and conditional form: "*if all the conditions assumed by the model* are present, *then* it *might* be that . . ."; for example: "it *may* be that foreign aid is the only way to achieve development, that the transformation of labor relations is the only way to escape stagnation," etc. The *logical form* of the conclusion has therefore changed completely. Where one had a statement of *necessity*, one now has a statement of *possibility*. But the change from *law* to *model* assumes that we have taken note of the "underlying implicit premises."

On the contrary, so long as the implicit remains implicit, one tends to believe that such a theory leads to the demonstration that in the social world there exist immutable relations. Thus illusion is part of the development of knowledge. The implicity as a law, that which is really just a model, is a mutable relation, that which is but a possible relation, and it makes us naturalize the human world. The normal course of evolution of knowledge thus produces powerful metaphysical illusions.

One could push these analyses further. The researcher must be seen as *active*. Far from contenting himself with *discovering* the socio-economic reality, he asks him or herself questions for which he already has an expectation of the answer. He sets his questions in frameworks of which he is more or less conscious. Thus he has a tendency to emphasize the spectacular cases. For example, White (1969) superbly showed that technical innovation can have radical transformational effects. He made this point notably with respect to the metal plowshare and the horse's bit. In both cases, the technical innovations spurred real social change: the pattern of population, migratory movements, political organizations, social relations, class systems and economic systems were in both cases revolutionized. Similarly, Mendras (1967) has shown in the case of France that the introduction of hybrid corn completely transformed French agriculture. The fine examples of this type are more easily identified and remembered than the more complex and equivocal cases. Therefore, we know less of the work of Epstein (1962) on southern India because here the innovation (irrigation) appeared to have equivocal effects: it provoked effects of modernization in the countryside, in certain cases and according to some measurements, but also effects of reinforcement in the most traditional aspects of society in other cases and according to other measurements. But attention tends to favor the simple cases. In the sphere of knowledge, as in the sphere of perception, one may talk, to explain these phenomena of effects, of *gestalt*.

It is gestalt's effects that explain that one gives particular attention to the case of "small cases—big effects," illustrated by the works of Mendras or of White. Generally speaking, they incite simplification. The dependence of one nation in relation to others can, in certain instances, create progress or stagnation, but one finds it preferable for dependence to be bad in all aspects, even though in certain cases, such as in Nigeria or Argentina at the turn of the century, dependence may have positive effects in regards to development (Boudon 1986a). The theory of cognitive dissonance applies here: one admits more readily that the effects of a situation are all of the same type.

In general, from every cause, or from almost every, negative effects may result. But this idea could easily be disturbing and irreconcilable in scientific thought. Similarly, contingency makes one uncomfortable and one prefers, in conformity with rules of what is sometimes called "magical thought," substantialist explanations to contingent explanations. Yet they are the hazards of the politics of the Counter Reformation which explain, at least in part, the correlation between Protestantism and Catholicism.

These *cognitive* phenomena are accentuated by different *social* factors. Thus the relationship between the producer and the user, or consumer of knowledge, tends to reinforce these illusions and these simplifications. This reinforcement is due to the fact that the policy maker accepts a scientific theory readily and with closed eyes as soon as it is the object of consensus in the scientific community. The need for action being pressing, he needs theories on which to base his theories. Naturally, he has not many resources—especially time—to test the current theories. Where there is a monopoly, he will readily accept these theories. According to Keynes, that is why bankers spend their time using economic theories which they do not understand. One usually trusts our societies to trust science. Even so, it is the most reliable way of thinking.

While on the subject of development, one must add that studies on the subject blossomed at the time the world was divided into two camps. On one hand, developmental problems were seen as arising from social engineering; on the other hand, they were seen as arising from revolutionary therapy. This ideological division made the *frameworks* in which scientific discussions developed more rigid. For the West, it has probably reinforced the *scientists*' side of social sciences. Currently, the sociologist perceives him or herself in a saint-simonian fashion, like a social engineer deserving, because of the nobility of his or her object, more consideration than an engineer of natural science. For the sociologist, this climate reinforced illusions and hyperboles normally arrived at through work and scientific discussion. All of this created simplifying visions of developmental phenomena, visions which were believed to be guaranteed by the authority of science and little attention was paid to those such as P. Bauer or A. Hirschman, who had insisted on singularity, contingency and the unpredictability of developmental processes.

CONCLUSION: FOR A PRAGMATIC POLICY

The deception produced by the social sciences on the subject of development, more than on any other subject, does not come from the fact that they have taught us nothing. On the contrary, the development period is perhaps one of the richest in social sciences. It is due to the fact that the climate in which they developed, just as the mechanics I have attempted to describe, have produced terribly distorted results. One thought one was finding immutable laws and miraculous recipes for political action. One confused law and model, the particular case and the general case, and promoted the interesting example to the rank of typical example. We thought we were getting rid of ineffectual theories, but really they were just theories that did not produce the desired effect.

From the moment one sees that the social sciences are productive of *models* rather than *laws*, one understands that they cannot directly guide political action. Because a model is a statement of the form, is the form "under the conditions of a model (that one can rarely describe in an exhaustive manner), if X, then Y." As one can never measure exactly the proximity between reality and a model, one never knows for certain if it is applicable. In summary, science can clarify, but not guide action, and the former can never be stripped of its uncertainty. Apparently, Chile made a good wager in taking advantage of the reversal of seasons to substitute for copper cash crops based on the needs and patterns of consumption of the Northern Hemisphere. Political action cannot be reduced to the application of techniques. It is a question of flair and imagination. The social sciences can explain the past, produce many models and examples, enrich the imagination and help to dispel false ideas. But, as distinct from natural sciences, they can produce neither "techniques" nor "recipes." The disillusion produced by the social sciences with respect to development carries, in the final analysis, a severe lesson of pragmatism.

References

Année Sociologique. 1991.

Bauer, P. 1971. *Dissent on Development.* London: Fakenham & Reading.

Berger, P. 1978. *Les Mystificateurs du Progrès.* Paris: PUF.

Bhaduri, A. 1976. "A Study of Agricultural Backwardness under Semi-Feudalism." *Economic Journal* 83(329):120-37.

Boudon, R. 1986a. *L'Idéologie.* Paris: Fayard [also Le Seuil 1992].

Boudon, R. 1986b. *L'Art de se Persuader.* Paris: Fayard [also Le Seuil 1992].

Boudon, R. (1984) 1991. *La Place du Désordre.* Paris: PUF.

Chazel, F. 1987. "L'Apport de Gérard de Gré." *Revue Français de Sociologie* 28(4):663-77.

De Gré, G. (1941) 1979. *The Social Compulsion of Ideas: Toward a Sociological Analysis of Knowledge.* New Brunswick: Transaction Books.

Eisenstadt, S. N. 1967. "The 'Protestant Ethic' Thesis in an Analytical and Comparative Context." *Diogenes* 59:25-46.

Eisenstadt, S. N., ed. 1970. *Readings in Social Evolution and Development.* Oxford: Pergamon.

Epstein, S. 1962. *Economic Development and Social Change in South India.* Manchester: Manchester University Press.

Habermas, J. 1986. *Théorie de l'Agir Communicationnel.* Paris: Fayard.

Hagen, E. 1970. *Structures Sociales et Croissance Economique.* Paris: Editions Internationales.

McClelland, D. 1961. *The Achieving Society.* Princeton, N.J.: van Nostrand.

Mendras, H. 1967. *La Fin des Paysans.* Paris: Sedeis.

Mill, John Stuart. 1974. *A System of Logic, Ratiocinative and Inductive.* London: Routledge & Kegan Paul.

Nurkse, R. 1953. *Problems of Capital Formation in Underdeveloped Countries.* Oxford: Blackwell.

Schneider, L. 1970. *Sociological Approach to Religion.* New York: Wiley.

Stoetzel, J. 1978. *Psychologie Sociale.* Paris: Flammarion.

White, L. 1969. *Technologie Médiévale et Transformations Sociales.* Paris: Mouton.

Chapter 12

HUMAN SOCIAL RELATIONS AND ENVIRONMENT CHANGE: A GLOBAL PERSPECTIVE

Akinsola Akiwowo

Ondo State University

The terms "human social relations" as used in the title of this paper convey two assumptions. One assumption is that human beings engage in uniquely meaningful human and transcendental forms of relationships which we do not find in most non-human communities. The second assumption is that there are also reciprocal relationships between our physical and supra-physical environments and the varied patterns of beliefs, social practices and knowledge systems among mankind. These two assumptions, however, are based, of course, upon a more fundamental belief, namely: the "psychic unity" of all groups and races of man. This unity has made it possible to locate a most severely challenging problem of our planet, Earth: how to heal an ailing Earth.

CONGRESS AS THE GATHERING OF TRIBES

At regular intervals of time and at selected centers of intellectual and cultural achievements, sociologists hold their World Congresses or what I choose to call otherwise "the gathering of the tribes." We are afforded precious opportunities, on such occasions, to be physically present at the gathering, to meet fellow sociologists from different national sociological traditions, and to discuss and share knowledge carefully garnered from different parts of the globe. All these form aspects of the processes of developing a universal knowledge which the discipline of sociology had given rise to since its birth and through its early years of nurture by Auguste Comte and Herbert Spencer, respectively.

As a result of our purposive "gatherings of the tribes," however, we, as sociologists, have developed over decades, amongst us, a quiet subconscious enlargement and broadened knowledge of humanity, the human society, and the planet Earth.

Many sociologists who had come to such congresses, however, probably might not have been giving full attention to a significant fact: namely,
that the discerning inhabitants of our host communities also are given,
perhaps, a once-in-a-lifetime opportunity to observe and meet an assortment
of human types who are members of our world sociological multi-cultural
and multi-lingual body. Imperceptibly, perhaps, from the beginning of the
opening of a plenary session to the last convocation to observe the ritual of
dispersal to our home countries, the discipline itself undergoes, gradually, a
transformation whose true intellectual characteristics and spiritual qualities
are probably beyond each one's immediate complete comprehension.

It is in this manner that Sociology, in my judgment, had come to
acquire the unique expressions of academic offsprings of new ideas which
some may see as "new heresies," or "orthodoxies," that are borne away by
those present at each congress. One such belief or orthodoxy is that mankind belongs to three distinctive worlds or social arrangements as well as
three distinctive ways of perceiving social realities, but one universal meth-
odology of knowing truths about human societies. I like to suggest for our
consideration another belief derived from a West African myth, which goes
thus:

> When existence began and *Olodumare* [divine origin] wanted to create man-
> kind, He prepared three pots of dye. In one pot He prepared a mixture of
> black dye. In another pot, He prepared a mixture of red dye, while in the third
> pot, He prepared a mixture of white dye. These dye preparations were from
> one group of ingredients except in the material used for coloration. *Olodu-
> mare* also made man from one lump of clay and one prototype. In one dye-
> pot, He dipped one human prototype, in another dye-pot, He dipped another
> human prototype, and in the third dye-pot He dipped another prototype.
> *Olodumare* was equally pleased with the resultant creation. He named the
> three dyed human prototypes, together, as *ENIYAN* (The Chosen One). It was
> in that manner that Man was made and placed on Earth.

From this account, we are informed that there are three pristine somatic
groups of one human prototype and one essential humanity. It is through the
harmony of the arrangement of each *somatic* hue that groupings of mankind
reach out, through a method, to fulfill their intellectual and spiritual potenti-
alities and aspirations.

Also, in another African mythical account, we learn why man was
called *The Chosen One*. A Nigerian philosopher, Moses A. Makinde
(1988),[1] in his discourse on morality and the will of God, identified "a vision
of an ideal state in which man is likely to be in the future if mankind pursued the course of moral excellence" which are spelt out fully in an oral

---

[1]See Makinde (1988) for a full treatise of this most interesting theme.

corpus of divinatory verses. The course of moral excellence which he draws our attention to contains certain conditions of living which, if mankind acts in accordance with, leads to a good end for all mankind. From an English translation of the original text, Makinde sourced the following conditions.

> They are wisdom so encompassing that we can use it to govern the earth; sacrifice—that is, the love of doing good to all our fellow human beings who stand in serious need of our help or who are in any form of need; the exertion of our energies to add one jot of goodness to the stock of goodness in the world without thereby losing our own natural goodness.

Makinde also presented this concluding statement of the translated version of the myth: "Behold, there are many good things in heaven which the earth has not yet possessed; but which, of certainty, the earth will come to possess!" But, it is human beings who must work to bring about the possession of the promised good things. Mankind cannot permanently run away from the task of creating the envisioned good state of living. We may, for a long duration of time, refuse or prevaricate; but we cannot escape our collective divine assignment, as the impacts of material experiences of life will force mankind back inevitably to the task. This will be so, because in the words of the text of the mythical account, "unquestionably, of all the offsprings of the Creator, man was the one chosen to bring goodness to the planet Earth." Hence, mankind's name is *E-ni-yan* (one that is chosen).

From this African cosmological view of mankind's destiny, it is believed that mankind, through periods of time, over millennia perhaps, would introduce to this world fresh and revolutionary ideas about ways of improving the quality of life of human and other "living things" throughout the world. The following signs may mark the coming into being of the universal spirit: the possession among mankind of knowledge of such considerable proportion and magnitude the sorts of which can be used to hold the world together. This vision of "the state of lofty existence" (Makinde 1988, p. 17) was most recently conceptualized as "unicity of humanity" by Professor Margaret Archer (1990) in her valedictory address as president of the International Sociological Association at Madrid, Spain.

In fact, the works of Martin Albrow (United Kingdom) (1987), Edward A. Tiryakian (United States) (1986) in recent times and of Norbert Elias (Germany) (1897-1990), before them, contain conceptual frameworks such as the "Internationalization of Sociology," "World Society," and "Globalization" which can be recommended as sociological approaches to the achievement of the ethical visions of world society.[2] In his contribution, Martin Albrow gives us this very useful definition of *globalization* as "those values which

---

[2]Some recent relevant works from Western writers are Wallace (1961), Albrow (1987), Tiryakian (1986), Bertaux (1990).

take the real world of 5 billion people as the object of concern, the whole earth as the physical environment. . ." (1987, p. 8).

Ecology of "Unicity" and Globalism

Recently, while reading an article by Sandy Greenberg in the *Topic* (Issue No. 186, n.d.), I came across a series of photographs depicting what is now called a *photohistory* of the different regions of our planet. The photohistory resulted from twenty-five years of space programs by the United States.[3] Sandy Greenberg made this interesting observation:

> That Earth is an interactive, interrelated entity—without boundaries, as the astronauts have observed—is increasingly apparent from space.
>
> Flooding in a coastal area of one country may have its roots in the deforestation taking place far upstream in another country. Drought and dust-storms on one continent may be tied to burning and destruction of tropical rainforests on another. The demise of fish and forests in remote areas can be traced to acid-rain from industrial pollution that does not stop at international boundaries. (Greenberg in *Topic*, Issue No. 186, n.d., p. 20)

This view of our world from space led me to think of the phrase *the ecology of unicity*, with apologies to Margaret Archer, and to conclude, with a firm personal conviction, that indeed we human beings increasingly are forming a world society, according to a principle which I called *asuwada* (Akiwowo 1986; Archer 1990). With reference to this principle, "creation is presented as a specific demonstration of the principle of *asuwada* (purposive clumping of diverse existences). The Earth is also seen as a haven for implanting and cultivating goodness" (Akiwowo 1986, p. 347). Furthermore, there is the view of our world from the earth below from which

> All things continue-in-being as communities, through the realms of nature from ants to elephants, from algae to whales, from plants to giant forest trees, man-made objects continue-in-being in communities or systemic wholes, from dyads to congregations, from families to nations. It is this community of creatures that is the substance of *goodness*. The whole earth is a macro-community in which human settlements of varied sizes and densities are micro-communities. (Akiwowo 1986, p. 352)

Such then is a view of the ecology of unicity from earth below. It is these ecological structures and functions which, in our judgment, form the "sodality among all elements in creation" (Akiwowo 1986, p. 353), and to which astronauts drew our attention.

---

[3]In addition to this issue of *Topic*, I wish to draw your attention to two very important issues of *Japan Pictorial Quarterly Magazine*: 13(2) (1990), whose theme is "One World, One Future," and 13(4) (1990), whose theme is "Saving the Earth." These two publications are down-to-earth, non-academic discussions of the same ecological issue treated by Sandy Greenberg. See also Revkin (1989) and Brown (1989).

I once introduced the phrase: "the implantation of wrong seeds in the proper soil" of cultures and ideas (Akiwowo 1988). The implanted "seeds" may be in the form of new maladaptive cultural traits or cultural trait complexes introduced into the cultural milieu of a country, or some contaminated waste products exported to some unsuspecting poverty-stricken dust farmers of a "developing nation" for burial in the soil of their land. The "seeds" may also be the destructive developments which result in the denuding of forests as sources of life-giving oxygen. Or it may be interpreted as fertilizers acting as water pollutants, or as robbers of life from the soils of different countries. We must add to that list the harmful effects of bush burning for wood as sources of rural energies, such as may be found in many parts of Africa; as well as the exposure of man and other aspects of nature to harmful rays from the sun, and the raising of the temperature of the earth by pernicious gases released into the atmosphere, resulting in the depletion of the ozone layer. The list of maladaptive "seeds" can continue.

But, we must remember the gentle but firm warning of Ralph Waldo Emerson ([1841] 1937), American poet, essayist and philosopher, when he wrote regarding the application of the law of compensation in world affairs:

> This law writes the laws of the cities and nations. It will not be baulked of its end in the smallest iota. It is in vain to build or plot to combine against it. Things refuse to be mismanaged long, *Res nolunt diu male administrari.* Though no checks to a new evil appear, the checks exist, and will appear. (pp. 88-89)

Emerson, though speaking one hundred and fifty years ago, is current today, when he said:

> Every thing in nature contains all the powers of nature. Every thing is made of one hidden stuff; as the naturalist sees one type under every metamorphosis, and regards a horse as a running man, a fish as a swimming man, a bird as a flying man, a tree as a rooted man. (p. 89)

It is such a thought as this which led the old wise men in some parts of Africa to caution, "When you cut down a tree in the forest, think of yourself in its place!" It is the same pervading spirit which has led a Nigerian musician, Ebenezer Obey, to sing: "When you sight a bird upon the branch of a tree, please, do not throw stones to kill it. For the affliction of the bird-child is like the affliction of the man-child." To understand the moral of the song further, we cull again this passage from Emerson's "Compensation."

> Every act rewards itself, or in other words integrates itself, in a two fold manner: first in the thing, or in real nature; and secondly in the circumstance, or in apparent nature. Men call the circumstance the retribution. The causal retribution is in the thing and is seen by the soul. The retribution in the circumstance is seen by the understanding; it is inseparable from the thing, but is often spread over a long time and so does not become distinct until after many years. The specific stripes may follow late after the offence, but they follow because they accompany it. (p. 90)

The "Stripes" of Global Environmental Pollution

In the light of Emerson's thought, and those of the African sage, the *stripes* of the cutting down of trees for timber are floods; those of burning bushes for agricultural or rural energy purposes are droughts, dust storms, and destruction of tropical rain forests; while those of acid rain or contaminated wastes from industries are destruction of fish life, whales, seals; and those of poaching are endangered wildlife such as elephants, tigers and lions in Africa. These and many other *stripes* from global environmental destruction may even yet take a decade or so to manifest. Indeed, as Joseph L. Fisher (1963), President of Resources for the Future, stressed: "No problem is of deeper concern to mankind than that of coming to terms with the natural environment so that it will support a reasonably satisfying way of life" (p. v).

A Perspective on Restructuring and Development[4]

I have come to the section of this paper where I see *restructuring* not in economic terms, but as taking place in man's viewpoints and ways of thinking about our planet, the planetary system of which ours is a member, and the entire human race. It is very necessary that sociologists be involved in improving our environments, by being able to see more and more the earth as a global home of mankind which we share with other living matters in equal rights to the environmental provisions of a "life-bearing" planet. Also, sociologists need to develop an interest in the factors which affect the earth's atmosphere which, in turn, affect human behavior and patterns of relationships in a psycho-social environment. What, for example, comprise destructive forces in nature? What clearly is nature? and Where do human beings fit in the scheme of this so-called nature? If nature is, as the dictionary says, "what something consists of" or "the essential character or quality of a thing," then sociologists may want to add to their knowledge what are the essential qualities of the Earth which make it life-bearing, including the life of Man. We may want to know, too, what Life consists of. As physical scientists continue to build increasingly more complex and costly telescopes to probe into space in order to broaden our knowledge of the essential characters of Mars, Jupiter, Uranus, and other planets within our solar system, what methodologies and devices can the social scientists come up with to increase our knowledge of the essential character of man, human society,

---

[4]I am grateful to my colleague, Sigismund A. O. Akinbulumo at the Department of Sociology, Ondo State University, Nigeria, who wrote to me most recently on this topic: "Alvin Toffler's idea of our planet being 'Global village' consequent upon advanced technological inventions—cybernetics, computer, fax, *et cetera*, has brought about the awareness of humanity's oneness and closeness within an ecosphere" (July 6, 1991).

and humanity? How else can we proceed to understand and tackle the essential characteristics of "the state of the world's health," as the interviewers of Lester Brown, the founder of Worldwatch Institute, Washington, D.C., have put it? Whatever forms of *restructuring* we may propose— economic or technological—we must return to the proper study of man. It is not enough to share the realization that the state of the world's health is our common concern. It is not enough, also, to agree intellectually with Buckminster Fuller that the successful operation of the "Spaceship Earth" rests upon our seeing it as "whole spaceship" and "our fate as common" fate (*Dialogue* 3 [1989], p. 10). We must accept and put to practice that whatever development policies we formulate should be for all mankind and the whole of the Spaceship Earth, not separate policies for different continents and people. As Edmund Husserl, philosopher, put it not too many years ago, individually and jointly, we need to accept the idea that

> Whatever holds good for me personally, also holds good, as I know, for all other men whom I find present in my world-about-me. Experiencing them as men, I understand and take them as Eco-subjects, units like myself and related to their natural surroundings. But this is in such wise that I apprehend the world-about-them and the world-about-me objectively as one and the same world, which differs in each case only through affecting consciousness differently. (White 1955, p. 109)

Social scientists in general and sociologists in particular, as we prepare to enter the 21st century, need to be encouraged to collect, examine, and analyze indigenous knowledge systems throughout the world which are concerned with Man and his earthly and non-earthly environments, and man's diverse "non-scientific" techniques of coping with the crises in Nature. The purpose of this is to greatly enrich our common human intellectual sources of resources of methods for studying environments, such as those developed by the Dogon of Mali in West Africa. Encouragement may be given in the form of support of transcultural, multi-lingual study of the relationships, if any, between the environmental condition of an area and the state of war or disturbance among mankind in the same area. Sociology, in the world today, has a lot to offer, too, to researches designed to discover the best means of community-based education whose objectives are environmental improvement, and the development of health-promoting behaviors.

If, as the call has gone out, sociologists are now expected to develop globalism as a disciplinary perspective, then we need to develop a sincere appreciation of the genuine efforts of sociologists who may be working from different national traditions for the purpose of contributing to the acquisition of reliable knowledge of human social relations worldwide. Again, while it is a welcome move to have sociologists discuss not only the problems and prospects of global human society, but also the improvements of the quality of life, sociologists as individual human beings must endeavor to increase contacts with other sociologists living and working in different regions of the world and with different intellectual inclinations. To do this, sociologists may need to be reminded of what they know very well about social interactions as forms of social processes. This is one of the responsibilities of such bodies as the International Institute of Sociology, namely: to institutionalize increased contacts among their members. One approach is the encouragement of an international teammate approach to the exploratory study of new frontiers of sociological knowledge of the global society. A recent example of this approach was the teammates approach of explorers of the Antarctic. An interesting account by Will Steger of these "six very different men from six very different countries" can be gleaned from the article, "Six Across Antarctica" (*National Geographic*, November 1990, pp. 67-93). These six men, Victor Boyarsky (Soviet Union), Geoff Somers (Great Britain), Qin Dake (China), Will Steger (United States), Kezio (Japan), and Jean-Louis Etienne (France), after an 8,700-mile journey, "most of them in blinding light and snow," had this to say:

> We had emerged from the interior of Antarctica with our friendship not merely intact, but deep and mature. This bond of true affection, woven in mutual hardship, had strengthened all of us. It had pulled us—six very different men from six very different countries—across this frozen land. Perhaps that was our biggest success; we proved in the end that we weren't very different after all. (p. 93)

The experiences of the six different men in the Antarctic contribute to our understanding of two sorts of knowledge: one whose root lies in "the development of sense contacts into knowledge of things," and another sort whose root lies in the "contact with the minds of other men, through communication, which sets going a process of thought and sentiment similar to theirs and enables us to understand them by sharing their states of mind." The first sort of knowledge Charles H. Cooley identified as "spatial and material knowledge," while the second sort he identified as "social knowledge" (Gittler 1952, p. vii).

The discovery, by the six explorers in the Antarctic, provides a contemporary illustration to the statement: "As a new system of human relations develops, it is inevitable that the people involved in it develop new patterns of thoughts and sentiments" (Gittler 1952, p. 222). If there is a great measure of truth in the above statement, then the training of a new generation of sociologists in the early decades of the 21st century may well begin with a teammate structure of research organizations in the areas of changes in human social relationships due to fluctuations in man's natural environment, and efforts to maintain a natural equilibrium in Earth's ecosystem.

In conclusion, I think it is proper that I return to the eschatological ethical evolutionary vision of life contained in the West African myth to which I alluded earlier, and to conclude on this positive note drawn from the English translation of a part of the text:

"This world you now experience is the locale of the state of the lofty experience," said Orunmila. "Here Man will live to possess a most comprehensive knowledge of everything on Earth, and there will be joy at all times; all human beings will live without fear of anything, without hatred or enemies, the attacks of snakes or similar evil animals; here Man will be free from the fear of death, sickness, suit in court, loss, wizardry or witch-craft, and from fear of *ESU*; there will be no fear of harm done to the body by drowning, fire, poisonous ivys, and poison; there will be no more fear of poverty or want. . . . *all these shall be, after Man must have learned to exercise his will power, good conduct, and wisdom, to the fullest.*" (Makinde 1988, p. 16)

This vision is predicated upon the belief: "Behold, there are many good things in heaven which the earth has not yet possessed; but which, of certainty, the earth will come to possess!" As sociologists, part of our tasks and function is to bring this vision to a realizable stage.

References

Akiwowo, Akinsola A. 1986. "Contributions to the Sociology of Knowledge from an African Oral Poetry." *International Sociology* 1(4):343-58.

Akiwowo, Akinsola Ayodele. 1988. "Indigenization of the Social Sciences and Emancipation of Thought." Valedictory Lecture delivered at Oduduwa Hall, Obafemi Awolowo University, Ile-Ife.

Albrow, Martin. 1987. "Sociology of One World" (an editorial). *International Sociology* 2(1):1-13.

Archer, Margaret S. 1990. "Foreword." Pp. 1-2 in *Globalization, Knowledge and Society: Readings from International Sociology*, edited by Martin Albrow and Elizabeth King. London: Sage Publications in association with the International Sociological Association.

Bertaux, Daniel. 1990. "Designing the World Competition." *International Sociology* 5(4):373-78.

Brown, Lester. 1989. "The State of the World": Interview with Lester Brown, founder of the Worldwatch Institute. *Dialogue* 85:11-16.

Emerson, Ralph Waldo. (1841) 1937. "Compensation." Pp. 85-104 in *Essays and English Traits*, with Introductions and Notes, Vol. 5, The Harvard Classics, edited by Charles W. Eliot. New York: P. F. Collier.

Fisher, Joseph L. 1963. "Foreword." In *Scarcity and Growth: The Economics of Natural Resource Availability*, by Harold I. Barnett and Chandler Morse. Washington, D.C.: Resources for the Future, Inc.

Gittler, Joseph B. 1952. "Preface." *Social Dynamics: Principles and Cases in Introductory Sociology.* New York: McGraw Hill.

Makinde, M. Akin. 1988. "African Culture and Moral Systems: A Philosophical Study." *Second Order, an African Journal of Philosophy, Special Issue: Ethics and African Societies*, New Series 1(2):1-27

Revkin, Andrew C. 1989. "Living with the Greenhouse Effect." *Dialogue* 85:24-31.

Tiryakian, Edward A. 1986. "Sociology's Great Leap Forward: The Challenge of Internationalisation." *International Sociology* 1(2):155-71.

Wallace, Anthony F. C. 1961. "The Psychic Unity of Human Groups." Pp. 129-63 in *Studying Personality Cross-Culturally*, edited by Bert Kaplan. New York: Row, Peterson & Co.

White, Morton. 1955. *The Age of Analysis: 20th Century Philosophers.* Mentor.

Appendix

A NEW PARADIGM FOR REGIONAL POLICIES: THE CHALLENGE OF HYOGO PREFECTURE

Toshitami Kaihara

Governor, Hyogo Prefecture, Japan

INTRODUCTION

To solve our environmental and natural resource problems, there has been a tendency to emphasize the natural science and technological perspectives. But, these problems are the result of human activities, and it goes without saying that changes in these activities represent the means to solve these problems.

Recently, in Japan, discussions of these problems have been frequent. In the newspapers, environmental problems, including such issues as atmospheric concentrations of carbon dioxide, have been discussed. Kuwait's burning oil fields are seen on television in every household, and deforestation of the Temperate and Tropical Zones has been a recurrent topic. Hence, the problems of our environment and natural resources have come to touch our everyday lives.

Partly due to mass media, for some of the Japanese people, recognition of and attitudes toward environmental and natural resource problems have changed quite significantly. More specifically, the attitudes that these problems should be the direct responsibility of the industries which develop and utilize our natural resources, as well as the responsibility of the central government, which establishes the policies which relate to these industries, and attitudes of indifference on the part of the people, have all changed. The attitude which held that the central government and these industries must make every effort, on their own, to solve these problems, has changed. Based on recognition that these problems relate directly to everyone's daily life—for example, everyday behavior such as daily purchases and consumption of the commodities and services of these industries—a new set of attitudes seems to be emerging. These new attitudes include the idea that we must consider the environment and natural resources when we think about our daily conduct.

I believe that these attitudinal changes among the Japanese people—that is, emerging recognition of the problem and its solutions—are quite healthy and desirable. Additionally, it is essential that these changes in outlook be adopted and accepted by the majority of the Japanese people; that recognition of the importance of environmental protection and natural resource preservation become a part of our everyday lives. I believe such change will come to represent one of the basic forces for action toward creation of a motive for the re-formation of norms for industrial activities and consequently for the re-formation of market frameworks, which, in turn, will improve the socio-economic structure. In these circumstances, that is, promoting such healthy and valid change for the benefit of society, the role of the regional government, being in charge of policies, must reflect closely the will of the citizenry and therefore will take on greater and greater importance.

HYOGO PREFECTURE AS A "MINIATURE" OF JAPAN

Hyogo Prefecture's area is about 8,400 km^2, which represents about 2.2 percent of Japan's total land area, meaning that Hyogo is the twelfth largest of Japan's forty-seven prefectures. Our population is 5.4 million, constituting 4.4 percent of Japan's total population, and therefore ranking us the eighth largest prefecture with respect to population. Using total production as an economic measure, our prefecture represents 4.1 percent of Japan's total production and therefore numbers fifth out of all prefectures in that respect.

Geographically, our northern coast faces the Japan Sea. During the winter, the mountain areas have a good deal of snow. Our southern boundary faces the Inland Sea of Seto and the Pacific Ocean, and here the temperature is mild. The population and most of the industries are concentrated in various cities along the coast of the Inland Sea, including Kobe City. Major industries in the prefecture include development and production of various types of electronic products and fine chemicals, steel and titanium mills, shipping industries, and production of instruments for oceanic development. Hyogo is one of the leading technological/industrial areas in Japan. Hyogo also has rich agricultural, forestry, and fishing industries. Hyogo Prefecture's population concentrates in the southern cities because of their advanced economic development. As a result, population densities in these southern cities are very high. On the other hand, the communities in the northern mountain areas are now sparsely populated and, because of rapid population outflow, are characterized by an elderly rural populace.

These geographical characteristics and our variety of socio-economic problems have led to Hyogo Prefecture's being called a "miniature of Japan."

THE BASIC PROBLEM FACING JAPAN'S REGIONAL SOCIETIES

I will now discuss the basic problem which the regional societies of our nation face, with specific reference to the current situation in Hyogo Prefecture. This basic problem has its roots in the policy of economic priority which our nation selected as a means to recover from World War II. The advanced degree of economic development subsequently achieved naturally has had significant impact on the regions of our nation.

In this situation, where economic activities had highest priority, the traditional social order, which restricted free enterprise activities and individuals' profit-making activities, was broken up. As part of this, the traditional type community, in which neighborhood associations formed the basic unit of the community, was rejected entirely.

With regard to basic human rights, which compose the basis of social norms, since claims for freedom and rights have continued to be emphasized, there has been a tendency for the prohibition of abuse of these rights, which is provided for equally in the Japanese Constitution, and responsibility for social welfare to be overlooked. Through this drift of public opinion and attitude, egocentric thought and behavior became rampant. This, then, became one of the causes for a loss of quality and warmth in community life, an attribute which the regional society is supposed to provide.

Another result of the economic priority has been a significant shift in population densities and locations. Due to economic development, the demand for labor in urban areas has increased dramatically, causing a sudden and massive surge of population movement from rural areas to urban areas. This phenomenon has seriously disrupted the community functions of the region's rural areas. At the same time, this phenomenon has negatively impacted the quality of life in the urban areas and created an ever-widening urban-rural gap. In these rural areas, abandoned houses are covered with weeds, while in the urban areas, concrete jungles have been built.

Yet another impact of the economic priority has been a trend toward standardization of the regions of our nation. In the course of Japan's advanced economic development, rapid consolidation of basic infrastructure, such as transportation, communication and information systems, has occurred. Japan's structure has been neatly ordered by centering everything around Tokyo; the result being that each region's characteristics and culture have eroded away.

To foreigners, Japan's image has become one of "Japan Corporation Limited," stemming from the standardization of its social structure and management organizations, not only with respect to ethnicity and language but also in the cultural sphere. Japan thus has come to be seen as an odd, economically oriented nation which places priority on the economy over all other elements, ultimately creating, I believe, a background for conflict between Japan and foreign nations.

As such, I feel strongly that our advanced economic development, which has provided great benefits for the Japanese, has resulted in losses of equilibrium among the residents living in any given region of Japan, among the regions themselves, and between Japan and other nations.

These situations, their impact on regional society, and their context within expanding means of mental/spiritual communication among the peoples of Japan and the world, raise the issue of the basic problem, which can be summarized as, "How do we put meaning into everyone's daily lives? How do we cooperate to solve the problems faced by our global society?"

THE NEW PARADIGM AS A BASIS FOR "RICHNESS OF MIND"

Essentially, local society is not gesellschaft, a profit-oriented society in which everybody is united by a common interest, but rather gemeinschaft, a communal society in which all members feel bonded by mutual dependence and trust. I believe gemeinschaft, which fosters mental and emotional stability, is the type of society which we need at present, a time when we need to see a change in values from materialistic richness to spiritual richness.

I believe that some elements of spiritual richness can be seen in a devout soul which is inspired by the mysteries of providence and spirit of the natural world, a warmth of nature which cherishes peace and harmony and desires to share one's own happiness with others, and a will to cooperate with family and friends for the betterment of the future. Without this "spiritual richness," then we cannot construct a truly rich quality of life. Using economic power alone, which we now have, it would be difficult for us to be respected among the world's societies.

In our nation, I believe now is the most important time to search seriously for a new paradigm for regional policy, a paradigm based on "spiritual richness," and to begin, as soon as possible, to make concrete efforts to establish a desirable regional society. Needless to say, this desirable society is one in which everyone's free ideas, innovations, thoughts and free activities are unrestricted, one in which everyone's activities are in total autonomous harmony. Although this may be a bit too theoretical, if we make a steady effort toward the goal of obtaining "spiritual richness," even if it begins as only a little drop of water, if it is gathered in a stream it can ultimately lead to a large river. In order to achieve this large river, I believe we should make every effort to develop regional policies based on these new ideas.

PUTTING THE NEW PARADIGM INTO PRACTICE

Based on this new way of thinking, in Hyogo Prefecture we have a unique plan to develop specific policies. I would like to introduce some of these by focusing on the following two examples.

Formation of a New Community: "A Residents' Movement"

The first issue concerns the formation of a new community or a new sense of community. People living in a given residential area should think about such things as their children's education, and should provide aid to families who need assistance (for example, elderly persons or families whose houses have burned down). Residents also should work together to protect their neighborhood's, town's or village's environment, relying on the input of the older leaders who know the area well.

This community function dwindled away after the second world war, given the circumstances of drastic population mobility at that time. To replace that community function, the role of administration expanded rapidly, and, as a result, the quality of administrative services improved. But, community identity weakened and the people came to rely more on these professional organizations, such as administrative organizations. Under these circumstances, solutions to problems in education, social welfare and the environment, for example—solutions which satisfy all the residents—cannot be achieved due to the varying characteristics of the problems in each of these areas.

I believe that right now there is a strong need for something that lies between the "Public Domain," which includes professional/administrative organizations, and the "Private Domain," which includes individuals and families. We need to establish and expand a third domain, the "Civic Domain," where any and all citizens can bring up problems, where we gather knowledge and think individually and collectively about the behavioral norms and practices inherent in the problem. In this "Civic Domain," if we make good use of our time and energy, gained through shortened working hours, we can form a new community based on "spiritual richness."

For this purpose, I have proposed open conferences, to be called "Prefectural Citizens' Forums," in which free discussions can be conducted, including the participation of invited experts. From the result of these discussions we can set goals for ourselves to initiate voluntary solutions to identified problems.

This proposal has received our citizens' understanding and support, as it involves more than just participation in policy formation, as has been the case up to now. It involves the more desirable target of community formation and gives prefectural residents, as the main constituents, pragmatic activities in which to be involved. At this point, I would like to talk about several examples.

1. The "Shopping for the Environment Movement" and the "Recycling Movement" contribute to the maintenance of the earth's environment through consumer behavior aimed at reducing waste through recycling. Women's groups are the principal initiators within this movement.

2. "500 Committee Members for Fostering Warm-Hearted People." This group of prefectural residents freely participates in activities oriented to the healthy growth of the prefecture's youth. Young people who will be the new leaders of the community grow up learning the principles of human character and human nature through the instruction of excellent teachers and intense discussions.

3. An appeal by a medical doctor who works in the prefectural hospital, "Can you save the life of the person you love?" became a widespread movement for learning cardio-pulmonary resuscitation (CPR) which can save the life of a person who experiences trauma such as a heart attack.

In addition, a "Community Welfare Volunteer System," consisting of 10,000 core members, has developed into a mutual assistance movement oriented to social welfare needs at the neighborhood level.

4. It is certainly important that everyone be able to participate freely and joyfully in these movements. Being oriented to this attitude, the prefectural residents have a great opportunity to facilitate participation, and in particular to provide opportunities for the elderly and physically disabled to enjoy sports and hobbies, to display the results of these activities in the community, and to exchange experiences. An event involving all 5.4 million prefectural residents, the "Fureai Festival," or "Event of Mutual Understanding," has been facilitated by a conception of ever-widening rings emanating from a central point.

I hope, from these series of community activities, that these rings will expand to re-form not only the community itself but also the sense of community; that the circles of people who share the same interests and concerns will become friends in a free atmosphere, thereby approaching the core of their problems, and wrestling with ideas to create practical solutions.

Correction of Japan's Regional Imbalance: Another Face of Japan

The second point I would like to discuss here is the re-formation of Japan's regional structure. Up to now, Japan has produced excellent industrial commodities by adding its own applied technologies to the science and technology introduced from the West. As a result, Japan has become the world's economic giant. Japan ranks second in GNP in the world, and its per capita GNP is very near the top. Japan has become the largest creditor power. The Tokyo area, which has played a principal role, has developed into a center for international financial information.

Nonetheless, Japan is still regarded as inscrutable by outsiders. Someone metaphorically said that Japan is like a "black hole," meaning that it has tremendous energy to absorb everything in its path: knowledge, technology, materials, etc. Another opinion holds that Japan just sells commodities to the world; that Japan should demonstrate not only economic power but also synergistic power, through its cultural heritage, as one means to solve the problems which the world faces.

Japan is a nation with a beautiful natural environment and a traditional culture. The excellent skills of the Japanese, a legacy of our traditional culture, persist today. Excellent technological and human resources exist, and therefore Japan can and should play a significant role in the world society, thereby making a significant contribution to world peace and human progress. This will mean focusing upon the Japanese culture, which has been hidden behind its economic prosperity, and revealing Japan's total existence to the world.

The ancient capitals of Kyoto and Nara, which have more than a thousand years of history, are found in the Kansai Region, which includes Hyogo Prefecture. This long history has carved the region as an area central to Japan's development and prosperity. Osaka, for instance, is a commercial capital which has supported Japan's economy for several hundred years. Kobe is a well-known international port. This region has a great accumulation of rich and traditional culture, as well as innovative academics, having originated most of Japan's Nobel Prize winners.

If Japan's economic center is located in the Tokyo area, the Kansai region can become another face of Japan, different from the Tokyo Region, and a center for Japan's unique culture. To facilitate the Kansai Region's becoming another face of Japan, the Hyogo Prefecture actively participates in this region's policies, with the goal of maintaining and enhancing Japan's originality in such fields as culture, art, science, technology, education and research. Specific examples of these regional policies include:

1. Kansai International Airport is currently under construction and will be completed in 1993. This airport will be open twenty-four hours a day, making it the first airport of its kind in Japan.

Other construction projects underway include building coastal roads to integrate the seaside districts, the urban areas and Awaji Island, which has a beautifully green environment. Part of this construction includes the Akashi Kaikyo Bridge which will be the world's longest suspension bridge.

Our prefecture is participating in the consolidation of the infrastructure of the Osaka Bay area, which is being developed as Japan's "front entrance," and is involved in several other projects, including helping to consolidate several new places for international interchange; promoting Japan's largest marina project, the "Nishinomiya-Ashiya Marina Project," which will revive the waterfront; promoting an urban renewal project in the Hanshin areas, which will include an international center for theater and the arts; and finally promoting the creation of several areas for international interchange, such as the coastal area around the Akashi Kaikyo and on Awaji Island which will involve a land connection with Kobe City.

2. In the western hilly area of Hyogo Prefecture, a new science park, Harima Science Garden City, is now under construction. This science city will have a large-scale synchrotron radiation facility for basic research for natural scientists from all over the world, in cooperation with the National Science and Technology Agency. This facility will be the largest of its kind in the world. It will emit super high intensities of radiated light to elucidate the structures of tissues and other substances at the molecular level. In this science city, we have also established the Science Department of the Hyogo Institute of Technology. In the inland areas, including this city, we are planning to establish the Hyogo Corridor for Research and Development, which will cater to basic science research and high technology and will be open to the world.

3. We are promoting the Hyogo Joint Summer Session at Sea for students from twenty-four different four-year colleges and universities. The ship sails throughout Asia and Oceania. We also have a Japanese Language Education System for foreign students, mainly from Asia. In addition, we promote the non-profit Pan-Pacific Information Network Plan.

4. The Statue of Liberty, which symbolizes "liberty" as the theme of human society in this century, was presented by France to the United States about a century ago. Today, on Hyogo Prefecture's Awaji Island which faces Osaka Bay, the French have initiated a movement to construct a large arch monument to symbolize "communication," which is seen as the theme of human society in the twenty-first century. This project is now underway as a joint national effort between Japan and France.

When the previously mentioned Akashi Kaikyo Bridge is completed in 1998, we will hold a large memorial and international event which will have the theme of communication. Plans for this event are already underway.

5. In addition to the "French-Japanese Friendship Communication Monument," we are beginning to examine the possibility of establishing an international research institute for the Problems and Policies of Peace. Even though

the end of conflict between the East and the West is in sight, we still see regional conflicts, such as the Middle East Gulf War, which can have tragic results. In this regard, I believe that Japan should make a progressive and active contribution to world peace. We must take partial responsibility for the creation of a new world civilization based on communication, in which shared knowledge, information, and technology engender peace and deepened mutual understanding.

As these projects progress, the uni-polar structure of Japan—with Tokyo at the top and a tendency toward regional standardization created by this structure—will be corrected, the result being a multi-polar national structure wherein the uniqueness of each region can survive. I believe this will lead to the realization of "another face of Japan." I want to see Hyogo Prefecture make every possible effort to accomplish these goals.

CONCLUSION

The issues and problems which I have been discussing represent the paradigm for the regional policies which we are considering and implementing as plans and actions for Hyogo Prefecture, based on that paradigm.

Although the problems of, and attempts at solutions to, our nation's regional societies which I have been discussing here might be thought of as uniquely Japanese problems, I suspect they may be shared by at least some other nations and their regions.

AUTHOR INDEX

SUBJECT INDEX